The B

TURNING POINTS
General Editor: Keith Robbins
Vice Chancellor, University of Wales Lampeter

This ambitious new programme of books under the direction of Professor Keith Robbins (already General Editor of Longman's very successful series Profiles in Power) *will examine moments and processes in history which have conventionally been seen as 'turning points' in the emergence of the modern world. By looking at the causes and long-term consequences of these key events, the books will illuminate the nature of both change and continuity in historical development. There are numerous titles in active preparation, and the following are already available:*

The End of the Ottoman Empire, 1908–1923
A.L. Macfie

The Paris Commune, 1871
Robert Tombs

The Bomb

Nuclear Weapons in their Historical,
Strategic and Ethical Context

BEATRICE HEUSER

LONGMAN
London and New York

Pearson Education Limited
Edinburgh Gate,
Harlow, Essex CM20 2JE, United Kingdom
and Associated Companies throughout the world.

Published in the United States of America by Pearson Education Inc., New York.

© Pearson Education Limited 2000

First published 2000

ISBN 0–582–29291–3 CSD
ISBN 0–582–29290–5 PPR

Visit our world wide web site at http://www.awl-he.com

British Library Cataloguing in Publication Data

A catalogue entry for this title is available from the British Library

Library of Congress Cataloging-in-Publication Data

Heuser, Beatrice, 1961–
The bomb : nuclear weapons in their historical, strategic, and
ethical context / Beatrice Heuser.
p. cm. — (Turning points)
Includes bibliographical references and index.
ISBN 0–582–29291–3 (hbk). — ISBN 0–582–29290–5 (pbk.)
1. Nuclear weapons—History. 2. Nuclear weapons—Moral and
ethical aspects. I. Title. II. Series: Turning points (Longman
(Firm))
U264.H48 2000
355.02'17—dc21   99–24935
                                            CIP

Set by 35 in 10/12pt Baskerville
Produced by Addison Wesley Longman Singapore (Pte) Ltd.,
Printed in Singapore

For
Julian Chrysostomides,
Admiral Marcel Duval,
Professor Robert O'Neill and
Professor Donald Cameron Watt

Contents

List of Figures		ix
List of Tables		x
Acknowledgements		xi
Introduction		1
1.	*A Turning Point of World War II?*	7
	A turning point in World War II	8
	Was the bombing necessary?	19
	The suffering of the victims	24
2.	*A Turning Point in Strategy?*	35
	Air strategy until 1945	35
	Air strategy in practice since World War II	65
	Nuclear strategies	85
3.	*A Turning Point in the Development of 'Total War'?*	102
	Definitions of 'total war' and the link with totalitarianism	104
	Have any wars prior to World War II been Total Wars?	114
	The war aims of the major powers in World War II	119
	Conclusions: What is the relationship between nuclear war and Total War?	131
4.	*A Turning Point in the Thinking about the Morality Of War?*	135
	Immorality of war	136
	Pacifism before the nineteenth century	139
	From the wars of the French Revolution to World War I	143

Socialist opposition to nationalist wars 145
Pacifism in the inter-war period 147
Hiroshima and Nagasaki 154
Peace movements directed by the USSR since 1945:
from political tool to political self-destruction 158
Anti-nuclear protests in Protestant cultures 162
War, nuclear weapons and non-Protestant cultures 175
Conclusion 189

5. *A Turning Point in the History of Warfare and
Inter-societal Relations?* 192
Human history and the history of warfare 193
Societal and cultural-ideological causes of war 207
Conclusions 222

Useful Further Reading 224
Index 228

List of Figures

Figure 1.1 The growth of certainty that Japan could
not win   11

Figure 1.2 The growth of unwillingness to continue
the war   12

Figure 1.3 The effect of strategic bombing on German
morale, resistance and countermeasures   84

Figure 4.1 US views on the use of the nuclear weapons
on Japan in 1945   183

Figure 5.1 Estimated growth of world population
in millions   200

List of Tables

Table 1.1 Bombardment of cities during the Second
World War   30

Table 1.2 Tonnage of bombs dropped   32

Table 1.3 Total deaths during World War II   33

Table 4.1 Attitude towards the peace movement   171

Acknowledgements

The most enjoyable part of writing a book, I feel, is to write the acknowledgements, as this is one of the few formal ways in which one can express gratitude, and make one's intellectual debts known publicly without embarrassment. I am very grateful to Professor Keith Robbins, the general editor of this series, for asking me to write this book. It gave me a welcome opportunity to put down reflections which had been going around in my mind since 1991, when I started to lecture at the Department of War Studies, King's College London. Since 1989, I had been studying the development of nuclear strategies, and over the past years I have been trying to put them in the context of the overall development of warfare and strategic thinking. It dawned upon me very quickly that preferences in nuclear strategy are not just a function of technology or geography, but also of beliefs and values.[1] Arguments about whether the use of nuclear weapons would be appropriate in certain circumstances are thus not merely functions of whether these weapons are available for use and can be carried to their targets: they are functions of many other considerations, such as whether the enemy can avenge such use by also using nuclear weapons, whether the world will be safe to live in after a nuclear exchange or even only a unilateral use, on whether one can live with oneself after the use of nuclear weapons. All this has alerted me to the different levels on which nuclear weapons have to be discussed, and I am grateful to be given this opportunity to articulate my thoughts. But I also wish to express my deep gratitude to Professor Robbins for all the advice he has given me over time.

1. On different preferences with regard to nuclear strategy, see Beatrice Heuser: *NATO, Britain, France and the FRG: Nuclear Strategies and Forces for Europe, 1949–2000* (London: Macmillan, 1997). For the nuclear strategies of the Warsaw Treaty Organisation, see Beatrice Heuser: 'Warsaw Pact military doctrines in the 70s and 80s: findings in the East German archives', *Comparative Strategy* Vol. 12, No. 4 (Oct.–Dec. 1993), pp. 437–57. On the influence of beliefs on these preferences, see Beatrice Heuser: *Nuclear Mentalities? Strategies in Beliefs in Britain, France and the FRG* (London: Macmillan, 1998).

There are some other friends and colleagues who deserve my thanks for comments on this book, and they include in particular Dr Philip Sabin at King's, Sebastian Cox, Head of the Air Historical Branch of the Ministry of Defence, and Marcellin Hodeir at the French Ministry of Defence's Air Historical Service (SHAA) who gave me most constructive advice on my chapter dealing with the development, theory and use of air power; Bruce Mann, to whose pages of challenging remarks and thoughtful criticism I was not always able to do full justice; and Dr Saki Dockrill and Dr Barrie Paskins, again at King's, who commented very helpfully on chapters on the end of the Second World War and on the evolution of anti-war movements respectively. I must emphasise that all opinions, where not credited directly to other works, are entirely my own, and all remaining errors are due entirely to my own inadequacies. Greatest thanks are due to my parents, who saw little of me during the years when my visits had to be short to save time for reading and writing, and to my husband who has made many sacrifices for my work and who has unselfishly encouraged me to keep at it, making very helpful comments, too, on the final chapter of this book.

This book is dedicated to Julian Chrysostomides, for her patient support of my earliest efforts in writing and reasoning and her continued encouragement since; to Admiral Marcel Duval both for all he taught me about French military thinking, and also for his personal efforts with regard to international reconciliation and for the values which he defends (and for which, in turn, I admire him boundlessly); to Professor Robert O'Neill, for his generous and vital support for my work; and to Professor Donald Cameron Watt, to whom, besides admiration for his personal values, I owe more of my fundamental ideas and views than I realised for a long time. These are three historians and a practitioner who have earned my unlimited respect. I regard myself as their – no doubt unworthy – disciple in many ways, and with this book I want to thank them, inadequately, for all they have done for me.

Introduction

How could I ever forget that flash of light!
In an instant thirty thousand people disappeared from the streets;
The cries of fifty thousand more
Crushed beneath the darkness.

Yellow whirling smoke became light,
Buildings split, bridges collapsed;
Crowded trams burned just as they were –
Endless trash and heaps of embers,
Hiroshima.

Then, skin hanging like rags,
Hands on breasts;
Treading upon shattered human brains . . .

The conflagration shifts . . .
Onto heaps of schoolgirls lying like refuse
So that God alone knew who they were . . .

Sankichi Tōge, 'August Sixth'[1]

In August 1945, two atomic bombs were dropped on the Japanese cities of Hiroshima and Nagasaki. This is without any doubt one of the most memorable events of twentieth-century history, arguably even of human history in general. The number of deaths inflicted in a split second was unprecedented in history, and the way in which the victims died – in consequence of a nuclear blast – was technically different from anything humans had experienced before. These terrible events are unforgettable, certainly, but are they a turning point in history?

To answer this question, we must first consider what we understand by 'turning point'. In dictionaries, the term is often equated with a watershed, with a transition or transformation which can be linked to one event, which revolves around one experience. The

---

1. Robert Jay Lifton: *Death in Life: Survivors of Hiroshima* (New York: Basic Books, 1967) pp. 441f.

1

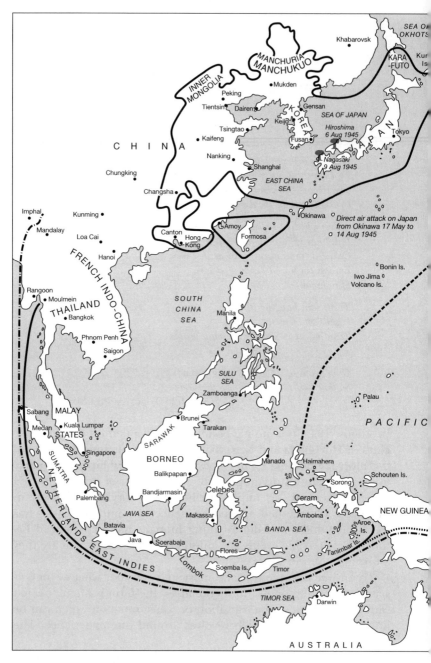

The war in the Pacific

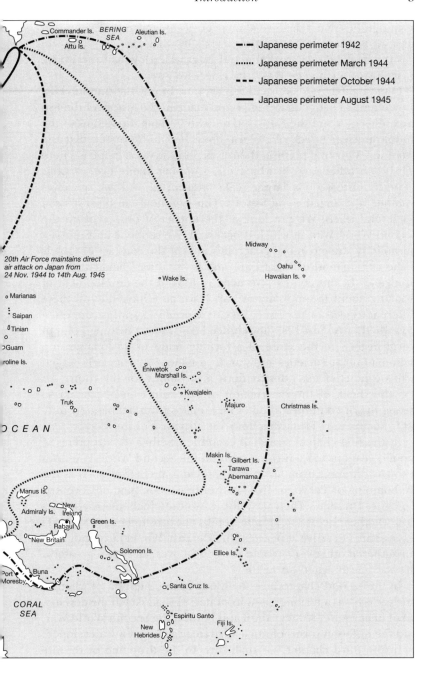

Commander Is.   *BERING SEA*   Aleutian Is.

Attu Is.

— · — Japanese perimeter 1942

· · · · · · · Japanese perimeter March 1944

– – – Japanese perimeter October 1944

——— Japanese perimeter August 1945

Midway

20th Air Force maintains direct air attack on Japan from 24 Nov. 1944 to 14th Aug. 1945

Oahu

Hawaiian Is.

Wake Is.

Marianas

Saipan

Tinian

Guam

roline Is.

Eniwetok

Marshall Is.

Kwajalein

Truk

Majuro

Christmas Is.

OCEAN

Makin Is.

Gilbert Is.

Tarawa

Abemama

Manus Is.

New Ireland

Admiraly Is.

Green Is.

Rabaul

New Britain

Solomon Is.

Ellice Is.

Port Moresby

Buna

Santa Cruz Is.

CORAL SEA

Espiritu Santo

New Hebrides

Fiji Is.

term signifies that a decisive change goes along with the event, that afterwards, there is 'no turning back'. In what way was there 'no turning back' after Hiroshima and Nagasaki? How had the world, or its history changed? Was it in a decisive way?

Quite deliberately, we shall discuss only briefly the undoubtedly fundamental change that 'the bomb' made in the history of the two Japanese cities and their inhabitants who became the victims of the double nuclear attack of August 1945. It is indisputable that the event was a turning point in their lives. But the main emphasis here will be on other ways in which the dropping of the two weapons changed history on a larger scale, indeed, we will ask ourselves whether it changed *world* history. This question can be discussed on several levels. We can look at the impact of this event on the Second World War, in which it occurred. We can look at its impact on military strategy more generally, and on the conduct of war. Is it the culmination of 'total war', and is 'total war' henceforth unthinkable? In this context, we need to look at the development of thinking about the morality of war. If we have looked at all these different aspects of the issue, we can proceed to address the question whether August 1945 does indeed constitute a turning point in world history, in the sense of a turning point in the relationship between human societies and war. Is 'total war' (particularly, waged with weapons of mass destruction) a possibility for the future, or was the shock of the destruction of Hiroshima and Nagasaki so strong that it continues to deter all humans from deliberately initiating such a war? From this flows the structure of this book.

In the first chapter, we shall examine whether the dropping of atomic weapons was a turning point in the Second World War. Was it totally different from anything that had gone before, such as the firebombing of Tokyo, or from conventional bombing of Coventry, Cologne, Dresden? Then we will turn to the much-discussed question whether the use of atomic bombs at Hiroshima and Nagasaki was essential to arrive at peace in the Far East. Would Japan not have surrendered otherwise? Would the cost in lives have been greater if the war had dragged on further?

In the second chapter, we shall look at the question of whether nuclear use was a turning point in strategy. I shall sketch the development of air power strategy until and beyond the Second World War, and the different forms of nuclear strategy subsequently developed.

In the third chapter, we shall turn to the dropping of the nuclear bomb as a manifestation of 'total war', examining how weapons of mass destruction relate to industrialised, centralised society.

Thinking about 'total war' preceded or predicted nuclear weapons. Might other weapons of mass destruction have taken the place of nuclear weapons? Might they still do so in future? How does this fit in with war aims such as the sparing of civilians, or the deliberate extermination of the enemy? Do nuclear weapons perhaps lead us to concentrate excessively on technology when we should have thought more about the phenomenon of 'total war'?

In chapter four, then, we shall consider thinking about the morality of war. Do nuclear weapons constitute a turning point in this context? Did the dropping of atomic weapons engender pacifist movements, or did these exist earlier? What impact did it make on pacifist movements, and are these the same as anti-nuclear movements? But we must also ask whether Western concepts of proportionality, of war as a last resort, and (more recently) of the desirability of avoiding civilian casualties have any relevance for cultures that have not experienced the American Civil War or the First and Second World Wars in the way Europeans, Americans, Russians and Japanese have.

Finally, in the fifth chapter, we shall examine whether nuclear weapons provided a turning point in warfare in general, and thus in world history. Are human beings naturally aggressive? Are human societies capable of adapting to the existence of the technology of mass destruction, whether by using it, or by avoiding it? The Third World War between NATO and the Warsaw Pact has not happened, and the fear of nuclear war clearly played an important rôle in its prevention. But is it not possible that a Third World War or a nuclear war (or indeed a total war fought with any other weapons of mass destruction) with catastrophic consequences for the rest of the globe will take place, albeit between different protagonists? What will warfare be like in the twenty-first century? And what will the role of nuclear weapons be?

The subject is a bitter one, especially where we are dealing with casualties in wars. I want to emphasise here that the problem of any comparison is that it can be misinterpreted as belittling the suffering of the individual. This is emphatically not the intention, and if on balance, the deaths of tens, hundreds or thousands are described in the following pages as 'small' in scale compared with the deaths of tens or hundreds of thousands, this is not to argue that violent death, or for that matter, natural death, is not the ultimate catastrophe for any creature or human being. Thus the numeric comparisons that are made do not subtract anything from the horror, the pain and the suffering of any individual victim of war or other brutality. Limited war, as defined in Chapter 3, is just as terrible for any of its victims as is 'total war', even though the difference in scale is of importance not only for moral reasons, but also because of the larger number of people who are made to suffer in the latter. It is with this in mind that this book should be read.

CHAPTER ONE

A Turning Point of World War II?

To Our good and loyal subjects: After pondering deeply the general trend of the world and the actual conditions obtaining in Our Empire today, We have decided to effect a settlement of the present situation by resorting to an extraordinary measure.

We have ordered Our Government to communicate to the Governments of the United States, Great Britain, China and the Soviet Union that Our Empire accepts the provisions of their Joint Declaration [unconditional surrender]. . . . the enemy has begun to employ a new and most cruel bomb, the power of which to do damage is indeed incalculable, taking the toll of many innocent lives. Should we continue to fight, it would not only result in an ultimate collapse and obliteration of the Japanese nation, but also it would lead to the total extinction of human civilization.[1]

This was the radio broadcast made by the Japanese Emperor on 15 August 1945, announcing Japan's surrender. As the end of war in the Far East, this was the end of the Second World War, and certainly a *caesura* in world history. But was the use of atomic bombs at Hiroshima and Nagasaki a turning point in the Second World War? Was it essential to bring the war to a close in the Far East? Or might Japan have surrendered soon anyway? This is the first issue we shall examine in this chapter, reflecting the main scholarly debate on the subject. The second will be whether the use of the bomb on Japan was indeed the most defining event of the Second World War and whether it stood out from other events and developments as the worst of its kind.

---

1. Text in Robert J.C. Butow, *Japan's Decision to Surrender* (Stanford, CA: Stanford University Press, 1954), pp. 1–3.

A turning point in World War II

While a majority of Americans still believe that on balance, drop-ping the atom bombs was the right decision to take,[2] a number of historians have questioned the necessity and morality of this deci-sion. They have conducted very detailed studies of the documenta-tion available that provides clues to the motivations of US President Harry S. Truman and his chief advisers. Until the end of his life, Truman himself repeated over and over that he stood by his decision, as, in his view, it had saved many more lives (mainly of American servicemen) than it cost in numbers of victims. Truman retro-spectively claimed to have thought at the time that, because of the determination of the Japanese military not to be taken prisoner and their willingness to incur death rather than surrender, the conquest of Japan on the ground would have resulted in further very high casualties for both sides.[3] Among the experts on the sub-ject, historian Herbert Feis has argued that this was indeed the main reason why Truman gave orders to drop the bomb.[4]

While Truman himself claims never to have lost a night's sleep over the issue,[5] some did, most notably historian Gar Alperovitz, who made the question of the President's motivation his own main subject of research over decades. Indeed, in 1965, with the Vietnam War fully under way, and its critics ever more interested in the origins of the Cold War which was so hot and deadly in South East Asia, Alperovitz published a historical blockbuster called *Atomic Diplomacy: Hiroshima and Potsdam*. In this he argued that Truman's main motivation was not to cut short the war in the Far East, but to impress Stalin with the military power America could command, lest Stalin might hope to take advantage of the inexperienced new US President in the post-World War II peace settlement. The book was grist to the mills of those (mainly Left-wing) critics of the US government who saw the Vietnam War as a further aberration of a continuous US policy which had sought confrontation with the

2. See Chapter 4.

3. For examples of later interviews with Truman and statements, see Sadao Asada, 'The mushroom cloud and national psyches: Japanese and American perceptions of the atomic-bomb decision, 1945–1995', in Laura Hein and Mark Selden (eds.), *Living with the Bomb: American and Japanese Cultural Conflicts in the Nuclear Age* (New York: East Gate Books/M.E. Sharp, 1997), pp. 179–82.

4. Herbert Feis, *Japan Subdued: The Atomic Bomb and the End of the War in the Pacific* (1961), revised and republished as *The Atomic Bomb and the End of World War II* (Princeton NJ: Princeton UP, 1966).

5. Asada, 'The mushroom cloud', p. 179.

USSR even when both had just emerged as victorious allies from the war against National Socialist Germany. The Cold War 'revisionists' thus saw a terrible logical link between the willingness of President Truman to kill one-and-a-half thousand Japanese civilians and his willingness to engage the Soviet Union in a conflictual confrontation, leading to the sacrifice of lives in the Korean War and now in Vietnam. Responsibility for the Cold War was thus assigned to Truman, his advisers and his successors, as much as, if not more than, to the Communist side.

A great debate ensued about every minor aspect of the atomic bomb decision, and the counsellors involved. Had there been serious alternative strategies discussed by the US government in 1945, and would these really have led to even greater casualties? Or was it a 'strange myth' that 'Half a million American lives [were] saved'?[6] Had General Dwight D. Eisenhower, Truman's successor as US President, really (as he later claimed) opposed the decision to use the bomb in 1945?[7] Was Truman's own decision not a bit of both, the hope of saving American GIs' lives *and* the hope of impressing Stalin?[8] The evidence has been gone through meticulously again and again, and a few hairs seem to have been split in the process.[9] In a very large collective research project, Gar Alperovitz reopened the issue and in 1995 published his old and new findings in *The Decision to Use the Atomic Bomb and the Architecture of an American Myth,* and provoked both ardent praise and angry responses, such as that by Robert James Maddox.[10] The debate is certainly not concluded. What are the main points raised by the historian-critics of the Hiroshima and Nagasaki decisions?

Let us begin with the development of the war in the Far East. The US Air Force had massively increased its bombing of the Japanese homeland in the winter of 1944–45. In November 1944, suburbs of Tokyo were for the first time subject to significant bombardment. In March 1945 came the great bombing of Tokyo

6. Rufus E. Miles, Jr., 'Hiroshima: the strange myth of half a million American lives saved', *International Security* Vol. 10, No. 2 (Fall 1985), pp. 121–40.

7. Barton J. Bernstein, 'Ike and Hiroshima: Did he oppose it?', *Journal of Strategic Studies* Vol. 10, No. 3 (Sept. 1987), pp. 377–89.

8. Barton J. Bernstein, 'Eclipsed by Hiroshima and Nagasaki', *International Security* Vol. 15, No. 4 (Spring 1991), pp. 149–73.

9. Correspondence: 'Marshall, Truman, and the decision to drop the bomb', Gar Alperovitz and Robert L. Messer vs. Barton J. Bernstein, *International Security* Vol. 16, No. 3 (Winter 1991/92).

10. Robert James Maddox, *Weapons for Victory: The Hiroshima Decision Fifty Years Later* (Columbia: University of Missouri Press, 1995).

with conventional ordnance which led to a fire-storm costing the lives of at least 88,000 people – a figure, as we shall see, that was comparable to the losses of Hiroshima and Nagasaki. Morale was declining rapidly; doubts about Japan's ability to win the war grew exponentially among the population.

The American conquest of the Pacific island of Iwo Jima in the last week of March allowed the US Air Force to deploy fighter planes there. These could henceforth accompany and protect bombers on their sorties to destroy targets on the Japanese mainland. On 1 April 1945 the Americans landed on Okinawa, which again gave them air bases closer to the Japanese mainland, further facilitating air bombardment of mainland targets.

As early as 6 April 1945 the US State Department received information that, via neutral Sweden, civilian members of the Japanese government had put out feelers to negotiate an armistice. The US minister in Stockholm reported that the Japanese would probably accept far-reaching conditions, but that 'The Emperor must not be touched. However, the Imperial power could be somewhat democratized as is that of the English [*sic*] King.'[11]

It must be noted in this context that Japanese culture inclined towards a deep veneration of the Emperor, even though this was a person whom, prior to the famous broadcast of 15 August 1945, ordinary citizens had never heard speak even on the radio, let alone seen in the flesh. The US Strategic Bombing Survey, for example, which was written up well after Hiroshima and Nagasaki in 1946/7, listed four factors as the most important in fuelling the determination of the Japanese to carry on the war, namely,

- Fear of the consequences of defeat
- Faith in the 'spiritual' strength and invincibility of the nation
- Obedience to and faith in the Emperor
- The black-out of information about the war.[12]

When during the survey, Japanese respondents were asked what changes should occur in the future, with the additional question: 'And what about the Emperor?', 69 per cent expressed the wish to retain him, 12 per cent would not answer, another 12 per cent said they could not 'discuss such a high matter' (both those refusing to answer and those who said they could not discuss this matter may

---

11. Quoted in Gar Alperovitz, *The Decision to Use the Atomic Bomb and the Architecture of an American Myth* (1995, this edn.: London: Fontana Press, 1996), p. 25.

12. *The United States Strategic Bombing Survey: The Effects of Strategic Bombing on Japanese Morale* (Morale Division, June 1947), p. 1.

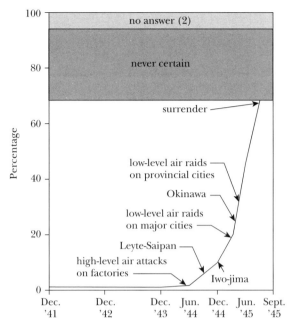

Figure 1.1   *The growth of certainty that Japan could not win*
Source: *The United States Strategic Bombing Survey: The Effects of Strategic Bombing on Japanese Morale* (Morale Division, June 1947)

have held the same view, namely that it was unthinkable for them to say anything against the Emperor). Only 3 per cent thought the Japanese should 'drop him'.[13]

It is thus crucial in this context that the Japanese were almost more concerned about the fate of their Emperor than about their own fate, and that the Allies did not convey the impression that while the Japanese government was seen as guilty of the war and as meriting punishment, the Emperor, as standing above actual policy-making, might be spared. As we shall see, the issue of the treatment of the Emperor would remain crucial in the following months.

Another key reason for Japanese reluctance to surrender was their fear of maltreatment at the hands of the Americans. The image which the Japanese had of the Americans was that they would show no mercy to the Japanese population, once they occupied Japan. The mass suicides of Japanese civilians on individual islands conquered by the Americans testify to this. It is interesting to note that the Japanese projected onto their opponents the attitude towards

13. *The Effects of Strategic Bombing on Japanese Morale*, p. 26.

12 *The Bomb*

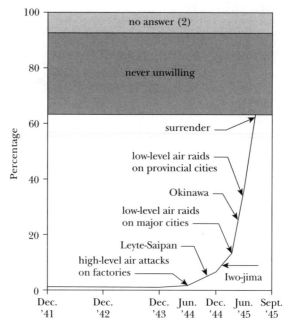

Figure 1.2 *The growth of unwillingness to continue the war*
Source: *The Effects of Strategic Bombing on Japanese Morale*

prisoners of war which they themselves showed in their treatment
of captured enemies – Japanese cruelty shown in Manchuria, China,
the Philippines, Indonesia and South East Asia beats any records
bar those set by the extermination camps of the Germans.

In mid-May 1945, after the defeat of Germany, further news of
Japanese peace feelers – again emanating from the civilian part of
the Japanese government – reached Washington via the Japanese
representation in neutral Switzerland and via Portugal, and there
were more reports of this sort in June and July.[14] These initiatives
were still vehemently opposed by the Japanese military leaders who
held to the samurai ethos of victory or death.[15] Japanese civilian
members of the government also negotiated with the Soviets in the
hope of seeking support there for better peace terms than they
expected to get from the USA, which continued to demand unconditional surrender.[16] This term had been adopted earlier during

14. Alperovitz, *The Decision*, pp. 26–7, 296.
15. Robert J.C. Butow, *Japan's Decision to Surrender* (Stanford, CA: Stanford University Press, 1954), pp. 103–11.
16. *Ibid.*, pp. 112–41.

the war by the Allied governments in order not to open the door to separate peace deals. Nevertheless, as early as at the Allied conference in Casablanca in January 1943, US President Roosevelt had given the impression that he did not want to destroy the populations of Germany, Austria, Italy and Japan, but merely their ideology and their leaders.[17]

The issue of unconditional surrender is so crucial because it seems that the fear that the USA would somehow depose the Japanese Emperor or worse was, next to the samurai ethos already mentioned, central to the Japanese government's hesitations about accepting the terms of Allied demands. Indeed, historian Dennis Wainstock has concluded, like several of his colleagues, that 'If the United States had given Japan conditional surrender terms, including retention of the Emperor, at the war's outset, Japan would probably have surrendered sometime in the spring or early summer of 1945, if not sooner.'[18] (At the very least, this would have supposed a statement of terms well in advance of the July 1945 Potsdam declaration, of course.) A contemporary observer, Hanson Baldwin, was one of the earliest critics of Truman's decision in noting only four years after the event that the US government was demanding *unconditional* surrender before the bomb was dropped twice; once the two Japanese cities had been annihilated, however, the USA conceded to Japan what the Japanese wanted most, namely the protection of their imperial family, terms of a settlement America could have secured without recourse to atomic bombs![19]

The Japanese peace feelers of May 1945 convinced Acting Secretary of State Joseph Grew that the Japanese would accept a *conditional* surrender.[20] The US–British Combined Intelligence Committee explained their view that one should try to find and communicate to the Japanese an interpretation of unconditional surrender, 'which did not involve the dissolution of the Imperial institution.'[21] The US Joint Chiefs of Staff echoed this when they noted, 'The concept of 'unconditional surrender' is foreign to the Japanese nature. Therefore, 'unconditional surrender' should be defined in terms

17. Alperovitz, *The Decision*, p. 37.
18. Dennis Wainstock, *The Decision to Drop the Atomic Bomb* (Westport, Ct.: Praeger, 1996), p. 132.
19. Hanson W. Baldwin, *Great Mistakes of the War* (New York: 1949), p. 92, quoted in Barrie Paskins and Michael Dockrill, *The Ethics of War* (London: Duckworth, 1979), p. 57; see also Barton J. Bernstein, 'Understanding the atomic bomb and the Japanese surrender', *Diplomatic History* Vol. 19, No. 2 (Spring 1995).
20. Miles, 'Hiroshima: the strange myth', pp. 124f.
21. Alperovitz, *The Decision*, p. 245.

understandable to the Japanese who must be convinced that destruction or national suicide is not implied.' [22] There seems to have
been support also among other leading figures in the War Department, but less so in the Department of State, where Assistant Secre-
taries Dean Acheson and Archibald MacLeish were particularly keen
to enforce the abdication of the Japanese Emperor whom they saw
in part as responsible for the war. US public opinion at the time
was also highly focused on Emperor Hirohito as the main culprit.
Against this background of opinion, President Truman initially
considered the matter but put off a decision on changing the surrender terms. Later, after the US test of the first atomic device on
16 July, he no longer felt the need to make concessions to Japan.[23]
Unconditional surrender, then, was the only terms offered to Japan.

The test occurred while in Potsdam, Harry Truman as the new
US President met for the first time Josef Stalin and two successive
British Prime Ministers (half-way through the conference, Winston
Churchill was replaced by Clement Attlee after the general election
in the UK had returned a Labour government). It is important
here to take a look at the situation in Europe, although the war
against Germany was over, for this was the stage at which the former
Allies were wrestling for control of the liberated countries. Although
they had agreed at their meeting in Yalta in February 1945 that free
elections were to be held throughout the liberated areas, the
elections in Poland in April 1945 had clearly not been 'free', and
the USSR had imposed the Communist government-in-exile. Two
months later, Stalin was trying to do the same in Bulgaria and
Rumania.[24] Therefore at the time of the Potsdam conference, the
US State Department advised the US delegation there that it should
'be made clear to Stalin that we cannot accord diplomatic recognition to regimes such as those in Bulgaria and Rumania until they
have been fundamentally changed in line with the [Yalta] Declaration on Liberated Europe'.[25] Indeed, on 17 July, the day after the
successful test of the first atomic device in the American desert,
Truman took up with fresh confidence the issue of free elections to
be held in Greece, Rumania and Bulgaria. The bomb was also felt

---

22. Miles, 'Hiroshima: the strange myth', pp. 124f. Specialists on Japanese culture
would argue, by contrast, that it would have taken a number of years to explain the
term of 'unconditional surrender', rooted, as it was, in European traditions of warfare, to the Japanese. I am grateful to Dr S. Dockrill for this comment.
  23. *Ibid.*, pp. 127f.
  24. Cf. Lynn Etheridge Davis, *The Cold War Begins: Soviet–American Conflict over
Eastern Europe* (Princeton, N.J.: Princeton U.P., 1974).
  25. Quoted in Alperovitz, *The Decision*, p. 253.

by the US delegation to be an asset in negotiations about the future of Germany.[26] It seems, however, that Stalin was either very poker-faced indeed or did not quite understand the relevance of the news when Truman proudly told him of the successful test of the American weapon.[27] There may thus have been a feeling – and Alperovitz's argument hinges on this – that Stalin would only truly be impressed by America's power if its possession of nuclear weapons were visibly demonstrated. Alperovitz ascribes this logic particularly to Truman himself and to his new Secretary of State, James Byrnes, the first among Truman's Cold Warrior advisers.

The historian Rufus Miles thinks that, at this stage, there were three alternatives to using nuclear weapons open in theory to (but not considered in practice by) the American administration. The first would have been a negotiated peace, spelling out that the person of the Emperor would not be touched.[28] As we shall see, this option was rejected.

The second option, according to Miles, would have been to continue with intensive conventional bombardment and with the blockade until 1 November 1945, which was the date foreseen for the American invasion of Kyushu. The United States Strategic Bombing Survey concluded in 1946 that under continuing conventional bombardment, Japan's leaders would have surrendered by the end of the year, probably even by 1 November, 'even if the atomic bombs had not been dropped, even if Russia had not entered the war, and even if no invasion had been planned or contemplated'.[29] It seems, however, that after the extremes to which Japanese soldiers had gone in order to continue to fight and not to surrender when US forces attacked Japanese-held islands, the US administration in the summer of 1945 found it difficult to believe a prediction of surrender by 1 November.

A third option for the US to follow, as Miles notes, was approved on 18 June by President Truman, namely an attack on Southern Kyushu in November 1945, an operation code-named OLYMPIC. Military leaders involved in the planning estimated that this operation would cost the USA as many casualties as the earlier conquest of Luzon (which had seen 31,000 casualties, including not quite 8,000 deaths). Miles argues, therefore, that military leaders did not fear the loss of 'half a million American lives'.[30] The fourth option was that of using the atomic bombs.

26. *Ibid.*, pp. 258f., 276–91.   27. *Ibid.*, p. 387.
28. Miles, 'Hiroshima', p. 129.   29. Quoted in *ibid.*, p. 131.
30. *Ibid.*, pp. 133–5.

Miles concludes that the option of avoiding the use of the atom bombs was never seriously considered either by President Truman or by Secretary of War Henry Stimson, but that both saw the bomb merely as a new and more decisive weapon which it was legitimate to use. In his view the excuse that the use of the bombs saved half a million of American lives was an *ex-post-facto* invention to counter moral qualms which neither Truman nor Stimson had in the summer of 1945.[31]

The US administration chose the fourth course. At the Potsdam conference, besides the issues concerning Europe, President Truman also sought to elicit a Soviet commitment to enter the war against Japan. Stalin had originally agreed at the Yalta conference that he would declare war on Japan as soon as the situation in Europe permitted. The Western governments continued to fear that if it did not enter into the war, the USSR might support Japanese conditions for an armistice against the USA's wishes.

At Potsdam, the following communiqué was jointly drafted and issued to the Japanese government (this is the Joint Declaration referred to in the Emperor's speech as quoted at the beginning of this chapter):

> The prodigious land, sea and air forces of the United States, the British Empire, and China, many times reinforced by their armies and air fleets from the West, are poised to strike the final blows upon Japan . . .

> The result of the futile and senseless German resistance to the might of the aroused free peoples of the world stands forth in awful clarity as an example to the people of Japan. The might that now converges on Japan is immeasurably greater than that which, when applied to the resisting Nazis, necessarily laid waste the lands, the industry, and the method of life of the whole German people. The full application of our military power, backed by our resolve, will mean the inevitable and complete destruction of the Japanese homeland . . .

> We call upon the Government of Japan to proclaim now the unconditional surrender of all the Japanese armed forces, and to provide proper and adequate assurances of their good faith in such action. The alternative for Japan is complete and utter destruction.[32]

The emphasis of the Potsdam communiqué to the Japanese government, in keeping with previous Allied policy, was thus again on

---

31. *Ibid.*, pp. 135–40.
32. Quoted in Robert Batchelder, *The Irreversible Decision, 1939–1950* (New York: 1961), p. 144, quoted in Barrie Paskins and Michael Dockrill, *The Ethics of War* (London: Duckworth, 1979), pp. 56f.

unconditional surrender, despite the advice given to Truman by some that this point should be toned down. It is also worth noting that it was not spelled out in the communiqué that complete and utter destruction might refer to a new weapon. But Japan had already experienced the firebombing of Tokyo, and the mere repetition of that suffering, imposed elsewhere, would have had the dimensions of the destruction of Hiroshima or Nagasaki (see below).

Co-operation with the Soviets had already proved to be difficult in many areas, and American leaders had mixed feelings about bringing the Soviets into the war in the Far East. Crucially, it was estimated by the US–British Combined Intelligence Committee that 'An entry of the Soviet Union into the war would finally convince the Japanese of the inevitability of complete defeat.'[33] It would also, however, lead to Soviet demands to be party to the peace settlement of Japan.

Gar Alperovitz, and, supporting him, Robert L. Messer, see as the most crucial factor in President Truman's decision to use the bomb the concern to force a Japanese surrender long before the Soviet Union could make a serious impact on the military situation in the Far East. There would thus have been a logical tension between the American desire to see the USSR enter the war to spread the cost of casualties incurred by the Allies in pushing Japanese forces out of the territories occupied by them, and the desire not to pay for such a sacrifice on the part of the Russians by giving them concomitant influence on the peace settlement. Alperovitz's analysis centres mainly on the importance of Secretary of State James Byrnes, who – and there is agreement on this point among some of Alperovitz's critics – wanted 'to end the war before the Soviets entered it and grabbed pieces of the Asian mainland'. Alperovitz argues that Byrnes was Truman's main adviser on all nuclear matters, and that he was determined early on to keep the Soviets in check. (Barton Bernstein, by contrast, thinks that this interpretation does not give enough importance to other individuals, including George Marshall, who, although harbouring some misgivings about nuclear use, in the summer of 1945 also urged it on the new US President.)[34]

The Japanese government at this stage in the summer of 1945 contributed further to the disaster that was in the making. It was

33. Alperovitz, *The Decision*, p. 227.

34. Gar Alperovitz and Robert Messer vs. Barton Bernstein, 'Marshall, Truman, and the decision to drop the bomb', *International Security* Vol. 16, No. 3 (Winter 1991/92), pp. 204–21.

still profoundly split between the military leaders, particularly the army generals, on the one hand, who wanted to carry on the war, and the civilian leaders on the other, who were pleading for capitulation. On 28 July Admiral Baron Kantaro Suzuki, head of the Japanese government, told a press conference in Tokyo:

> I consider the joint proclamation of the three powers to be a rehash of the Cairo Declaration. The government does not regard it as a thing of any great value; the government will just ignore it [or, 'will withhold comment', in Japanese: *mokusatsu*]. We will press forward resolutely to carry the war to a successful conclusion.[35]

The military leaders still had the upper hand. As even *Newsweek* knew, secretly, parts of the Japanese government were desperately trying to initiate negotiations in Moscow to prevent the Soviet Union from entering the war, putting forward terms for a negotiated peace.[36] But it was the military leaders who controlled the armed forces, and it is difficult to see how the Allies could have negotiated with only parts of the Japanese government, as long as its key members with direct command of the armed forces were not willing to accept the consequences of such negotiations.

Even before Suzuki's press conference, on 25 July 1945, President Truman had issued orders to USAF chief General Spaatz to use a nuclear weapon 'after about' 3 August, weather conditions permitting. As no formal, public proposal for a negotiated peace was made by the Japanese government, these orders were executed. On 6 August 1945, at 8:15 a.m. a single atomic bomb was dropped by the aircraft sentimentally named *Enola Gay* after the mother of one of its pilots; through the effects of the bomb, equally sentimentally called *Little Boy*, Hiroshima was obliterated.

Whether as an effect of the first use of the bomb or not, on 8 August, at 5 p.m. Moscow time, the USSR declared war on Japan. The following night, Red Army units invaded Manchuria to dislodge the Japanese occupation forces (the Kwantung army). Still Washington saw no sign of a Japanese surrender.

On the following morning, 9 August, at 11 a.m. local time, Nagasaki was wiped out with a second atom bomb cheerfully called *Fat Man* by its constructors; two other targets, one a more clearly military one (Kokura Arsenal), had been excluded because of the poor weather conditions in the target area. The US government had

35. Quoted in Alperovitz, *The Decision*, p. 407; see also there for a discussion of the term '*mokusatsu*'.
36. *Ibid.*, p. 411.

originally intended that the first atom bomb used on 6 August would be followed by the dropping of a second atom bomb on 11 August, weather permitting. But when the weather turned, the date of nemesis for Nagasaki was brought forward to 9 August.

Was the bombing necessary?

When he had received news of the destruction of Hiroshima, Foreign Minister Togo asked for an exceptional audience with the Emperor, who agreed with him that Japan had to surrender. The other members of the government were summoned to a meeting on 8 August, but the army leaders declared that it was impossible for them to make time for such a meeting before 9 August. The 'Big Six' members of the government finally met in the presence of the Emperor at 10:30 a.m. on 9 August – as the Red Army was advancing in Manchuria. During the meeting, the bombing of Nagasaki was announced. Unprecedentedly, the Emperor addressed the representatives of his government assembled in his presence – normally meetings in his presence would be observed by him in dignified silence – and asked them to accept the Allied request for a surrender. On 10 August, the Japanese government's representatives in Sweden and Switzerland received the following text:

> The Japanese Government are ready to accept the terms enumerated in the Joint Declaration which was issued at Potsdam on July 26 . . . with the understanding that the said Declaration does not comprise any demand which prejudices the prerogatives of His Majesty as a sovereign ruler.[37]

After a further exchange of notes, Japanese surrender came into force on 15 August 1945 (Japanese time). It was announced to silent crowds throughout Japan by the Emperor himself in the radio broadcast from which we have quoted above, the first any Japanese Emperor had ever made.[38]

Had the bombing of Hiroshima and Nagasaki been necessary to achieve this goal? In 1946 the US Strategic Bombing Survey was carried out, under a commission which included Paul Nitze as one of its vice-chairmen, and J. Kenneth Galbraith. The survey of 'The

---

37. Quoted in *Ibid.*, p. 417.
38. For a very vivid account of the Japanese government meeting on 9 August and the reasons for the delay of the surrender, see Wainstock, *The Decision to Drop the Atomic Bomb*, pp. 95–119.

Effects of Strategic Bombing on Japanese Morale' concluded that it would not have been necessary to drop the atomic bombs to secure Japan's surrender. Nevertheless, it concluded with regard to the strategic bombardment of the Japanese home islands with conventional ordnance that it 'produced great social and psychological disruption and contributed to securing surrender prior to the planned invasion'. Indeed, 'Military reverses and air raids were said by the Japanese to have been the most important factors in causing them to doubt victory or to become certain that Japan could not win.'[39] This is how the effects of strategic bombing on Japanese morale were described by an American team of researchers:

> From the standpoint of the politics of surrender – and by August 1945 politics was the key – the atom bombing of Hiroshima and Nagasaki was not essential. From its studies of Japanese resources, military positions, and ruling class politics, the Survey estimates that the government would have surrendered prior to 1 November and certainly before the end of the year, whether or not the atomic bombs had been dropped and Russia had entered the war. In the 10 to 15 weeks between the actual and probable surrender dates, the air attack from the Marianas, augmented by the Okinawa-based forces, would have reached a new high. Furthermore, morale probably would have continued its already steep decline to complete demoralization. In any case, the mounting aerial bombardment, the growing production and economic crisis, and declining morale in August and September [1945] would have weakened the position of the die-hard militarists in the ruling coalition, and added urgency to the maneuvers of the conservative peace faction, faced with the threat of a completely disorganized and grumbling populace.[40]

Gar Alperovitz's research has shown that, in accordance with the findings of the Strategic Bombing Survey, the majority of US military leaders at the time considered the war finished even before the bombs were dropped. Few naval officers, if any, recorded the opinion at the time that the atomic bombing was needed from a military point of view. By contrast he claims that many, particularly Admiral Leahy, 'were revolted at the slaughter of non-combatants'.[41]

Although the American air forces had a vested interest in this new weapon which was to make them incomparably stronger than before, Alperovitz's research has found a similar picture in his research on air force officers: they took some time to warm to the

---

39. *The Effects of Strategic Bombing on Japanese Morale*, p. 1.
40. *Ibid.*, p. 4.   41. Alperovitz, *The Decision*, p. 332.

new wonder weapons, unhappy that it was a small team and the Manhattan project, not their overall efforts, which led to the sudden end of the war in the Pacific. The US Army Air Forces' commander in China at the time, Major General Claire Chennault, thought it was Russia's entry into the war that proved decisive for Japan's decision to surrender, while the great Cold War hawk Major General Curtis LeMay in September 1945 told the *New York Herald Tribune* that 'The atomic bomb had nothing to do with the end of the war at all'. The commander of the US Army Strategic Air Forces in the Pacific, General Carl Spaatz, who himself relayed the orders to bomb Hiroshima and Nagasaki, made it known that he personally 'felt Japan would surrender without the use of the bomb', and did not understand why the second bomb was used.[42] Gar Alperovitz quotes copious evidence to show, from memoirs written years later and even confidences they made soon after the destruction of these two Japanese cities, that key army figures like General MacArthur and the Army Chief of Staff, General George Marshall, were equally opposed, at that stage, to the use of nuclear weapons. Nevertheless, in August 1945, they did not raise their voices to counsel Truman against the choice of targets for the atomic bombing.[43] While it was their clear duty to obey their President, it was also their duty to consider whether any tasks they were performing

42. *Ibid.*, pp. 335–7, 343–5. It is worth reflecting briefly on why Nagasaki was bombed. There are two obvious bureaucratic reasons. The scientific-bureaucratic organisations which had produced two different prototypes of bombs, *Little Boy* and *Fat Man*, were keen on testing both, and the choice of the target area in Nagasaki – deliberately away from the port which had been bombed previously, to get a clearer picture of the effects of the atomic bombing – follows a systems analyst's logic detached from the human or political effects of this action. Moreover, it was planned to assemble further bombs as early as possible, which would have been used against further city targets, had the Japanese government not surrendered. We know with the benefit of hindsight that the timing of the bombing of Nagasaki, on 9 August, was too soon after that of Hiroshima, on 6 August, to allow the Japanese government to react. Had the bombing of Nagasaki continued to be scheduled for 11 August, as originally planned before being changed because of weather conditions, a decision to surrender on 9 August might have intervened, obviating the need to drop the second bomb. Again, bureaucratic-procedural considerations (the sense that the mission, once ordered, must be executed, and that its timing, chosen for good political reasons, was changed for technical reasons, without concern for the question whether this still made sense politically) seem to have prevailed over any fundamental reassessment of the mission in changed circumstances. One could speculate, too, that Byrnes and others who were concerned about Soviet influence did not want the Japanese surrender to come immediately after the Soviet declaration of war, but wanted it to be seen to follow an American action. None of these reasons for proceeding with the bombing is easy to approve morally and dispassionately.
43. Alperovitz, *The Decision*, pp. 350–65, and Alperovitz and Messer vs. Bernstein, 'Marshall, Truman, and the decision to drop the bomb'.

were in accordance with international conventions of which their country was a signatory such as the fundamental obligation to distinguish between combatants and non-combatants, and to advise the President of it, if this was not the case.[44]

Barton Bernstein, by contrast, argues that most evidence of this kind is retrospective. Focusing particularly on the person of Dwight D. Eisenhower, supreme Allied commander in Europe during the latter phase of the Second World War, first SACEUR of NATO, and later Truman's successor as US President, Bernstein argues that he was silent about the issue of the A-bomb in 1945, and only later began to claim that he had been opposed to it, just as most of the military men who later insisted on their own disapproval of this decision seem to have developed this view retrospectively.[45] Bernstein himself found that a few men, including General George Marshall and the scientists who worked on the bombs, at least initially assumed that they would be used against Japanese forces, rather than civilians.[46] Nevertheless, it seems that most top decision-makers, even if they had received some details about the devastating effects of the atomic test on 16 July, had to be confronted with the bomb's impact on civilian lives in reality before they began to give deep thought to its other implications. After all, as we shall see below, the casualties resulting from Hiroshima and Nagasaki did not differ decisively in quantity from the victims of other mass bombing of Japan (particularly of the Japanese capital), and even of Dresden. The results of the American Strategic Bombing Survey made in the following year cast doubt on the effects the pain thus inflicted had on the enemy's actual preparedness to surrender. (We will discuss this matter further in Chapter 2.) Rather contradictorily, the evidence of the US Strategic Bombing Survey suggests that, on the one hand, Japanese morale had declined to the point of disintegration even prior to the destruction of Hiroshima and Nagasaki, while on the other hand, the Japanese population outside the cities that had suffered most from the bombing were extremely surprised and shocked at the Emperor's broadcast announcing the decision to surrender.

So why did Truman insist on bombing the two cities? Gar Alperovitz has shown persuasively that at least for James Byrnes,

44. On the Hague Conventions, see Chapter 4.
45. Bernstein, 'Ike and Hiroshima', pp. 377–89. Bernstein does not criticise them for developing qualms retrospectively, but argues that there is little evidence to substantiate their claims that they opposed the bombing *at the time*, as they have retrospectively claimed.
46. Bernstein, 'Eclipsed by Hiroshima and Nagasaki', p. 154.

the Soviet factor was of utmost importance. Moreover, it is clear that Truman, his advisers and many other Americans perceived some analogy between the Japanese surprise attack on Pearl Harbor (without a declaration of war) and the bombing of Hiroshima and Nagasaki, again without any direct warning. The attack without warning on US military ships and the attack without warning on unprotected civilian populations may seem two very different events from the perspective of any outsider. This perception of an analogy was prevalent in the USA at the time, however, and is thus important in reconstructing the motives of the US decision-makers.[47] Moreover, it seems to be a perception widely shared by Americans[48] – themselves still reeling from the national trauma of Pearl Harbor – which has coloured their strategic thinking ever since. And while perhaps at the time nobody believed that *half a million* American lives would be lost in a piecemeal conquest of Japan, there is no reason to dismiss Truman's expression of concern over the haemorrhage of American lives and his earnest desire to cut American losses back to the very minimum. If there still had to be victims in this war, they should be on the side of the enemy, who, after all, had started the war – not a sentiment easy to condemn.

The question still remains whether the bombing was necessary. One of Alperowitz's chief critics, Robert James Maddox, continues to argue that it was: in his view, not only uncertainty about the fate of the Emperor, but the samurai tradition mentioned above, stood between the Japanese military and surrender, and the latter was not something the Americans could have changed through negotiations.[49] Yet majority opinion among historians and indeed many military eyewitnesses is today that it is doubtful that the nuclear use was totally necessary.[50] Even in 1954, Robert Butow concluded in his study *Japan's Decision to Surrender* that Hiroshima and Nagasaki, together with the Soviet entry into the war, 'did not produce Japan's decision to surrender, for that decision – in embryo – had long been taking shape'. They did, however, incite the Emperor to break out of the conventions which barred him from actively participating in government, and this unprecedented decision on his part in itself could only have been brought about by a cataclysmic event.[51]

47. Asada, 'The mushroom cloud', p. 181.
48. *Loc. cit.*
49. Maddox, *Weapons for Victory*, p. 146; and p. 8.
50. Cf. J. Samuel Walker, 'The decision to use the bomb: a historiographical update', *Diplomatic History* Vol. 14, No. 1 (Winter 1990).
51. Butow, *Japan's Decision to Surrender*, p. 233.

The most convincing interpretation is perhaps that of Saki Dockrill and Lawrence Freedman, who emphasised the shock effect of the atomic bombs in catalysing the crucial decision-making process in Japan, pushing the Emperor into overcoming the sacred rituals of imperial behaviour which barred him from intervening directly in politics and imposing a decision on 'his' government.[52] Counter-factual speculation about the unfolding of events in the absence of the use of the atomic bombs can never be taken as evidence, and our benefit of hindsight cannot ever fully allow us to understand the thoughts in the minds of Truman and others in the summer of 1945. It is thus difficult to see the bombs as anything but decisive weapons in the Pacific War, or as anything but weapons that would hasten an American victory, with fewer American losses than a continuation of conventional fighting would have brought.

Our overview of the historiography of the end of the Second World War in the Pacific has shown that in the view of most historians, the bombing of Hiroshima and Nagasaki influenced the timing of the Japanese surrender. But the question of whether it was an indispensable condition for the victory of the USA over Japan remains hotly debated among the specialists on the issue.

The suffering of the victims

Let us turn to another aspect of the rôle of Hiroshima and Nagasaki in the Second World War: the suffering of the victims. How outstanding a feature of the war were these particular two instances? How different were they from the fates of other civilian victims of violence?

Certainly, the experience of the citizens of these two cities differed in some aspects from the experience of other bombardments. The British mission to both sites after the end of hostilities recorded the following:

> Eye-witnesses in Hiroshima were agreed that they saw a blinding white flash in the sky, felt a rush of air and heard a loud rumble of noise, followed by the sound of rending and falling buildings. All also spoke of the settling darkness as they found themselves enveloped by a universal cloud of dust. Shortly afterwards they became

---

52. Lawrence Freedman and Saki Dockrill, 'Hiroshima: a strategy of shock', in Saki Dockrill (ed.), *From Pearl Harbor to Hiroshima: The Second World War in Asia and the Pacific* (London: Macmillan, 1994), pp. 191–211.

aware of fires in many parts of the city . . . The bomb exploded near its centre over a point approximately 300 yards from the T-shaped double bridge which is a conspicuous feature of Hiroshima; and thence spread its destruction with great uniformity . . . On August 6th, the authorities in Hiroshima were making preparations to meet what they believed to be a threatened incendiary attack; they were not prepared for a holocaust.

Nor were the authorities or citizens of Nagasaki better prepared:

> The few previous attacks on Nagasaki had been aimed at the ship-yards, so that most of the damage from them is outside the area of atomic bomb damage. As in Hiroshima, the initial blast damage done by the atomic bomb was followed by extensive fires, which here spread somewhat more slowly . . . Nagasaki presents the appearance of a city struck by a brief but tremendous hurricane.

The British team surveyed the effects, both immediate and medium-term, of the bombing:

> Both in Hiroshima and in Nagasaki, the scale of the disaster brought city life and industry virtually to a standstill. Even the most destructive conventional attacks, the incendiary raids on Hamburg in the summer of 1943 and on Tokyo in the spring of 1945, had no comparable effect in paralysing communal organization. Witnesses report a panic flight of population, in which officials and civil defence personnel joined, abandoning even the rescue services. All large-scale effort had to await the return of population, which was slow; there were still only 140,000 people in each city at the end of November [1945]. Even the clearance of debris and the cremation of the dead trapped in it do not seem to have been begun for more than a month, and members of the [British] Mission still stumbled upon undiscovered skeletons.[53]

Those killed in the conflagrations are variously said to have numbered between 70,000 and 90,000 in Hiroshima (with a later calculation of numbers, produced by the Peace Memorial in Hiroshima, given as 200,000, including long-term victims) and between 35,000 and 40,000 in Nagasaki (with a high estimate of 79,000).[54] At least as many people were severely burnt or irradiated or both; some died months or even years later in consequence of their exposure to the bomb. The victims in Hiroshima were not only Japanese, but

53. The British Mission to Japan, *The Effects of the Atomic Bombs at Hiroshima and Nagasaki* (London: HMSO, 1946), pp. 2f.
54. See table below; and for specific figures on Hiroshima and Nagasaki, see also Wainstock, *The Decision to Drop the Atomic Bomb*, pp. 87, 92.

included thousands of Korean prisoners sent to Hiroshima to per-
form forced labour; the population of Hiroshima prior to 6 August
1945 had been somewhere between 350,000 and 400,000, including
45,000 such Koreans.[55] An equally sad irony is that there were perhaps just under 5,000 Americans in Hiroshima – mainly children of
US citizens of Japanese origin living in Hiroshima, where they had
been sent by their parents who meanwhile were mostly interned in
camps within the USA.[56]

An American psychologist, Robert Jay Lifton, later wrote a study
based on interviews conducted with eyewitness-victims. Many of the
descriptions of being surrounded by death, fire, chaos, of streets
littered with corpses and bodies buried under piles or rubble, of over-
crowded hospitals and dispensaries, where these still existed, could
be from any other site of bombing – Tokyo, Hamburg, Dresden . . .
There were differences, however. These included the unprecedented
experience of the explosion – 'there was a flash . . . A kind of flash
I had never seen before, which I can't describe'[57] – and the effects
of irradiation on the survivors. One victim recounted, 'My father
smelled terribly because a foul matter came out of his wounds. I
remember complaining about the bad smell . . . and my own legs
began to swell and pain . . .'[58] There are frequent accounts of victims no longer feeling those parts of their skins and faces which
were burnt, irradiated and which melted away into blood and slime.[59]
The victims' skin often came off in large patches. Nausea was also
frequent (here the account of another survivor): 'The eight-year-
old [of the family] began to complain that her stomach was hot –
and she threw up – a dark liquid like coal-tar . . . and then the baby
began to throw up also . . .' Both subsequently died.[60] A further
survivor was badly injured herself: 'I had the sensation that my
whole body had been split . . . and asked my friend whether anything had happened to *my* face . . . [She] cried out to me and said
that I too had been burned . . . I touched my face and the skin stuck
to my finger . . . And when I touched my nose, I had no sensation

55. Lisa Yoneyama, 'Memory matters: Hiroshima's Korean atom bomb memorial
and the politics of ethnicity', in Hein and Selden (eds.), *Living with the Bomb*, p. 205.
56. Rinjiro Sodei, 'Were we the enemy? American Hibakusha', in Hein and Selden
(eds.), *Living with the Bomb*, pp. 232–59.
57. Robert Jay Lifton, *Death in Life: Survivors of Hiroshima* (New York: Basic Books,
1967), p. 23.
58. *Ibid.*, p. 41.
59. Hiroshima Peace Culture Foundation, *Eyewitness Testimonies* (Hiroshima: HPCF,
1991).
60. Lifton, *Death in Life*, p. 43.

of my nose but my finger felt something swollen and hot . . .'[61] All these effects of radiation had not been experienced before; the effects of the long-term consequences of irradiation and of subsequent lingering radioactivity created unprecedented fears. People who had initially supposed that they had escaped the terrible consequences of the nuclear blast found later that they had in reality been mortally affected:

> My daughter was working with her classmates at a place a thousand meters from the hypocenter . . . [On 7 August] she had no burns and only minor external wounds . . . on the fourth of September she suddenly became sick . . . She had spots all over her body . . . Her hair began to fall out. She vomited small clumps of blood many times. Finally she began to bleed all over her mouth. And at times her fever was very high . . . After ten days of agony and torture she died on September fourteenth . . .[62]

Those who survived were scarred for life both psychologically and physically. People with a whitish-yellow area of overgrown scar tissue disfiguring hands and particularly faces, the keloid, were to be found everywhere in Hiroshima. The keloid became the symbol of the *hibakusha*, the victims of the atom bomb.[63] The bomb also overshadowed their relationships with others. Thirty gravely handicapped babies were born to mothers who had survived the blast in Hiroshima while already pregnant, and were recognised as late victims of the blast; other cases were more difficult to assign exclusively to this cause.[64] Subsequently, people from Hiroshima and Nagasaki continued to fear that they would have disfigured, mutated children; people from other areas were afraid to get married to *hibakusha* as children from such marriages might be blighted by the long-term effects of radioactivity. *Hibakusha* themselves blamed subsequent illnesses on the effects of the nuclear blast, or feared them excessively, simply because others were known to have died of them.[65]

It is clear that the nationwide trauma suffered by the Japanese on account of the atomic bombing had lasting effects even on the minds of those who had not been directly affected. One macabre manifestation of this trauma is the series of disaster films produced by the Japanese cinema industry over the following years about the monster Godzilla which threatened and devastated Japan at regular

---

61. *Ibid.*, p. 175.   62. *Ibid.*, p. 59.   63. *Ibid.*, pp. 173–81.
64. Edward Pilkington, 'The day the black rain fell', *The Guardian* (3 August 1995).
65. Lifton, *Death in Life*, chs. IV and V.

intervals. Godzilla was dangerous less because of its height of 50 metres than because it had been irradiated by the H-bomb and spat nuclear fire of destruction on its victims – an allegorical attempt to represent the abstract notion of a nuclear threat.[66]

New generations of Japanese have grown up with a national trauma of anonymous persecution through artificially created horrors. On the whole, the Japanese seem to have internalised the identification with the *hibakusha*, but most seem not to reflect on the causality of the incineration of Hiroshima and Nagasaki: to this day, the link between Japanese expansionism, the atrocities committed by Japanese forces in China, the Philippines, and South East Asia and the attack on Pearl Harbor (dwarfed in terms of human suffering by the enormity of other Japanese military action) are rarely dwelt on as contributing factors. For the Japanese, the atom bombing thus seems to have acquired a meaning independent of time, space, causality of human action or even specific responsibility (unless it is interpreted vaguely as something white foreigners inflicted upon the Japanese). The 'Spirit of Hiroshima' is invoked as a timeless, general and unconditional condemnation of war and commitment to peace, regardless of cause or justification. Even for most Japanese, Hiroshima is thus almost an ahistorical phenomenon, linked only to an event of 6 August 1945, but not to the developments which started with the bombing of Pearl Harbor in 1941, if not with the Marco Polo Bridge incident in 1937 or even with the Japanese invasion of Manchuria. While the atomic bombing is regarded in Japan as the epitome of human suffering, it is compared with Auschwitz, rather than with the bombing of Hamburg or Dresden, and it is bizarrely taken out of the historical context of the Pacific War.[67]

For us, however, the question remains to what extent the use of atomic bombs on Hiroshima and Nagasaki differed from the firebombing of Tokyo, or from conventional bombing of Coventry, Rotterdam, Cologne or Dresden. To reflect on this question, let us glance at a comparative statistic of deaths through bombardment.

In 1940, 1,150 Germans were killed in air raids; in 1941 the figure was 3,253, and in 1942 it was 6,825. In 1943 it is assumed to have been 100,000, in 1944 – 180,000, and in 1945 – 115,000. Total German air raid victims thus numbered 406,000, including *Wehrmacht*,

---

66. Olivier Mauraisin, 'La saga Godzilla', *Le Monde* (25 Aug. 1997).
67. Ian Buruma, *The Wages of Guilt: Memories of War in Germany and Japan* (New York: Meridian/Penguin, 1995).

police, forced labourers and POWs.[68] In the bombing of Hamburg of 24 July–2 August 1943 (day and night, involving many hundreds of bomber sorties), 6,200 out of 8,382 acres of the city's buildings were destroyed, 42,600 people were left dead, 37,000 injured. A memorandum by Bomber Harris to Churchill on the results of the strategic bomber raids, written on 3 November 1943, noted that the following twenty cities had been 'virtually destroyed': Aachen, Barmen, Bochum, Cologne, Dortmund, Düsseldorf, Elberfeld, Emden, Essen, Hamburg, Hanover, Kassel, Köln-Deuz, Krefeld, Mannheim, Mühlheim, Mönchen-Gladbach/Rheydt, Rostock, and Remscheid; eighteen cities had been 'seriously damaged': Berlin, Bremen, Duisburg, Frankfurt, Hagen, Kiel, Karlsruhe, Lübeck, Mainz, Munich, Nuremberg, Oberhausen, Osnabrück, Rüsselsheim, Saarbrücken, Stettin, Stuttgart and Wilhelmshaven; and nine further cities had been 'damaged': Augsburg, Brunswick, Darmstadt, Flensburg, Friedrichshafen, Jena, Leipzig, Leverkusen, and Wismar.[69]

Accounts of the bombing of Tokyo are not actually very different from those of Hiroshima and Nagasaki, minus the suffering caused by the effects of radiation. A firestorm was caused in Tokyo as in some German cities, but was particularly devastating in Tokyo in view of the high percentage of houses built of wood, paper and highly combustible materials, rather than stone and bricks. A vivid summary of the 9 March 1945 bombings, which took two hours and resulted in the loss of only 14 US planes, is given by Dennis Wainstock, based on memoirs and other eye-witness accounts:

> On the ground, it was an inferno. Those who did not die in the flames choked to death or were trampled to death by escaping mobs. The winds whipped the fires into tornadoes of flames, racing from district to district 'leaping streets, firebreaks, and canals at dazzling speed' [according to the memoirs of an eye-witness]. Panic-stricken crowds tried to cross the bridges that crossed the Sumida River; many fell into the river and drowned, or were crushed to death . . . 'Fanned by the gale then prevailing,' said Marquis Kido, lord privy to the seal, 'the air bombings developed to an unexpected disaster.'[70]

The firestorm – one US pilot remembered, '[w]e headed into a great mushroom of boiling, oily smoke, and in a few seconds were

---

68. Olaf Groehler, 'Strategic air war's impact on German civilians', in Horst Boog (ed.), *The Conduct of the Air War in the Second World War: An International Comparison* (Oxford: Berg, 1992), p. 284.
69. Manfred Messerschmidt, 'Strategic air war and international law', in Boog (ed.), *The Conduct of the Air War in the Second World War*, pp. 306f.
70. Wainstock, *The Decision to Drop the Atomic Bomb*, p. 7.

TABLE 1.1   *Bombardment of cities during the Second World War*

City	Date of bombardment	Number of deaths
Rotterdam	14 May 1940	900
Coventry	14/15 Nov. 1940	554
Hamburg	24 July–2 Aug. 1943	42,600 (see above)
Berlin	3 Feb. 1945	22,000
Dresden	13/14 Feb. 1945	34,000
Tokyo	9/10 March 1945	88,800
Hiroshima	6 Aug. 1945	70,000 (90,000)
Nagasaki	9 Aug. 1945	35,000 (40,000)

Source: Der grosse Ploetz: Auszug aus der Geschichte von den Anfängen bis zur Gegenwart 31st edn. (Würzburg: Verlag Ploetz, 1991), pp. 876–916; for figures for Tokyo, Hiroshima and Nagasaki, see Laura Hein and Mark Selden, 'Commemoration and Silence', in Hein and Selden (eds.), *Living with the Bomb*, p. 4, and Wainstock, *The Decision to Drop the Atomic Bomb*, pp. 7, 87, 92.

tossed 5,000 feet into the air'[71] – the burnt bodies, the corpses in the river, all this does not read much differently from the events in Hiroshima and Nagasaki, and the casualty figures were comparable.

Even when it comes to intention, there is not much difference: the bombing of Warsaw by the *Luftwaffe* in 1939 was conducted on the following instructions from the General Staff: 'It will be important to achieve extensive destruction in the densely populated parts of the city during the first attack.'[72]

The conclusion is inevitable that the bombing of Tokyo by conventional means comes in the same category as that of Hiroshima, and surpasses the suffering of Nagasaki, and in this bleak reckoning, Hamburg and Dresden are not far behind. The difference is of course that, technically, only one aircraft was needed to inflict hell upon Hiroshima and Nagasaki, while hundreds of bomber sorties were needed for the 'conventional' destruction of Tokyo. And while the atom bombs of the Second World War were enormously powerful weapons compared with the conventional ordnance used, they were minuscule compared with the hydrogen bombs developed from the 1950s.

During the Second World War, 'over 1,500,000 tons of bombs were delivered to Germany by the Allies, of which clearly the largest portion came in the last two years of the war. Some 300,000 Germans

71. *Ibid.*, p. 8.
72. Quoted in Groehler, 'Strategic air war's impact on German civilians', p. 282.

were killed in the air raids and 780,000 seriously injured. Of the tonnage delivered, over 600,000 tons belonged to the USAAF, and about 900,000 to RAF Bomber Command. Close to 500,000 tons of the latter were devoted to the 'area' offensive.'[73] Before Hiroshima and Nagasaki, over 160,000 tons of ordinary bombs had been dropped on Japan, killing some 225,000 people and wounding another 640,000, mostly in the last nine months.[74]

The aerial bombardments during the Second World War shifted the effects of the war from the combatants to the civilians, who suffered more than in many previous wars, and certainly more than in any war experienced by these populations within living memory. The economic planners of the Second World War on all sides had planned on a more 'total' involvement of the population in the war effort, and on a more 'total' mobilisation of the industry. Only the National Socialists elevated this to a principle of Darwinian contest among the races (see Chapter 3). But the effects of this 'totalisation' of warfare were felt in all occupied countries, and also in Britain. The following table gives some indications of the proportions of civilians among the deaths of the populations of some of the belligerent countries (where known). In Poland, for example, by far the largest proportion of civilian victims died in *concentration camps*, and that number was tens of times larger than that of the victims of nuclear bombing. In Russia, civilians died in mass shootings, concentration camps, through starvation or collateral effects of the actual fighting. The Japanese invasion of China in 1937 is said to have resulted in the death of at 150,000 Chinese in Nanking alone – mainly civilians, killed at close range by the Japanese, with handguns, bayonets, or even swords.[75] These horrifying figures give an idea of what the most common mode of death was for civilians in the Second World War, with Hiroshima and Nagasaki coming relatively low down on the list.

How unique and outstanding was the suffering of the inhabitants of Hiroshima and Nagasaki, compared with those of other devastated cities? The bombing of the two Japanese cities was certainly special in that it was the last instance of massive bombardment and large-scale killing of the Second World War. For Americans

---

73. Quester, *Deterrence before Hiroshima*, p. 158; for a higher figure of the victims of German bombing raids, which includes military victims, see Groehler, 'Strategic air war's impact'.

74. Quester, *Deterrence before Hiroshima*, p. 171.

75. This is the number of victims buried by special teams according to R.J. Rummel, *China's Bloody Century* (New Brunswick: Transaction Books, 1991), p. 145.

TABLE 1.2   *Tonnage of bombs dropped*

German bombs dropped on UK	
1940	36,000 t
1941	21,860 t
1942	3,260 t
1943	2,298 t
1944	9,151 t
1945	761 t
Allied bombardment of Germany and German-occupied areas	
1940	14,600 t
1941	35,500 t
1942	53,755 t
1943	226,500 t
1944	1,188,580 t
1945	477,000 t
Tokyo, 9 March 1945	1,783 t incendiaries
Hiroshima	14,000,000 t = 14 kt
Nagasaki	21,000,000 t = 21 kt
For comparison:	
US LGM-30F *Minuteman II* ICBM	1,200,000,000 t = 1.2 Mt
Soviet SS-11 *Sego* ICBM	1,000,000,000 t = 1 Mt
US bombardment of Vietnam, 1962–1973	8,000,000 t
Gulf War 1991, Coalition bombardment of Iraq	85,000 t

Source: Der grosse Ploetz, pp. 876–916; and for specific figures on Hiroshima and Nagasaki, see also Wainstock, *The Decision to Drop the Atomic Bomb*, pp. 87, 92. For Vietnam figures: E.J. Tilford, *Setup: What the Air Force did in Vietnam and Why* (Alabama: Maxwell Air Force Base, 1991), p. 293, quoted in C.D. Coulthard-Clark, 'The air war in Vietnam: re-evaluating failure', in Alan Stephens (ed.), *The War in the Air* (Fairbairn, Australia: RAAF Base, 1994), p. 167. For Gulf War Figure: G. Waters, *Gulf Lesson One – The Value of Air Power: Doctrinal Lessons for Australia* (Canberra, 1992), quoted in C.D. Coulthard-Clark, 'The air war in Vietnam: re-evaluating failure', in Stephens (ed.), *The War in the Air*, p. 167.

and Europeans at the time, these were just two in a long series of reports of bombings which they had read in the press for the previous years, and if anything, they were eclipsed by the happy news of Japan's surrender. For most ordinary people, it took years for the significance of nuclear use to sink in – a Gallup poll conducted in

TABLE 1.3   *Total deaths during World War II*

Japan	1,800,000, of whom 600,000 civilians
China	4,300,000 (victims of conquest of Nanking by Japanese in 1937: variously estimated between12,000 and 300,000)
Philippines	1,000,000
Germany	5,250,000, of whom 500,000 civilians
USSR	20,600,000, of whom 7,000,000 civilians[76]
Poland	4,520,000, of whom 4,200,000 civilians, plus 1,500,000 (mainly civilian) victims in the Polish regions occupied by the USSR.
Britain	386,000, of whom 62,000 civilians
France	563,000, of whom 350,000 civilians
USA	259,000
Italy	330,000 (civilian figures not given)
Victims of the Holocaust	4,200,000–5,700,000 (est.)
Approx. total number of deaths in World War II	50,000,000

Source: Der grosse Ploetz, pp. 916, 946. Figures for France, China and the Philippines: Le Monde des Editions & The Economist: *La Deuxième Guerre Mondiale, récits et mémoires* (Paris: Le Monde, 1994).

Britain in December 1945 asked respondents about the changes brought about in their view by the splitting of the atom. Only 4 per cent expected changes in international relations and in warfare.[77]

Hiroshima and Nagasaki only stand at the top of a long list of cities which were more or less laid to waste in that war, and in terms of sheer numbers, the victims of Hiroshima and Nagasaki were by far surpassed by the numbers of human beings who were systematically killed during this war – not through aerial bombardment, but

76. High estimates for civilians killed (including through Stalinist terror, deportations, in camps and in transit) go up to 24.5 million, see R.J. Rummel, *Lethal Politics: Soviet Genocide and Mass Murder since 1917* (New Brunswick: Transaction, 1990), p. 179.
77. Christopher Driver, *The Disarmers: A Study in Protest* (London: Hodder & Stoughton, 1964), p. 16.

in gas chambers and mass shootings. This is not a book about the Holocaust or the Japanese atrocities committed in what Japan called the 'Greater East Asian Co-Prosperity Sphere', but quotations from eyewitness accounts of the Holocaust, of the rape of Nanking, or of air raids on Tokyo, Hamburg or Dresden are as defining of the Second World War as the events of 6 and 9 August 1945 in Japan. In the short-term perspective of the Second World War and the suffering of its victims, Hiroshima and Nagasaki contributed to a horrible pattern and stood out as the last bombings of the war. Otherwise, they were sadly not unique in the number of casualties, and if at all, then barely, in the quality of their suffering. They were merely a facet of the much larger phenomenon of 'total war', as we will show in the following chapters.

CHAPTER TWO

A Turning Point in Strategy?

Strategically, atomic bombing is part of aerial bombing as we already
know it, amplifying its effects, but retaining the main characteristics.
The new weapon has thus, to a greater or lesser degree, the features
of a normal air power weapon, its properties, its possibilities and its
limitations, its strength and its weaknesses . . .
(Admiral Raoul Castex, writing in 1945)[1]

This chapter will discuss how nuclear strategy developed from conventional strategy, and more specifically, from air power strategy.
We thus need to look both at the development of air power strategy
until and beyond the Second World War, and at the development
of nuclear strategy since 1945. This chapter therefore has three
sections, addressing three questions: how did the bombing of Hiroshima and Nagasaki differ (if indeed it did) from the principles of
conventional air bombardment as developed to that point? How
did conventional air strategy develop after the invention of nuclear
weapons? And how did nuclear strategy develop after August 1945?

Central to these questions will be the rôle of city bombing, and
the rationales given for and against adopting it. It is in the following chapter that we will seek to relate these rationales to concepts
of 'total war', and to the underlying ethical precepts on the basis of
which this form of war is advocated, condoned or condemned.

Air strategy until 1945

Until the advent of the aircraft, the occupation of land, through pain-
staking advances on the ground, had been a central and unavoidable

1. Raoul Castex, 'Aperçus de la bombe atomique', *Revue Défense Nationale* No. 9
(October 1945).

feature of war on the European landmass. The challenge was to break through enemy defences to occupy areas beyond them. The First World War was the extreme example of this: as the warring factions, more and more equal numerically and in terms of resources through the alliances they formed, mobilised their entire industries and populations, warfare had moved further and further towards stalemate, towards 'matériel battles' (*Materialschlachten*), as the Germans called them, in which the industrial resources of all opponents were thrown into the scales and slowly ground up on the battlefields, without allowing either side to make substantial territorial gains.

The aircraft promised the strategic revolution which would overcome this strategic impasse. It was thus a revolutionary new weapons system, a revolution in military technology, which could usher in a new era of warfare. The invention of aircraft, like that of a number of other weapons and weapons systems which constituted a breakthrough in technology and strategy, created the hope that this would be a 'decisive weapon', of the sort that would permit one's own side to win wars, suffering fewer losses than the enemy.

Periodically, weapons systems had produced such changes in warfare. Promising (or 'decisive') weapons or weapons systems included crossbow, longbow, gunpowder, pikes used in close formation, breech-loading rifle, machine-gun and tank, as well as chemical and nuclear weapons, and later, precision-guided munitions. Aircraft thus stood in a tradition of discoveries, and strategic thinkers were prepared for the idea that they might change warfare decisively, as other weapons systems had before. Indeed, they were looking for new decisive weapons. The appalling carnage of the First World War had led strategists to search systematically for new possibilities offered by any new inventions: they all agreed that the experience of the last war must not be repeated, and that in the event of a future war, the aim must be to win without accepting losses similar to those of 1914–18. While some focused on armoured vehicles as holding out the hope of making warfare shorter and more decisive in future, others concentrated on the new possibilities created by air power. How could the aircraft – with its great mobility, its flexibility and its growing reach – be put into the service of such a strategy?

EARLY ADVOCATES OF POPULATION TARGETING

Air power doctrine developed over a very brief period of time. The First World War saw the first serious casualties inflicted from the air, with well over a thousand (mainly civilian) casualties inflicted on England.[2] This left the British with an almost obsessive preoccupation with air strikes on towns and cities, to the point of arguing, absurdly, that 'England is still more vulnerable to attack by air than her neighbours.'[3] (This obsession was paralleled only by the fixation on air strikes in the USA from the late 1950s, while the other countries of Europe were much more vulnerable to and therefore preoccupied with ground-based attacks and invasions.)

But no sooner had aircraft been used in war than most of the fundamental ideas were shaped which have ever since been applied to air power, and later to nuclear strategy. One of them concerns the distinction between tactical and strategic targets. Tactical targets are usually taken to be targets that directly affect the outcome of battles on the ground or at sea. Tactical air support thus means the use of air power to support the operations of ground forces in the battle area or just beyond.

Strategic targets fall into another category. In his seminal work on the conventional origins of thinking on nuclear deterrence, George Quester has identified three crucial aims of strategic air operations: the first being the 'rapid infliction of great pain on civilian populations', and the second the hope that through *indirect* employment of air power against enemy military assets, not directly in the battle area, one 'might impose greater losses on the military forces of the defended territory than on the invading forces'.[4] The third aim was to disable the enemy's military means not at its cutting edge, but where it drew its physical fighting strength: the war industry, fuel, transport.

The third aim overlapped with the first: industrial areas are peopled by civilians, not only by metal workers in tank factories, but also by their families, and transport nodes tend to be found in cities. This is a crucial factor for our understanding of how air strategy shifted progressively from targeting purely *military* assets (Quester's aim No. 2) to targeting the industries which supplied armed forces and the transport lines through which they were supplied (Quester's aim No. 3) to that of targeting civilian populations in big cities (Quester's aim No. 1).

2. Malcolm Smith, *British Air Strategy Between the Wars* (Oxford: Clarendon, 1984), p. 17.

3. Sir Frederick Sykes, *From Many Angles* (autobiography) (London: Harrap, 1942), p. 561.

4. George H. Quester, *Deterrence before Hiroshima: The Airpower Background of Modern Strategy* (New York: John Wiley, 1966), p. 1.

The aim of inflicting pain on civilian populations was already spelled out in late 1914 in a memorandum by the Deputy Chief of the German Naval Staff, Rear-Admiral Paul Behncke, who urged air attacks with aeroplanes and Zeppelins on London, Dover, Portsmouth, Plymouth and Glasgow from bases on the Belgian and French coasts, arguing that they promised 'considerable material and moral results'.[5] And while Behncke thought that '[b]uildings of historic value, monuments, etc. are to be spared as far as possible', he concluded: 'We dare not leave untried any means of forcing England to her knees, and successful air attacks on London, considering the well-known nervousness of the public, will be a valuable measure.'[6] Also in late 1914, Fleet-Admiral Tirpitz, the German naval commander, proposed that in view of

> the great fragility and vulnerability of our airships, all available ships should be concentrated on London . . . The measure of the success will lie not only in the injury which will be caused to the enemy, but also in the significant effect it will have in diminishing the enemy's determination to prosecute the war, which will be greater than if the bombs are scattered singly.[7]

Was this an advocacy of population targeting or of government targeting (what would later be called 'decapitation')? We cannot be certain as to whether Tirpitz had thought it through and come down either way by 1914, while Behncke, as we have seen, was already advocating exploiting the 'nervousness of the public' in general. While Chancellor Bethmann-Hollweg worried about the 'unfavourable impression' Zeppelin raids would make 'on apparently undefended places',[8] the argument nevertheless prevailed that the undermining of civilian morale through bombardment might lead to domestic opposition in Britain to the continuation of the war. Indeed, Britons at first seemed to panic when exposed to German bombardment during the First World War. Lloyd George, later British Prime Minister, remembered a morning in July 1916 when

> a large fleet of German aeroplanes reached central London and dropped a number of bombs on the City and south of the Thames, killing and wounding numbers of people and causing a great deal of material damage. There was grave and growing panic amongst the population in the East End where the attack had taken place. At the slightest rumour of approaching aeroplanes, tubes and tunnels were

---

5. Quoted in D.H. Robinson, *The Zeppelin in Combat* (3rd edn., Henley-on-Thames: G.T.Foulis, 1971), p. 50.
   6. Quoted in *ibid.*, p. 52.   7. Quoted in *ibid.*, p. 54.   8. *Ibid.*, p. 65.

packed with panic-stricken men, women and children. Every clear night the commons around London were black with refugees from the threatened metropolis.[9]

(The famous and influential Italian air power strategist Giulio Douhet extrapolated from such experience that repeated bombing was intolerable and most likely to break down a population's moral resistance and to persuade them to accept surrender.[10])

Reprisals against enemy cities were considered by the British government during the First World War, but on balance it was judged that large numbers of aircraft could not be spared from their commitment to close air support for the forces on the ground, and that isolated raids would only make the Germans feel more vindictive. The British general Frederick Maurice was sceptical about bombing 'civil populations', because of the threat of retaliation, the danger that one's own population would be subject to reprisals. He did not think civilian casualties could be avoided altogether, as they would result from collateral damage to targeting 'railway junctions and stations, arsenals, centres of supply, and other places of military importance'. 'But such attack will be different in nature and effect from one which makes the civil population its chief target.'[11]

Not all British planners were so concerned to avoid city bombardment. In September 1917 Major Lord Tiverton, later one of the RAF's chief planners, was speculating about the 'moral effect' of targeting industry and workers from the air; in August 1918 he asked for a list of targets to be drawn up, selected to include mainly workers' quarters in large towns.[12] A memorandum of January 1918, sent by the Chief of the Imperial General Staff in London to the British military representative at the Supreme War Council, gave the gist of British government policy on bombing operations as follows:

> The policy intended to be followed is to attack the important German towns systematically . . . It is intended to concentrate on one town for successive days and then to pass to several other towns, returning to the first town until the target is thoroughly destroyed,

    9. David Lloyd George, *War Memoirs* vol. II (London: Odhams Press, n.d.), pp. 1104–5.
    10. Giulio Douhet, *The Command of the Air*, trans. Dino Ferrari (New York: Coward-McCann, 1942), pp. 276–8.
    11. Frederick Maurice, *British Strategy* (London: Constable, 1925, reprinted 1940), p. 70.
    12. Tami Davis Biddle, 'British and American approaches to strategic bombing: their origins and implementation in the World War II combined bomber offensive', in *Journal of Strategic Studies* Vol. 18, No. 1 (March 1995), p. 93.

or at any rate until the morale of workmen is so shaken that output
is seriously interfered with ... Long-distance bombing will produce
its maximum moral effect only if the visits are constantly repeated at
short intervals, so as to produce in each area bombed a sustained
anxiety. It is this recurrent bombing, as opposed to isolated and
spasmodic attacks, which interrupts industrial production and under-
mines public confidence.[13]

Indeed, at the time of the peace conferences after the First World
War, a memorandum circulated to the British Cabinet by the military noted:

These German officers and men are to be tried in time of peace
before a court exclusively composed of their ex-enemies for acts
which do not differ from those ordered to be carried out by the
Royal Air Force upon German towns. The orders given included
directions to bomb German towns (where any military objective was
situated), to destroy the industrial activities there by bombing during
the day, and to weaken the morale of the civilian inhabitants (and
thereby their 'will to win') by persistent bomb attacks which would
both destroy life (civilian and otherwise) and should, if possible,
originate a conflagration which should reduce to ashes the whole
town and thereby delete a whole centre of industrial activity.[14]

On the basis of this memorandum the British Cabinet decided not
to indict German airmen for bombing raids conducted during the
war.

With the armistice, British interest in city bombardment had by
no means disappeared. Major E. Childers and his collaborators,
who conducted a survey of the effects of bombing on Belgium after
the Great War, concluded that 'it is a simple deduction from experience to say that with the progress in air science that seems likely
to continue, it will be possible in a few years ... for a powerful
military nation ... to obliterate cities in a night and produce the
stunning moral effect necessary to victory'.[15]

The debate within British government and military circles was
complex, however. Not only were there those advocating city bombardment and those counselling against it for moral reasons. There

    13. Quoted in H.A. Jones, *The War in the Air* (Oxford: Clarendon Press, 1935),
Appendices, p. 26.
    14. Quoted in Klaus Maier, 'Total war and German air doctrine before the Second
World War' in Wilhelm Deist (ed.), *The German Military in the Age of Total War*
(Oxford: Berg, 1985), p. 211.
    15. Quoted in Biddle, 'British and American approaches to strategic bombing',
p. 97.

were also some who were unconvinced that it would produce the desired effect. General Milne, Chief of the Imperial General Staff, was sceptical about city bombing in order to target enemy morale, as '[t]he air raids on London, unpleasant as they were, had no result except to harden the Nation's will to war and they certainly exercised no deterrent effect on the many other large towns in England which were quite unaffected by the treatment suffered by London'.[16] Indeed, Lloyd George remembered,

> the undoubted terror inspired by the death-dealing skies did not swell by a single murmur the demand for peace. It had quite the contrary effect. It angered the population of the stricken towns and led to a fierce demand for reprisals. [17]

Nevertheless, in the inter-war period the chief of the RAF, Marshal Sir Hugh (later Viscount) Trenchard, and Air Vice-Marshal Sir Frederick Sykes,[18] who both preceded and succeeded Trenchard as Chief of the British Air Staff, proposed that city bombing should be elevated as the RAF's mission. Sykes drew up a document in December 1918, entitled 'Air Power Requirements for the Empire'. In Sykes' view, 'The objectives of [air] striking forces will be nerve centres, the armies and navies of the opponent, the population as a whole, his national *moral[e]*, and the industries, without which he cannot wage war.'[19] While for Sykes population bombing arguably came after targeting governments (or whatever else might be implied by 'nerve centres') and armed forces, Trenchard clearly prioritised population bombing. In 1928, during his second period as Chief of the Air Staff, he wrote his famous memorandum for the Chiefs of Staff Sub-Committee on the rôle of an air force in times of war, and this deserves to be quoted at length. It emphasised air attacks on the 'vital centres of communication and production of war munitions', explaining that the 'objective of air action is to paralyse the enemy's production centres of war munitions of all sorts and to interrupt the whole of his transport and communication'. 'The aim of the Air force is to break the means of enemy resistance through attacks on targets chosen as most appropriate for the reaching of this aim.'[20] (Elsewhere, Trenchard wrote: 'direct

16. Text in Charles Webster and Noble Frankland, *The Strategic Air Offensive Against Germany* (London: HMSO, 1961), IV, p. 80.
17. Lloyd George, *War Memoirs*, II, p. 1105.
18. Malcolm Smith, '"A matter of faith": British strategic air doctrine between the Wars', *Journal of Contemporary History* Vol. 15, No. 3 (July 1980), pp. 405–21.
19. Sykes, *From Many Angles*, p. 561.
20. Text in Webster and Frankland, *Strategic Air Offensive*, IV, pp. 71–6.

air attack on the centres of production, transportation and communications must succeed in paralysing the life and effort of the community and therefore in winning the war'.[21])

In his 1928 memorandum, Trenchard noted:

> In my view, the object of all three Services is the same, to defeat the enemy *nation*, not merely its army, navy or air force. For an army to do this, it is almost always necessary as a preliminary step to defeat the enemy's army, which imposes itself as a barrier that must first be broken down. It is not, however, necessary for an air force, in order to defeat the enemy *nation*, to defeat its armed forces first. Air power can dispense with that intermediate step, can pass over the enemy navies and armies . . .[22]

> It will be harder to affect the morale of an Army in the field by air attack than to affect the morale of the Nation by air attacks on its centres of supply and communications as a whole . . . These are the points at which the enemy is weakest. The rifleman or the sailor is protected, armed and disciplined, and will stand under fire. The great centres of manufacture, transport and communications cannot be wholly protected. The personnel, again, who man them are not armed and cannot shoot back . . .[23]

Trenchard pondered whether it was reconcilable with the draft Hague Conventions[24] on the Conduct of War to bomb civilian populations. He argued that the primary purpose of such raids would not be to kill civilians, but to achieve the legitimate aim of destroying the enemy's means of waging war – the factories producing aircraft, tanks and other military equipment, the depots where they were stocked, the railway depots, docks and harbours and the transport links. Of course there would be collateral casualties, but he claimed to believe that these could be limited. 'What would be illegitimate, being against the humanitarian imperatives', Trenchard conceded in his memorandum, 'would be the blind bombing of a town with the only aim of terrorising the civilian population.' But he claimed that it was another matter altogether to terrorise the workers in munitions factories, with the aim of getting them to lay down their work and go on strike. They were part of the war effort as much as soldiers, sailors or airmen. The bottom line of his argument was thus that terrorising workers in munitions factories by

21. Quoted in R.J. Overy, 'Air power and the origins of deterrence theory before 1939', *Journal of Strategic Studies* Vol. 15, No. 1 (March 1992), p. 75.
22. Text in Webster and Frankland, *Strategic Air Offensive*, IV, p. 72, my italics.
23. *Ibid.*, pp. 74f.   24. See Chapter 4.

attacking their homes (but how was this possible without the 'collateral damage' of the deaths of many of their families?) was not only permissible but a key aim. The recognition that such a course might in fact result in more horror and destruction than implied in other parts of the memorandum comes across in the passage in which Trenchard admonished his colleagues to stifle qualms, for the enemy would most certainly resort to such measures: 'In a battle for life and death, all available arms have always been used, and will always be.' It would be nice, he added, to have a restriction of the use of air warfare, but he did not believe that such a restriction was practicable.[25]

Trenchard's apparent concerns about legal considerations must be offset against his blatantly chauvinist views: still with the French in mind as the possible enemy in a future war, Trenchard had written earlier that 'though there would be an outcry' in Britain if British towns were bombed, 'the French in a bombing duel would probably squeal before we did. That was the really final thing. The nation that would stand being bombed the longest would win in the end.'[26] (He was still indulging in similar comparisons, this time between the British and the Germans, again favourable to the British 'mentality', in 1941.[27]) This was not very different from the thinking of the German air theorist Dr Robert Knauss, who was well-liked by the National Socialist régime: Knauss wrote in May 1933 on the need for a 'German Air Fleet':

> Terror-bombing of enemy capitals or an air offensive against industrial areas will produce moral collapse so much earlier, the weaker national cohesion is, the more the urban masses follow materialistic interests and the more these masses are divided by socio-political tensions.

For Knauss this implied that it was the (as he thought, materialistic) British, rather than the Germans, who would cave in first under air bombardment.[28] Albert Speer after the war thought that unlike the Germans, 'Other peoples, as perhaps the Italians, would have certainly collapsed under a similar series of night attacks and would have been unable to undertake further war production.'[29] But Knauss,

25. Text in Webster and Frankland, *Strategic Air Offensive*, IV, p. 72.
26. Quoted in Biddle, 'British and American approaches to strategic bombing', p. 99.
27. *Ibid.*, p. 116.
28. Quoted in Maier, 'Total war and German air doctrine', p. 213.
29. Text in Webster and Frankland, *Strategic Air Offensive*, IV, p. 383.

Speer and Trenchard were not the only ones thinking in such Social Darwinist categories.[30]

Nor were the recommendations for air strategy which they derived from this thinking limited to them. Trenchard for one was well aware of French Marshal Ferdinand Foch's views about air power: Foch, who had been the Supreme Allied Commander during the First World War, had noted: 'The potentialities of aircraft attacks on a large scale are almost incalculable, but it is clear that such attack, owing to its crushing moral effect on a Nation, may impress the public opinion to a point of disarming the Government and thus becoming decisive.'[31] This idea that one could bomb the enemy's population into rising in rebellion against the government, which became so important in British and American thinking, was thus shared also in France. It was further shared by Giulio Douhet in Italy, who argued that by surmounting the obstacle of the front line, where the enemy's ground forces were concentrated, aircraft could carry the war far into the enemy's territory and attack his cities, his civilian populations at home. For Douhet the main task for the air force was now the heavy bombing of the enemy's civilian populations, with everything else subordinated to this.

> By virtue of this new weapon, the repercussions of war are no longer limited by the farthest artillery range of surface guns, but can be directly felt for hundreds and hundreds of miles over all the lands and seas of nations at war. No longer can areas exist in which life can be lived in safety and tranquillity, nor can the battlefield any longer be limited to actual combatants. On the contrary, the battlefield will be limited only by the boundaries of the nations at war, and all of their citizens will become combatants, since all of them will be exposed to the aerial offensives of the enemy. *There will be no distinction any longer between soldiers and civilians.*[32]

Taking his own ideas to their logical extreme, Douhet increasingly convinced himself that bombardment from the air was so powerful and so unbeatable a weapon that ground forces were at best needed for supplementary mopping-up operations, but were no longer needed to defeat the enemy. He began to advocate the scaling down of army and navy, which would no longer have crucial rôles to play in future war.[33]

---

30. Biddle, 'British and American approaches to strategic bombing', p. 102.
31. Foch quoted by Trenchard in his memorandum, in Webster and Frankland, *Strategic Air Offensive*, IV, p. 75.
32. Douhet, *The Command of the Air*, pp. 9–10, my emphasis.
33. *Ibid.*, p. 30.

Douhet's thinking had an important impact beyond the frontiers of his own country, including on US concepts of strategic bombardment.[34] But several contemporaries of Douhet developed similar ideas, quite probably independently. These included in Britain (apart from Trenchard and Sykes) the military writer J.F.C. Fuller; in the USSR Mikhail Vassilievitch Frunze, and in the USA William Mitchell. What all these men had in common was the experience of the First World War, and they were determined to do their best to avoid any repetition of that experience. They tended to welcome aircraft as a wholly beneficial innovation, assuming that future war involving air bombardment of cities would result in fewer deaths – at least among the combatants – than World War I. Some even persuaded themselves that absolute numbers of deaths could be reduced in this way. In the words of Fuller,

> If a future war can be won at the cost of two or three thousand of the enemy's men, women and children killed, in place of over 1,000,000 men and incidentally several thousands of women and children, as was the case in France during the recent war, surely an aerial attack is a more humane method than the existing traditional type.[35]

Captain Basil Liddell Hart, another British strategic thinker who like Fuller would become more famous for his advocacy of the development of tank warfare, also praised the options created by air warfare. Just as in the Trojan War Paris had killed the near-invulnerable Achilles by homing in on his one vulnerable spot, countries might now attack their enemy's cities, their civilian populations, as the weakest part of his society, in view of 'the panic and disturbance that would result from a concentrated blow dealt by a superior air fleet'.[36] Extrapolating from the reactions in British cities to air raids during the First World War, he concluded:

> Provided that the blow be sufficiently swift and powerful, there is no reason why within a few hours, or at most days from the commencement of hostilities, the nerve system of the country inferior in air power should not be paralysed. A modern state is such a complex and interdependent fabric that it offers a target highly sensitive to a sudden and overwhelming blow from the air.[37]

34. Bernard Brodie, *Strategy in the Missile Age* (Princeton, N.J.: Princeton University Press, 1959), p. 73.
35. J.F.C. Fuller, *Reformation of War* (London: Hutchinson, 1923), p. 150.
36. B.H. Liddell Hart, *Paris, or the Future of War* (London: Kegan Paul, Trench, Trubner & Co.: 1925), p. 45.
37. *Ibid.*, pp. 46f.

In the Soviet Union, thinking was also devoted to the possibilities created by air warfare. Mikhail Vassilievitch Frunze was one of the leading figures there. He participated in the October Revolution in Moscow in 1917 and became Commissar of War after Trotsky, opposing the return to a classical army which both Lenin and Trotsky wished. One of his most famous works is called *Front and Rear in the War of the Future*, originally published in the year of his death, 1925. In it, he emphasised that 'the outcome of the war will be decided not only on the front but also on the lines where the civilian forces of the country are found': this, he pointed out, had become possible not least through the development of the air force. The air force could be decisive, totally changing any earlier notions of where the 'front' and where the 'hinterland' of military action was. Again, we find in his writing the idea that the whole population had to be mobilised in such a war, and was at the same time its target.

A.I. Egorov, who shared Tukhachevsky's interests, became Chief of the Red Army Staff; but he influenced the 'Provisional Directives for the Organisation of Battle in Depth' adopted by the Soviet General Staff in 1933 with a greater emphasis on the bombing of industry, and thus, by implication, of cities. One of the directives read:

> In the event of an attack on the USSR by a capitalist power or Coalition ... the task of our air forces is to strike at the roots of mobilisation and at the concentration of enemy armies, and to destroy the economic-industrial life of whole regions, primarily those of military significance.[38]

In the writing of Douhet, Sykes, Trenchard, Fuller, Liddell Hart, Frunze and Egorov one thus finds two key ideas which foreshadow thinking about nuclear weapons: the idea (explicitly welcomed) that one could use aircraft (later nuclear weapons) against enemy civilian populations and industry which in an industrial age constituted what Clausewitz would have called the 'centre of gravity' of the enemy's war effort; and the idea that air power (later nuclear weapons) in itself might decide the war, rendering the other services of the armed forces unimportant or considerably less important. (Trenchard and Sykes, typical products of the British bureaucratic system with its penchant for silencing internal opposition by pre-emptively countering its arguments, glossed over this last point, denying that they thought the air force could win a war on its own, even if all their other *dicta* suggest that they were quite convinced

38. Quoted in R.A. Mason and John W.R. Taylor, *Aircraft, Strategy and Operations of the Soviet Air Force* (London: Jane's, 1986), p. 127.

that the air force would henceforth be the decisive weapon[39]. What all four strategists had in mind was clearly another major war, in which all sides would fight with full strength, drawing on all their industrial and manpower resources.

The rationale for the attacks on Hiroshima and Nagasaki thus existed well before the invention of nuclear weapons, and it existed among British, German, French, Italian and Soviet military leaders, that is in most technologically advanced civilisations, no matter what their generally prevailing ideology – democracy, fascism or communism. It was thus not limited to the more authoritarian societies, or to those which generally valued human life less. Instead, it was an international trend among some military thinkers, whose thinking arguably developed along similar lines, separately from the ethics and ideals of their own societies. In more countries than just in Germany (where the military of the 1918–33 Weimar Republic has been described as a state within the state), at least sections of the military leadership thus seem to have held beliefs distinct from the ethos of society at large.

DETERRENCE AND OTHER USES OF THE AIR FORCES

There were other possible ways of reflecting upon the utility of air power. In the USSR, key ideas of Frunze's were taken up and developed further by other thinkers within the Soviet Armed Forces, including Mikhail Tukhachevsky, Director of Red Army Ordnance, who was later executed in the purges. Tukhachevsky was fascinated by the opportunities offered by the use of aircraft over long distances: to attack enemy installations far behind the front line, and to transport soldiers far into enemy territory.[40] He, for one, was not interested in population bombing.

We find alternative ideas also in the writing of the US aviation pioneer William Mitchell. It is perhaps not accidental that it was an American who, not having taken part in the many years of trench warfare in Flanders, was less fixated in his thinking on the idea of using aircraft to strike at the enemy's population centres. Admittedly, Mitchell shared with Douhet, Sykes, Trenchard and Frunze the excitement about the idea that through air warfare 'the whole country becomes the frontier'. Yet in other respects, his approach differed. One of his most important books was published in the year he was dismissed from the US armed forces, and its title was

39. Malcolm Smith, *British Air Strategy Between the Wars* (Oxford: Clarendon, 1984), p. 66.
40. Quoted in Mason and Taylor, *Soviet Airforce*, p. 156.

*Winged Defence: the Development and Possibilities of Modern Air Power
– Economic and Military.*[41] Here Mitchell argued his case that the
air force was not a mere auxiliary service to other forces, but had
decisive missions of its own, not tied directly to those of other
services. Like Douhet, he emphasised the effect of paralysis which
both thinkers imagined the threat of bombardment would bring to
a society. Unlike Douhet, Trenchard, Sykes and Frunze, Mitchell
hoped that this would work, on many occasions, without the loss of
too many lives. Writing from an American perspective, and despite
what must have been his knowledge of the losses to European countries caused by the Great War, he was impressed by the relatively
smaller losses the USA had suffered in the First World War than in
the American Civil War. His conclusion was that wars were becoming less bloody, the further one was away from the battlefield.
Therefore, he thought, air warfare did not necessarily have to be
particularly cruel. Indeed, he nurtured the hope that civilian casualties could be kept relatively limited. He thought that the threat of
bombardment might in itself be enough of a coercive measure to
make the enemy's population do one's will, to paraphrase Clausewitz.
The targeting he advocated also aimed less at the populations than
at production centres – and here he was unduly optimistic about
bomber crews being able to differentiate between the two.

One of the British strategists most closely associated in the 1950s
with the advocacy of strategic use of nuclear weapons, the later
Chief of the RAF Sir John Slessor, was also interested in using
aircraft in missions other than city bombing. Writing in 1936, when
still a wing commander, he extensively studied the small air operations of the First World War to draw from them conclusions about
the ideal army of the future, in which 'the long-range [air] striking
force, which from behind the cover of the frontier defences will
carry the war into the enemy's country, [will] cut the communications behind his fighting troops, and co-operate with the armoured
force in the counter-attack'.[42]

Early explicit criticism of city bombing strategies can also be found
in Britain. Here it came both from some of Trenchard's colleagues
within the military, such as, at least initially, Charles Portal, who
later had a stellar career comparable to that of Trenchard within
the RAF, and from individuals outside the armed forces. Once the
Second World War was underway, however, Portal was won over to

41. (New York, 1925).
42. J.C. Slessor, *Air Power and Armies* (London: Humphrey Milford/Oxford University Press, 1936), p. 215.

the cause of city bombing, provided an impact on the German war effort could be demonstrated.[43] Other critics were more persistant in their views, and produced arguments based on moral or practical considerations. One of the chief British critics of nuclear strategy, Labour MP Philip Noel-Baker, was afraid even before the Second World War that mutual bombing would 'obliterate the civilisation in which we live'.[44] Another British critic, Jonathan Griffin, even in the inter-war period spoke of a 'balance of terrors', because he thought it would not hold but lead to disaster, since both sides would be tempted to strike first.[45] Griffin was not alone in his mistrust of the balance of terror: at the Disarmament Conference in 1932, US President Herbert Hoover still proposed the abolition of the bomber.[46] (As later with nuclear weapons, the argument won out that there was no point in abolishing the bomber, because it could always be replaced by civil aviation adapted in wartime.[47])

Other criticism was levelled at the city bombing idea for more technical reasons, crucially, the fear of reprisals by the country so attacked. All sides studied possibilities of defence against enemy air attacks, but were initially quite pessimistic. General Smuts mused in September 1917, in response to night attacks:

> [T]he only proper defence is offence. We can only defend this island effectively against air attacks by offensive measure, by attacking the enemy in his air bases on the Continent and in that way destroying his power of attacking us across the Channel.[48]

The pessimism of many early air strategists about the ability to defend against bomber planes was matched by their concomitant optimism about the chances of aircraft penetrating into enemy air space in most conditions. In 1921 Douhet asserted that

> Nothing man can do on the surface of the earth can interfere with a plane in flight, moving freely in the third dimension. All the influences which have conditioned and characterised warfare from the beginning are powerless to affect aerial action.[49]

43. Biddle, 'British and American approaches to strategic bombing', p. 103.
44. Philip Noel-Baker, 'A national air force is no defense', in Storm Jameson (ed.), *Challenge to Death* (New York: E.P. Dutton, 1935), quoted in Quester, *Deterrence before Hiroshima*, p. 88.
45. Jonathan Griffin, *Glass Houses and Modern War* (London: Chatto and Windus, 1938), p. 75, quoted in Quester, *Deterrence before Hiroshima*, p. 73.
46. Quester, *Deterrence before Hiroshima*, p. 74; see also Basil Collier: *A History of Air Power* (London: Weidenfeld and Nicolson, 1974), ch. 3.
47. Prime Minister Stanley Baldwin, HofC Deb. (10 Nov. 1932), col. 631–8.*
48. Quoted in Jones, *The War in the Air*, V, p. 493.
49. Douhet, *The Command of the Air*, p. 9.

Writing in the mid-1920s, his American colleague William Mitchell also thought that no means could be found to shoot down aircraft. Mitchell and Douhet did not foresee the development of radar and the contribution that early warning of an air raid could make to allowing societies to function despite the constant fear of air raids. Neither spent much time thinking about the possibility of attacking enemy air forces while still on the ground on enemy air strips. Trenchard in 1928 thought that it would be much more sensible to destroy the industry that produced aircraft than to try to target existing aircraft on their airfields, or to engage in wasteful air battles. Prime Minister Stanley Baldwin addressed the House of Commons with a famous speech in 1932, in which he expressed his fear that '[t]he bomber will always get through'. From this he concluded, like Smuts before him: 'The only defence is in offence, which means that you have to kill more women and children more quickly than the enemy if you want to save yourselves.'[50]

Even at the time, there were people who doubted that getting one's 'retaliation' in first (in other words pre-empting an enemy attack through a counter-attack) would work (quite apart from worrying about its morality) – and who thought that threatening reprisals was not enough, perhaps, to prevent an enemy from attacking one's own cities. General E.B. Ashmore, who had commanded London's air defences during the First World War, did not think any threats of retaliation were comforting; instead, he wanted to promote air defences.[51] Given the development of radar and anti-aircraft munitions fired from the ground ('FLAK', from the German *Flug Abwehr Kanonen*, anti-aircraft guns), air defences became much more effective than was foreseen by Douhet, Mitchell, or even Baldwin. When dealing merely with conventional ordnance, air defences could make a very decisive difference, as the Second World War would show. We shall see, however, that this reasoning did not necessarily hold for nuclear ordnance.

These and indeed earlier examples demonstrate that it was not the entire military leadership of the Western liberal democracies and the USSR (or indeed Germany, as we shall see presently), who supported the deliberate targeting of civilian populations, and welcomed the option of city bombing that aircraft created. And it would be as unfair to associate all RAF leaders with the views of Trenchard as it would be to suppose all the leaders of the *Luftwaffe*

50. Hof C Deb. (10 Nov. 1932), col. 631–8.*
51. Quester, *Deterrence before Hiroshima*, pp. 68f.

subscribed to Hitler's racism. But the disquieting fact remains that whatever attitudes the respective air forces had in the inter-war period, high moral standards, where they existed, did not survive long into the actual Second World War. Germans, Britons and Americans equally resorted to city bombing.

THE PRACTICE: INTER-WAR USE OF AIR POWER AND STRATEGIC BOMBING IN WORLD WAR II

Aircraft were used against civilian populations as much as against armed forces in several smaller wars in different parts of the globe between the First and Second World Wars.[52] Air power was used extensively in the Spanish Civil War; the main casualties being inflicted by powers external to the conflict: the German, Italian, and Soviet air forces who used the Spanish conflict as an occasion to perfect their own air forces' performance. Most memorably, on 26 April 1937, German aircraft bombed the small town of Guernica on a market day, killing perhaps 500 civilians, leaving many wounded,[53] causing public revulsion comparable to that associated now with Hiroshima and Nagasaki. Indeed, until Europe experienced worse in the Second World War, 'Guernica' was the symbol of the criminal abuse of air bombardment and of the civilian suffering evoked now by Hiroshima and Nagasaki. Pablo Picasso's famous painting became a visual reference to this event, still immediately recognisable by a large European public at the end of the twentieth century.[54]

City bombing was not actually the preferred strategy of the German *Luftwaffe* in the Spanish Civil War: Guernica was a small town, not a major city, and it was bombed because it was a transport node. The German air force took away from this experience the lesson that the most profitable form of bombing was air support for ground operations, not so much in the form of close air support by fighter planes, but joint operations, where army and air force co-operated with closely harmonised military aims. It was mainly other

52. Malcolm Smith, *British Air Strategy Between the Wars* (Oxford: Clarendon, 1984), p. 44.

53. Figures give here are from James S. Corum, 'The Luftwaffe and the coalition air war in Spain, 1936–1939', *Journal of Strategic Studies* Vol. 18, No. 1 (March 1995), p. 71; the number of deaths has variously been estimated as between that figure and 1,700, with many more wounded, see Ed Vulliamy's article 'For whom does the bell toll now?' *The Guardian* (15 July 1995).

54. See Martin Rowson's illustration in *The Guardian* (15 July 1995) for Ed Vulliamy's article 'For whom does the bell toll now?'

forces who contributed to the bombing of big cities in Spain during
this period, above all the two Spanish forces themselves (e.g. the
Nationalists bombed Malaga and Badajoz, the Loyalists bombed
Seville, Saragossa, Cordoba and Oviedo), and the Italians (e.g. with
the bombing of Barcelona), who followed the Douhetian preference for the bombing of urban targets.[55] The Italians also targeted
civilians as much as barely armed combatants in the Italian war of
conquest of Ethiopia (Abyssinia), October 1935–May 1936. British
forces used a similar strategy in controlling Britain's Middle Eastern dependencies in the 1930s. Japan used its air forces (under
army and navy command respectively) against China from 1937 to
1939, bombing Beijing, Shanghai, Nanking, Hankow and Chungking, each time inflicting large numbers of casualties.

Turning back to the European theatre, under the influence of
Sir Hugh Trenchard, the RAF developed the doctrine which put
great emphasis on the targeting of population centres. The RAF's
doctrine was enshrined in the *Royal Air Force War Manual*, Part I:
Operations. It was first drawn up in this form in 1928, and the version which held for British operations during the Second World
War was the updated version of February 1940. An RAF staff exercise of March 1933 aimed to break enemy morale by 'striking at
targets located in thickly populated areas'.[56] The RAF *War Manual*
of 1935 noted 'that the air offensive should strike at the "nerve
centres, main arteries, heart and brain" of an enemy economic and
administrative system, with the aim of "weakening his resistance
and his power to continue the war"'.[57] In 1939 the RAF argued:

> It is of the utmost importance that, when we do initiate air action on
> a serious scale, we must be allowed to do so in the most effective way
> and against those objectives which we consider will have the greatest
> effect in injuring Germany, unhampered by the inevitable fact that
> there is bound to be incidental loss, and possibly heavy loss of civil-
> ian life.[58]

In the February 1940 version, war was described as a nationwide
concern which equally required a nationwide effort, i.e. it had to
involve the entire population and economy. Similarly, the will on
both sides to persevere in the war effort was crucial, and defeat was
defined as the loss of the will to defend oneself on the part of the

55. Corum, 'The Luftwaffe and the coalition air war in Spain', pp. 68–90.
56. Quoted in Biddle, 'British and American approaches to strategic bombing',
p. 103.
57. Overy, 'Air power and the origins', p. 83.   58. Quoted in *ibid.*, p. 84.

people or government. This state of affairs could be reached, it was argued, through outright defeat of the armed forces, but also through a blockade which might lead to unrest among the population, or war-weariness caused by large-scale internal destruction. War would thus become a contest of morale – and the morale of the British was regarded as an asset, indeed as a weapon in the war effort, just as much as the air force was itself. The RAF's bombers were regarded as the principal means of waging air warfare, and offensive bombing raids were seen as the main task of the air forces. For this purpose, targets were to be selected which would undermine the enemy's will to resist. Undermining the morale of the enemy, by terrorising the enemy population with what came to be known as 'strategic bombardments', thus became crucial to RAF doctrine.

On the eve of the Second World War, British military planners assumed that the Royal Air Force would mainly serve to interdict and destroy the enemy's production centres and morale, both essentially co-terminous with enemy cities.[59] Targets for RAF bombardment were to be chosen to fit in with the overall war plan or 'grand strategy' of Britain. The historian Malcolm Smith has summarised RAF planning as based on the assumption that '[a]ir power should leap over the enemy defences and proceed straight to the vital centres on which the ability to wage war depended, thus creating the preconditions for the defeat both of the enemy army and air force in a general advance.' Nevertheless, the Trenchardian theory also allowed the possibility that 'mass long-range attack by bombers' might in itself give Britain decisive superiority over her enemies, with surface forces merely occupying the defeated territory. Thus 'Trenchardism blurred the classical analytical distinction between "tactical" and "strategic" . . .'[60] Or, one might say, it blurred the distinction between the air force as auxiliary to the ground forces (by destroying the enemy's cities, the wells of industrial and human resources from which reinforcements flowed) and the air force as decisive force which would extinguish the enemy's vital powers by taking war to the heart of his society. Whether this meant targeting the government, the main urban populations, or the houses and families of munition workers, the effects were largely indistinguishable (except that in targeting Hamburg or the Ruhr, one was clearly not targeting the German government).

59. Biddle, 'British and American approaches to strategic bombing', and W. Hays Parks, '"Precision" and "area" bombing: Who did which, and when?', in *Journal of Strategic Studies* Vol. 18, No. 1 (March 1995).
60. Smith, *British Air Strategy*, pp. 269f.

When the Second World War broke out, the RAF did not resort immediately to strategic bombing, even though its doctrine emphasised it so greatly. Opponents of Trenchard's emphasis on city bombing had made their impact on British planning. The 'Inskip Report', named after the Minister for the Co-ordination of Defence, Sir Thomas Inskip, put the emphasis for the RAF on air defence rather than on trying to effect a 'knockout blow' against Germany.[61] Initially, the Western air plans selected militarily relevant targets only.

But the heavy losses incurred by the RAF in December 1939 when following this choice of priorities posed the question of how to cope with enemy air defences. The RAF decided to move to night operations, and this in turn ruled out accurate bombing, as the night-targeting capability of bombers was still poor. Precision attacks against small military targets were thus impossible. A whole range of different targets was experimented with, but given the technical limitations, the prioritisation of inanimate targets still resulted in massive collateral civilian damage. Webster and Frankland have commented on the impreciseness of the language used by British air power strategists from the very beginning until way into the Second World War: aims such as the 'breakdown of morale', the 'final collapse' of Germany, 'general dislocation' or 'internal disruption' of its workforce particularly in the war-relevant industries could not be translated into distinct targeting patterns. The United States Special Observer Group in London were critical of this, being told at the end of 1941 that the RAF's aim was to attack German morale by means of 'the disruption of transportation, living and industrial facilities of the German population'. No attempt was made any longer to pretend that old people and children could somehow be spared in these attacks.[62] On 14 February 1942, Bomber Command, with the support of Prime Minister Winston Churchill, completed the shift to population targeting.[63] Air Chief Marshal Sir Arthur Harris, who was appointed to head the British strategic air command about a week later, strongly supported this turn away from concentrating on military land campaigns and towards concentration of 'our air power against the enemy's weakest spots' – their cities, 'the vital part of Germany'. He noted: 'The utter destruction of Lübeck and Rostock, the practical destruction of Cologne . . .

---

61. Biddle, 'British and American approaches to strategic bombing', p. 105. Inskip did not change British production priorities from the production of bombers to the production of fighter aircraft, however, as Sebastian Cox has pointed out to me.
62. Webster and Frankland, *Strategic Air Offensive*, I, p. 298.
63. Biddle, 'British and American approaches to strategic bombing', p. 117.

point the certain, the obvious, the quickest and easiest way to over-whelming victory.'[64]

Only now was the doctrine as spelled out in the *Royal Air War Force Manual* implemented. While the decision preceded the appoint-ment of Air Marshal Harris to the command of these operations, they were carried out under him, even after further improvements of navigation and targeting mechanisms from 1944 in turn im-proved the feasibility of precision bombing. Greater accuracy in its own performances did not prevent vulnerability to enemy defences, however: the RAF in its attack on Nuremberg on 30/31 March 1944 lost 107 of the aircraft used. The battle of Berlin campaign cost the RAF 1,117 of its aircraft.[65]

City bombing was not uncontested on the Allied side. Even in 1944, there were some disagreements between 'Bomber' Harris and RAF Chief of Air Staff, Air Chief Marshal Sir Charles Portal, and also Eisenhower's deputy, Air Chief Marshal Sir Arthur Tedder, over bombing priorities. The US British Canadian Combined Chiefs of Staff wanted as 'First Priority [targets]: Petroleum Industry, with special emphasis on petrol (gasoline) including storage'. Second would come transport systems: rail, canal, and military plant. The British government, at the recommendation of Sir Solly (later Lord) Zuckerman, then scientific adviser to Tedder, tried to target mainly transport nodes, particularly railway marshalling yards (which may have been the principal target in the bombing of Dresden). Fuel depots turned out to be one of the most effective selected targets. Harris, however, was tired of attempts to single out particular eco-nomic or fuel targets. Having found previous efforts on the part of the RAF to target them inconclusive, he criticised the Ministry of Economic Warfare (MEW) who 'in the past have never failed to overstate their case on [targeting] "panaceas", e.g., ball bearings, molybdenum, locomotives, etc., in so far as, after the battle has been joined and the original targets attacked, more and more sources of supply or other factors unpredicted by MEW have become revealed'. Instead, he saw city bombing as the way most decisively to affect the German war effort.[66]

Meanwhile Tedder implicitly criticised both Harris's city bomb-ing preferences and 'panacea' targeting, that is targeting sites which

64. See Webster and Frankland, *Strategic Air Offensive*, I, pp. 341f.

65. John McCarthy, 'Did the bomber always get through? The control of strategic air space 1939–1945', in Alan Stephens (ed.), *The War in the Air 1914–1994* (Fairbairn, Australia: RAAF Base, 1994), p. 87.

66. 12 Dec. 1944, quoted in Air Vice Marshal Tony Mason, *Air Power: A Centennial Appraisal* (London: Brasseys, 1994), p. 56.

are identified as so crucial to the enemy's war effort that the latter might collapse through their loss:

> As I see it, there are two methods of ending this war, one is by land invasion and the other is by breaking the enemy's power and control behind the lines. I, myself, do not believe that these two courses are alternative or conflicting. I believe that they are complementary. I do not believe that by concentrating our whole Air effort on the ground battle area we shall shorten the war. Nor do I believe that we would shorten the war by putting our whole Bomber effort against industrial and political targets inside Germany . . . The various types of operations, should fit into one comprehensive pattern . . .[67]

Harris was not the only one to put his faith in city targeting, though. Other British military planners predicted that due to food shortages and the strains of the war effort, the German morale was undermined, 'and for this reason *also* will be liable to crack before a nation of greater stamina [!].' [68]

It was seen as all the more disappointing on the British side that post-war assessments ranked the effects of these bombing raids on civilian resistance to the National Socialist régime as negligible. Indeed, the arms production of Germany increased steadily until the summer of 1944. The British Bombing Survey Unit concluded after the Second World War:

> In so far as the offensive against German towns was designed to break the morale of the German civilian population, it clearly failed. Far from lowering essential war production, it also failed to stem a remarkable increase in the output of armaments.[69]

The pessimism of the surveys conducted by the British immediately after the Second World War into the effects of the bombing raids on Germany has been questioned by several historians, and in particular by Richard Overy. He has argued that whatever the shortcomings of the effects compared with the expectations, by 1944 bombing had become the main problem for the German home front, and the diversionary effects – including Germany's struggle to keep up with bomber and fighter production, and the concomitant effects on the German war economy – contributed crucially and cost-effectively to Germany's complete defeat.[70] Nevertheless,

67. Webster and Frankland, *Strategic Air Offensive*, IV, p. 290.
68. Text *ibid.*, p. 190, italics mine.
69. British Bombing Survey Unit, *The Strategic Air War Against Germany, 1939–1945* (London: HMSO, 1946), p. 79.
70. Richard Overy, *War and Economy in the Third Reich* (Oxford: Clarendon Press, 1994); Richard Overy, 'World War II: the bombing of Germany', in Stephens (ed.), *The War in the Air*, pp. 113–34.

the chief Allied hopes were not fulfilled: Germany only capitulated when the country was totally flooded by Allied forces overrunning it from East and West, and when its capital Berlin was physically taken by the Soviets; moreover, German armed forces fought bitterly until this very last point, inflicting enormous losses on the Allies (particularly Russia) as they advanced, right up to the final battles of 1945.

While the German minister of military supplies and transport, Albert Speer, initially thought Germany would cave in under the pressure of city bombing, retrospectively, he reckoned that it was the American attacks, concentrating on industrial targets, which 'caused the breakdown of the German armaments industry' while the night attacks by British bombers 'did not succeed in breaking the will to work of the civilian population.' He thought that the latter had failed because the pressure was gradually stepped up rather than being applied suddenly and without mental preparation, which allowed the victims to adapt and improve their defences, and also because 'The powers of resistance of the German people were underestimated and no account was taken of the fatalistic frame of mind which a civil population finally acquires after numerous air raids.'[71]

Turning to Germany's air force, the *Luftwaffe* (literally, 'air weapon') was created much later than the air forces of Britain, the Soviet Union and even the USA, because the Versailles Peace Treaty had barred Germany from developing large forces and a full range of military equipment. It was thus only in 1935, when the *Luftwaffe* itself was formed, already under Hitler and Hermann Goering, that a German doctrinal statement was formulated. The individual most commonly associated with this doctrine is General Walther Wever, the *Luftwaffe's* first Chief of Staff, who died in 1936. The doctrine itself was called *Luftkriegführung* (Conduct of Air War). It emphasised, just as Douhet and other early thinkers had, the ability with air power to 'carry the war from the beginning against the enemy's homeland [and to] attack his military power and the morale of the enemy population at the root'.[72] There was, however, a profound difference from Douhet's thinking. The strategic purposes of the *Luftwaffe* were described as follows:

9. The task of the armed forces (*Wehrmacht*) in war is to break the enemy's will. The will of a nation finds its strongest embodiment in

71. Text in Webster and Frankland, *Strategic Air Offensive*, IV, p. 383.
72. For this and all following quotations from *Luftkriegführung*, see Williamson Murray, 'A tale of two doctrines: The *Luftwaffe's* 'Conduct of Air War' and the USAF's Manual 1–1', *Journal of Strategic Studies* Vol. 6, No. 4 (December 1983), pp. 84–93.

the *armed forces*. Therefore, *the destruction of the enemy armed forces is the foremost goal of war.*

10. The task of the *Luftwaffe* is this: Through its conduct of the air war within the framework of overall strategy to serve this goal. Through battle against the enemy air force [the *Luftwaffe*] weakens the enemy's armed forces and at the same time strengthens one's own armed forces, the population, and [one's] living space.

Through intervention in operations and combat on land and at sea the *Luftwaffe* supports the army and navy.

Through attacks against the sources of support for the enemy's armed forces and the support structure [linking] industry to the front the *Luftwaffe* seeks to weaken the enemy's armed forces.[73]

Attacks on the infrastructure were thus by no means ruled out, but the argument that the enemy's workforce and more general population *per se* should be the prime target was not made. Which of the above tasks – close air support, or targeting of 'support structure' – should have priority, it was said, should be decided in view of '[t]he enemy, the weather, the time of year, the disposition of the [enemy's] country, the popular character and one's own military power'. The doctrine of 1935 cautioned that while air strikes against enemy industry could be of decisive importance, such a campaign might also take 'a long time to take effect and therefore carries the danger that it would come too late to influence the struggle on land and at sea'.[74]

The doctrine thus specified three tasks for the German air forces: first, the constant battle against the enemy's air force, in order to protect Germany's own vital centres and to enable ground forces on land and at sea to continue to operate in relative safety from air strikes. Secondly, 'operational air war' was the task of supporting ground forces, particularly on land, in battle. This aspect was exercised by the *Luftwaffe* particularly in the Spanish Civil War. Thirdly, the *Luftwaffe* was tasked to fight against the lines of supply of the enemy's armed forces.

The term 'strategic bombing' was imported into German terminology from British and American theoretical writing. The *Luftwaffe* doctrine of 1935 still described this sort of city bombing as exceptional:

The attack on cities with the purpose of [creating] terror against the civilian population should be rejected on principle. If the enemy

---

73. Murray, 'A tale of two doctrines', p. 87, my emphasis.   74. *Ibid.*

executes terror attacks upon undefended open cities, then reprisal attacks can be the only way to make the enemy stop . . . this sort of air warfare. The choice of timing will thus be determined above all by the precedent of an enemy terror attack. [One's own] attack must in any case clearly express the character of a reprisal.

The logic of this tied in with the initial statement that the enemy's armed forces were the strongest incarnation of the enemy's will to exist:

Thus it is the first aim of warfare to bring down the enemy armed forces, not the civilian population. It is the task of the *Luftwaffe* to serve this aim through conducting the war in the air in the context of the overall warfare, i.e. not as in Douhet, [trying to bring about victory] on its own.[75]

Thus oddly enough, the first air doctrine of the Third *Reich's* air force, under the influence of Wever's thinking, was set considerably less on bombing population centres than Douhet's thinking, or even than the strategy of the RAF. This did not mean that the more restrained aims of the *Luftwaffe* were shared throughout its officer corps, let alone by the National Socialist régime, or indeed by the Chief of the Air Staff, General Jeschonnek.[76] Warsaw was bombed mercilessly at the beginning of the German invasion of Poland, and in 1939 the commander of the *Luftwaffe's* Second Fleet, General Felmy, specifically wanted to attack London and other British cities in raids of terror bombing. He thought the British prone to hysteria because of the reactions to the Munich crisis in September 1938, when sandbags had been piled up in front of public buildings in London and slit trenches had been dug in parks, and he concluded: 'It is beyond any doubt that a city like London can be struck with such fear that the government would be subject to enormous pressure.' Only the range of German aircraft was insufficient to carry out his plan immediately; he thought Germany needed airbases in the Netherlands to attack London from the air effectively.[77]

Germany virtually began the war on the Eastern front with the strategic air attack on Warsaw which had the clear object of instilling terror. By contrast on the Western front, its air raids on Rotterdam

75. Quotations in Horst Boog, 'Der strategische Bombenkrieg: *Luftwaffe*, Royal Air Force und US Army Air Forces im Vergleich bis 1945', *Militärgeschichte* Vol. 2, No. 2 (2nd quarter 1992), p. 21.
76. Williamson Murray, 'The Luftwaffe before the Second World War: a mission, a strategy?', *Journal of Strategic Studies* Vol. 4, No. 3 (Sept. 1981), pp. 261–70.
77. Maier, 'Total war and German air doctrine', pp. 216f.

in May 1940, and on Paris and Marseille in June 1940 aimed mainly at military-industrial targets. When the battle of England began, Goering and General Jeschonnek, disregarding the 1935 doctrine, wanted to target the living quarters of workers. Moreover, during the war itself, the reprisal attacks became targeted primarily at places of great emotional value to the enemy: after the bombing and resulting incineration of the historical cities of Lübeck and Rostock by Allied air raids in the spring of 1942, Hitler ordered raids on some of Britain's most beautiful cities. Soon after, the whole idea of selective reprisals was scrapped completely on the German side; later the V-1 and V-2 missile raids targeted mainly cities, including Antwerp in Belgium and of course London. Thus the relatively high moral standards – in aiming to avoid population targeting – set by the 1935 air doctrine were not applied in practice.[78]

In the US, Mitchell's concern to avoid targeting cities was not universally shared among air power thinkers. An American survey conducted after the First World War had concluded that

> Bombing for moral[e] effect alone . . . which was probably the excuse for the wide spread of bombs over a town rather than their concentration on a factory, is not a productive means of bombing. The effect is legitimate and just as considerable when attained indirectly through the bombing of a factory.[79]

Nevertheless, in the US Air Service Tactical School 1926 manual on bombardment we read:

> *Against industrial centers.* Industrial centers, especially those devoted to the manufacture of war matériel, are important strategical targets . . . particular sub-targets should be selected and each plane or formation should be assigned a certain building or group of buildings to destroy. It is wrong to send out planes simply to drop their bombs when over a large target . . .

> *Against political centers.* The bombing of political centers is prohibited by the laws of warfare. However, since they are the nerve centers of the nation, they are apt to be important targets for bombardment in reprisal for attacks made by the enemy on such centers in our own country.[80]

---

78. Boog, 'Der strategische Bombenkrieg'.

79. Quoted in Biddle, 'British and American approaches to strategic bombing', p. 108.

80. United States Army, Air Service Tactical School, *Bombardment* (Washington: U.S. G.P.O., 1926), pp. 63f., quoted in Quester, *Deterrence before Hiroshima*, p. 72.

The *Manual of Combined Air Tactics*, produced in the US in 1926, included the following passage: 'The objective is selected with a view to undermining the enemy's morale . . . Such employment of air forces is a method of imposing will by terrorising the whole population of a belligerent country.' Like the British and the Germans, the manual's authors used the Clausewitzian concept of imposing one's will on the enemy as the main aim of war.[81] US strategic literature of the 1930s reflects the conviction that reprisals against the enemy's population centres must not be ruled out.[82]

A targeting priority aiming to bring down industrial targets rather than civilians is reflected in US air power strategy at the beginning of the American involvement in the Second World War, as codified in a plan written by the Air War Plans Division, 'AWPD-1' of August 1941. It emphasised selective attacks against 'key node' targets vital to the German war economy, such as electric power stations, transport nodes, fuel depots and the aircraft industry.[83]

American planning was influenced by the generally much better flying conditions in large parts of the United States (where there is better visibility than in Europe), by the wider spaces (where targets could be isolated more clearly) and by the relative absence of air defences in considerations about bombing raids. The Americans therefore dreamt of ideal scenarios of precision bombing, which would also, it was thought, produce the greatest cost-effectiveness of bombing raids. It was claimed that the American Norden tachometric bomb-sight was so accurate that it could help 'drop a bomb in a pickle barrel from 25,000 feet' – a tall story indeed.[84] In reality, the technological limitations of the time dictated that such raids be flown at low altitude and during the time of best visibility, i.e. during day-time. This led to the devastating losses of American bomber fleets in their attacks on the industrial targets of the German city of Schweinfurt on 17 August 1943 (60 bombers destroyed, a 19 per cent loss rate) and 14 October 1943 (again 60 bombers destroyed, this time 26 per cent loss rate).[85]

Originally, the USAF also tried to identify 'panacea targets' for their strategic bombing. During the Second World War, these targets

81. Extract quoted in Overy, 'Air power and the origins', pp. 75f.
82. *Ibid.*, p. 84.
83. Biddle, 'British and American approaches to strategic bombing', pp. 117f.
84. Alan Stephens, 'The true believers: air power between the wars', in Stephens (ed.), *The War in the Air*, p. 65.
85. McCarthy, 'Did the bomber always get through?', p. 87.

were mainly identified as the enemy's military industry; the United
States made particular efforts to hit ball bearings factories, which
were thought to have a crucial effect on all the other sectors of the
German industry. (Schweinfurt was home to ball bearing factories,
hence the US commitment to bombing it, despite the high loss
rates.) Quantitatively, the American targeting of specifically industrial sites had a greater impact on the German war effort than
British city bombing, but the American bombing also inflicted huge
collateral damage and thus created significant numbers of casualties
also among the civilian populations. European weather conditions,
and experiences such as that over Schweinfurt, led to a degenera-
tion of American targeting until it was virtually indistinguishable in
its result from British practice. Thus for example, shortly before
the air attack on Berlin planned for 3 February 1945, the Commander of the 8th Air Force, asked General Carl Spaatz, the Commander
of the U.S. Strategic Forces:

> Is Berlin still open to attack? Do you want priority oil targets hit in
> preference to Berlin if they definitely become visual [*sic*]? Do you
> want center of City in Berlin hit or definitely military targets, such as
> Spandau, on the Western outskirts?

In reply, Spaatz instructed him to 'hit oil if visual assured; otherwise, Berlin – center of City.' As the day scheduled for the mission
was overcast, the latter course was chosen, resulting in an air attack
estimated to have killed 25,000 people.[86] By February 1945, the
USAF had effectively moved to the sort of area bombing that was
quite indistinguishable from British practice.[87]

Thus the historian Tami Davis Biddle has concluded: 'While
participation in the infamous Dresden raid (of 13–14 February 1945)
is generally cited as evidence of the American slide to terror bombing, the USAAF's stated aim point for that raid – the railroad marshalling yards – was considered by planners to fall within the rubric
of selective targeting (under the general category of communications targets).' She has argued that if, due to weather and visibility,
'the distinction between American and British bombing in the European theater was not always apparent, it is nonetheless true the
Americans remained committed to the *theory* supporting selective

86. Mark Clodfelter, *The Limits of Air Power: The American Bombing of North Vietnam*
(New York: the Free Press, 1989), p. 6.
87. Cf. Richard G. Davis, *Carl A. Spaatz and the Air War in Europe* (Washington DC:
Center for Air Force History, 1993).

bombing'.[88] Nevertheless, the effects of US raids were difficult to distinguish from British city bombing, and the raids carried out at the end of the war targeted cities outright – as the firebombing of Tokyo in March 1945 demonstrated. Hiroshima and Nagasaki simply took large-scale city bombing one technical step further, by substituting one single aircraft for the whole air fleet previously needed to destroy a big city. The shock effect of this concentration and speed of destruction was new; the suffering caused, was not.[89]

Turning to the air forces of the other main protagonists of the Second World War, the Japanese entered the war still with two separate air forces, designed to support the army and navy respectively. Other than in the Sino–Japanese war, where Japanese air forces resorted to extensive bombing of Chinese cities, Japanese air operations were more directly operational (in the sense of supporting the operations of the army and the navy respectively) than those of the Western powers.[90] While the unannounced Japanese attack of December 1941 on US shipping, on purely military targets, broke international conventions on the conduct of war since it preceded the Japanese declaration of war, Pearl Harbor was in a different category, as air operations go, from the German bombing of Coventry or Warsaw, the British and American bombing of Hamburg, Cologne and Dresden, and the US bombing of Tokyo, Hiroshima and Nagasaki. The Japanese attacks on Chinese cities, by contrast, conducted mainly by surface forces, measured up to the horrors of Western strategic bombing raids.

The Soviet Air Force had gained some early combat experience during the Spanish Civil War, but also by intervening in the Sino–Japanese war of 1937–39 on the side of the Chinese against the Japanese forces. Targeting undertaken here by Soviet aircraft, as in the Soviet campaigns of the Second World War, was purely designed to support the operations of ground forces, and to counter Japanese air forces directly. During the Second World War, air power was used predominantly in this way by the Soviet Air Force in its campaigns to resist the German invasion code-named *Barbarossa*. Even during the final stages of the war in the East, when Soviet forces were pushing forward towards Germany's capital with enormously disproportionate losses of manpower, the Soviet leadership

88. Biddle, 'British and American approaches to strategic bombing', p. 125.
89. See Chapter 1.
90. Basil Collier, *A History of Air Power* (London: Weidenfeld and Nicolson, 1974), ch. 11.

left it mainly up to the British and the Americans to bomb Berlin from the air.[91] Tactical and operational support for the other forces, the pre-emptive destruction of the enemy's war materials, and the use of air forces to airlift troops over long distances (practised not very impressively in the USSR's invasion of Finland from November 1939 until early 1940),[92] remained the main missions of Soviet air power doctrine until the end of the Soviet Union. Long-range bombers developed by the USSR until 1945 were ineffective, and it was only after copying the American B-29 that the USSR developed such a capability after the Second World War.

To conclude our observations of the development of air power strategy up to Hiroshima and Nagasaki, the deliberate targeting of civilians and the bombing of cities was not unique to America's first nuclear strategy, nor indeed was it unique to America's air power strategy. The Japanese, Italians, Germans, and the British had applied this strategy even before the Second World War, and during that conflagration, cities were bombed particularly by the *Luftwaffe*, the RAF and the US Air Force. One cannot help agreeing with Richard Crossman, a British philosophy don, one-time civil servant and later Labour minister, who described the nuclear weapon as the logical development of Western civilisation, the 'logical fulfilment of the strategy of area bombing evolved by our own Bomber Command and employed by the Americans in their fire-bomb raids against Japanese cities'.[93]

Nevertheless, the US Air Force General Orvil Anderson, in his controversial conclusion of the official US survey *Air Campaigns of the Pacific War* (1947), which provoked strong reactions, predictably, from the US Navy, wrote:

> Before World War II the growth and development of air power was restricted by concepts of surface warfare which visualized the air weapon as an ancillary force. Air power entered the war under this handicap and by slow evolutionary steps, each based on hindsight,

91. General Walter Schwabedissen, 'From Barbarossa to Stalingrad'; Peter Williams, 'From Stalingrad to Berlin', both in Asher Lee (ed.), *The Soviet Air and Rocket Forces* (London: Weidenfeld and Nicolson, 1959). Only in March 1945, when Soviet ground forces were drawing close to Berlin, were Soviet bombers allocated in support of this campaign; see Mason and Taylor, *Soviet Air Force*, p. 129.

92. See e.g. George Schatunowski, 'The Civil War to the Second World War', in Lee (ed.), *The Soviet Air and Rocket Forces*.

93. Richard Crossman, 'Western defence in the 1960s', *Journal of the RUSI* Vol. CVI (August 1961), pp. 334f.

emerged as the primary force. Air power was the dominant combat force of the war against Japan and was decisive in that –

Air power dominated its own element.

Air power dominated naval warfare.

Air power dominated ground warfare.

Air power possessed powerful and independent logistical capabilities.

Air power established effective area interdiction by occupation of the air space over an objective area.

Air power was capable of forcing the capitulation of an enemy without surface invasion.[94]

The conclusion he drew from this argument was that henceforth, particularly in the nuclear age, the air force must be the dominant part of any armed forces. But even this fervent advocate of air power left open the question whether the air force would henceforth be the mere agent of delivering nuclear weapons, or whether it would play the key conventional rôle in any future conventional war.

Air strategy in practice since World War II

How, then, did conventional air power strategy develop after Hiroshima and Nagasaki? Air forces were soon called upon to assume conventional rôles once more. France found herself tied down in war in Indochina right from the end of the Second World War, and Britain became involved in the Malayan insurgency in 1948; in both cases, helicopters were first used systematically for transportation and reconnaissance, which the Americans had experimented with in the Pacific War. In Algeria, France first used helicopters to bomb villages, an employment developed conceptually by Colonel Brodin, studied by US observers, and applied by the USA, on the basis of a further development of Brodin's work, in the Vietnam War.

Aircraft continued to be used in all missions. The Greek Civil War resumed in 1946, with British, and later US, involvement, and extensive use of air power. Pakistan and India came to blows over Kashmir in 1947–49, and the first Arab–Israeli war took place in 1948/9. 1950 saw a new fairly large-scale war erupt on the Korean peninsula, the first since 1945 that had extensive international involvement. Only half a decade after the end of the Second World

---

94. Quoted in David MacIsaac, *Strategic bombing in World War II: the story of the United States Strategic Bombing Survey* (New York: Garland, 1976), pp. 130f.

War, it was thus clear that air strategy found further *conventional* application. In the following we will examine whether the invention of nuclear weapons was a significant turning point in this context.

SOVIET STRATEGY

Of the major powers, the Soviet Union perhaps showed greatest continuity in its military doctrine. Marxism-Leninism taught that technological innovations did not in themselves fundamentally alter the nature of warfare, *ergo*, nuclear weapons could not do so. But the damage inflicted by enemy nuclear weapons on the USSR and its allies had to be minimised for Socialist society to survive. Therefore, the main principle of Soviet strategy, until the end of the Cold War, was an emphasis on the early destruction of enemy nuclear weapons, before these had been used against Soviet or Warsaw Treaty Organisation (WTO) member states' territory. In this context, Soviet official strategists for most of the time distinguished less between nuclear and conventional forces than between different delivery vehicles.

In the first two decades after the Second World War, the Soviet Union could not match the British and American strategic bomber forces.[95] Initially, Stalin claimed to be unimpressed by the effects of atomic bombs.[96] He articulated an important principle of Soviet doctrine, which was respected throughout the history of the Soviet military, with the partial exception only of the 1960s: namely, that all weapons systems and branches of the armed forces had to be seen as a complementary panoply which could only *jointly*, according to an overall plan, achieve victory. As the Sovietologist Mark Miller summed up Soviet reactions, 'The Soviets argued that the "terror bombing" of Germany had little impact on the overall Nazi war effort. Western theories of air power and strategic nuclear bombing were, therefore, denigrated as "adventuristic and anti-scientific".'[97]

Indeed, the Commander-in Chief of the Soviet Air Forces, Marshal of the Air Force Vershinin, in 1949 publicly distanced Soviet thinking from the aberrations of 'bourgeois' air power strategists:

---

95. David M. Glantz, *The Military Strategy of the Soviet Union: A History* (London: Frank Cass, 1992), ch. 6; Kenneth Whiting, 'Post-war strategy', in Lee (ed.), *The Soviet Air and Rocket Forces*, p. 89.

96. Interview in *Pravda*, 25 September 1946, quoted in Mark E. Miller, *Soviet Strategic Power and Doctrine: The Quest for Superiority* (Washington: Advanced International Studies Institute, 1982), p. 3.

97. Miller, *Soviet Strategic Power and Doctrine*, p. 3.

The doctrines of Douhet, Fuller, and their German proponents have been fully refuted, namely, that in modern conditions war may be won solely by means of a strongly developed and abundantly equipped Air Force or Tank Force [Fuller's and de Gaulle's dream!], or by both taken together . . . The victory of the Soviet Armed Forces in the Fatherland War showed that the wars of the machine epoch are a lengthy and ruthless competition between all the forces and resources of the belligerents and that a war can be won solely by means of all the armed services brought to perfection, whose co-ordinated operations are ably organised . . . Douhet's [ad]venturous ideas . . . emanate from the completely distorted view that the outcome of a war can be settled by one kind of weapon alone. History has proved the reverse more than once.[98]

The post-Second World War development of Soviet grand strategy can be divided roughly into three periods: the first – 1946–60 – was dominated by the wish to out-arm the United States (and from 1949 its North Atlantic Treaty partners) on a conventional level, while trying to catch up with a nuclear weapons programme. From 1960, or shortly before, until the late 1960s, initiated by Nikita V. Khrushchev, we can identify a second phase, during which the Soviet leadership put much more emphasis on its own nuclear forces. These were built up rapidly once the Soviet Union, as the first power to do so, had tested an intercontinental missile in 1957. It was nuclear 'rocket forces', rather than air forces, which were accorded the main rôle in this potential drama, according to the bible of Soviet strategy of that period, a co-authored work called *Military Strategy*, and the targets would be the enemy's ground forces, aircraft, (nuclear) missiles and other nuclear weapons.[99]

The rationale behind this shift (which was accompanied by significant reductions in the manpower of the Soviet armed forces), is reflected in a forecast made even in 1955 by the then Commander-in-Chief of the Soviet Air Forces, Air Chief Marshal Zhigarev, who explained that bombers were more expensive to build and more vulnerable to attack when on the ground than missiles, which were more easily controlled, needing fewer numbers of maintenance crew to operate them.[100]

98. Marshal of Aviation K.S. Vershinin, 'Speech on the Occasion of Air Force Day, 16 July 1949', *Pravda* (17 July 1949), quoted in Raymond L. Garthoff, *Soviet Military Doctrine* (Glencoe, Ill: Free Press, 1953), p. 175.

99. V.D. Sokolovsky *et al.*, *Soviet Military Strategy*, 1968 edn., Harriett Scott (ed.), (London: Macdonald and Jane's, 1975 (originally *Voennaia strategiia* Moscow: Voenizdat, 1968)), p. 202.

100. Quoted by Mason and Taylor, *Soviet Air Force*, p. 135.

The targeting of the Soviet rocket forces was primarily directed
against the nuclear weapons of NATO powers ('counter-force' targeting, in Western strategists' jargon), and against related communications systems which were needed to command, release and
direct NATO nuclear forces.[101] The Soviet Union thus preferred
a 'counter-force' strategy, which inevitably assumes that enemy
weapons have not yet been launched and can be destroyed on the
ground or on their delivery platforms at sea. It is thus a 'first strike'
strategy, a feature which was carried by Soviet doctrine into its
subsequent phase.[102] Marxist-Leninist military doctrine did not distinguish neatly between defensive and offensive operations. As an
authoritative work of 1981 argued, 'in a nuclear-missile war victory
over the forces of the enemy Coalition is possible only under conditions of a decisive offensive directed at his total destruction'.[103]

Nevertheless, Soviet doctrine also included the targeting of industry and other non-military targets (called in the West 'counter-
value' targets). The 1968 edition of the *Military Strategy* addressed
the question of the 'main military-strategic goal of war': was it de-
feating the enemy's armed forces as in previous wars, or the wiping
out of targets in the enemy's rear with the purpose of undermining
his war effort? The answer it gave was that both had to be done
simultaneously, in order to deprive him, as quickly as possible, of his
military, political and economic means of pursuing the war. What
the 'annihilation and destruction' of the enemy's economic means
implied for the chances of survival of enemy populations in heavily
industrialised areas was not spelled out.[104]

By and large, Soviet military thinkers saw civilian casualties as
incidental to the main aims of Soviet strategy:

> The most important task is to correctly determine economic objec-
> tives and vulnerable points, and to deliver strikes to those targets
> where it will lead to disorganisation of the enemy economy. The
> objective is not to turn the large economic and industrial regions
> into a heap of ruins (although great destruction, apparently, is un-
> avoidable), but to deliver strikes which will destroy strategic combat

---

101. Miller, *Soviet Strategic Power and Doctrine*, pp. 86–8, 106–8.
102. On the question of how a first strike operational doctrine could be squared
with Brezhnev's 'no first use' declaration, see Beatrice Heuser, 'Warsaw Pact military
doctrines in the 70s and 80s: findings in the East German archives', *Comparative
Strategy* Vol. 12, No. 4 (Oct.–Dec. 1993), pp. 437–57.
103. N.N. Azovtsev, *V.I. Lenin I sovetskaya voyennaya nauka* (Moscow, 1981), 1981
edition of *V.I. Lenin and Soviet Military Science*, p. 32, quoted in Miller, *Soviet Strategic
Power and Doctrine*, p. 210.
104. Sokolovsky *et al.*, *Soviet Military Strategy*, p. 202.

means, paralyse enemy military production, making it incapable of satisfying the priority needs of the front and rear areas and sharply reduce the enemy capability to conduct strikes.[105]

During this phase of Soviet strategy, the air force continued to be trained for (tactical) ground-support operations, of course, so its eclipse was far from total. Indeed, the Soviet Union continued to develop 'all types of armed forces and branches', and to train and equip them for 'modern battle, . . . operations, and . . . war as a whole'.[106]

In the late 1960s, research into guided precision munitions promised the dawn of a new military revolution and ushered in a new phase in Soviet doctrine. The Commandant of the Gagarin Military Academy, Marshal S.A. Krasnovskiy, wrote a treatise on air power in 1967, in which he emphasised that notwithstanding the utility of the nuclear strategic rocket forces, aircraft were preferable for a host of missions, due to their flexibility and manoeuvrability, particularly as the technology of air-launched missiles and precision-guided bombs was beginning to be anticipated.[107] Also in the period 1967–69, changes in NATO strategy involuntarily signalled to the USSR that NATO might take a long time to resort to the use of nuclear weapons.[108] This led the Soviets to conclude that there was a chance of securing Soviet strategic objectives with conventional weapons only, without either side resorting to nuclear weapons.[109] Henceforth, in the third phase of Soviet strategic thinking, which lasted roughly until the end of the Cold War, the Soviet military leadership developed for the Warsaw Pact complete sets of parallel plans and exercises, which assumed that fighting would either take place in a 'nuclear environment' or in a 'conventional environment' only.[110] A textbook for the use of military academies spelled

105. Colonel M. Shirokov, 'Military geography at the present stage', *Voyennaya mysl'* No. 11 (Nov. 1966), p. 59, quoted in Miller, *Soviet Strategic Power and Doctrine*, p. 225.

106. Marshal of the Soviet Union A.A. Grechko, 'V.I. Lenin and the building of the Soviet armed forces', *Kommunist* No. 3 (February 1969), p. 23, quoted in Miller, *Soviet Strategic Power and Doctrine*, p. 78.

107. S.A. Krasnovskiy, 'Air power' in *Military Thought* No. 3 (March 1967), quoted in Mason and Taylor, *Soviet Air Force*, p. 137.

108. For the development of NATO strategy, see Beatrice Heuser, *NATO, Britain, France and the FRG: Nuclear Strategies and Forces for Europe, 1949–2000* (London: Macmillan, 1997), ch. 2.

109. My periodicisation differs slightly from that of Glantz, *The Military Strategy of the Soviet Union*, pp. 188–213.

110. Various sub-sets provided for responses to the use of chemical weapons, and presumably also for their employment, as the USSR had large stocks.

this out in 1971: 'In working out methods of conducting battle in conditions of nuclear war, Soviet military science does not exclude the possibility of conducting combat operations with the use of only conventional means of fighting.'[111] Targeting preferences, at least on an operational and tactical level, were moving back towards counter-force priorities. Now aircraft gained a new and emphatic importance: capable of delivering both nuclear and conventional ordnance, they played the key rôle alongside missiles in all planning for massive attacks on NATO nuclear forces that were waiting to be launched.[112] In the words of the *Soviet Military Encyclopaedia* of 1984:

> Long-range aircraft are a component of the Soviet Air Forces designed to strike against military installations deep in the enemy's rear and continental and ocean theatres and to carry out operational and strategic aerial reconnaissance ... The strike systems comprise various types of airborne missiles and bombs including those with nuclear charges.[113]

Moreover, aircraft were prepared to take *Speznaz* (special operations) forces or air-landing units to their targets, potentially far behind the front, preparing for operations if necessary even in isolation from the main body of Warsaw Pact forces, a form of operations which harked back to Tukhachevsky's thinking in the early 1930s. Even in 1966, thought was given to the way in which airborne forces could be used in conjunction with nuclear strikes.[114] Even in a nuclear environment, Marshal Krasnovskiy envisaged aircraft supporting ground forces, including units which might find themselves isolated from other Warsaw Treaty Organisation forces behind enemy lines (the antecedents of the Operational Manoeuvre Group). Aircraft should in such circumstances ensure their logistic supplies allowing them to carry on their operations, and evacuate casualties.[115] Such operations would be exercised from the 1970s and 80s by Warsaw Pact Forces.

The actual warfare in which Soviet forces found themselves involved during the Cold War, however, stayed well clear of nuclear

---

111. Quoted in Mason and Taylor, *Soviet Air Force*, p. 159.
112. Heuser, 'Warsaw Pact military doctrines', pp. 437–57.
113. Quoted in Mason and Taylor, *Soviet Air Force*, p. 137.
114. Cols. I.I. Andrukhov and V. Bulatnikov, 'The growing role of airborne troops in modern military operations', *Military Thought* No. 7 (July 1966), quoted in Mason and Taylor, *Soviet Air Force*, p. 156.
115. Krasnovskiy, 'Air power', quoted in Mason and Taylor, *Soviet Air Force*, pp. 158f.

use: in their invasions of Hungary and Czechoslovakia, in the Korean War, where Soviet fighter pilots engaged in dogfights with US planes, and in Afghanistan, the Soviets differentiated as scrupulously between nuclear and conventional weapons as did the West.

CONVENTIONAL USE OF AIR POWER SINCE 1945

After the Second World War, US air power thinkers returned to their earlier interest in targeting specific sections of enemy infrastructure and military concentrations. Technology made possible emphasis on the sort of precision bombing which William Mitchell had dreamed of, and on the avoidance of collateral damage and civilian casualties. Coupled with this, the quest for the 'panacea targets' continued, as we shall see. Nevertheless, any planning for the 'operational' and 'tactical' use of the US Air Force was overshadowed throughout the Cold War by planning for 'strategic' use of air forces, defined as aimed at destroying 'the essential elements of the nation's total organisation for waging war . . . as distinct from its deployed military forces'.[116] And such use of air power was now usually linked with nuclear weapons.

The Korean War (1950–53) saw significant US conventional air action. The US air power specialist Robert Pape has identified three phases. The first was aimed exclusively at North Korea and consisted mainly of World War II-type bombardment of several cities, including the North Korean capital, Pyongyang.[117] The second strategy was aimed both at North Korea and at China, but not implemented: nuclear threats were used with the purpose of bringing about an armistice, but did not succeed in doing so.

In May 1951, the US moved to its third air strategy, which focused mainly on air interdiction, i.e. the targeting of enemy military forces in the rear of the battle area. Drawing on lessons and experiences of the Second World War, the American Commander-in-Chief of the UN forces, General Douglas MacArthur, in surprise attacks destroyed substantial numbers of North Korean airports, including aircraft on the ground. The US Air Force thenceforth tried to maintain this air superiority and to interdict enemy use of aircraft.[118]

---

116. 'Theater air forces in counter air, interdiction and close air support operations' USAF Manual 1–7 of March 1954, quoted in Clodfelter, *The Limits of Air Power*, p. 30.
117. Robert A. Pape, *Bombing to Win: Air Power and Coercion in War* (Ithaca: Cornell University Press, 1996), p. 144; see also Clodfelter, *The Limits of Air Power*, p. 17.
118. Jeffrey Grey, ' "Definite limitations": the air war in Korea 1950–1953', in Stephens (ed.), *The War in the Air*, p. 146.

MacArthur then applied World War II tactics of attempting to cut the communications and supply lines of the North Koreans by attacking transport lines far in their rear (concentrating particularly on bridges). Nevertheless, RAF observers noted early on that US bombardment of the North did little to reduce the North Koreans' capacity to fight, not least because they relied much less on logistic support and infrastructure than the Germans had done in most campaigns of the previous war.[119] After ten months of attacks on enemy supply lines in the early phase of the war, wasteful of US aircraft and manpower, the forces under United Nations command, led by the USA, switched to a new strategy, termed 'Air Pressure Strategy'. Its aims were, first, not simply to swamp the skies but to try to inflict as many losses on the Chinese MiG-15s as possible while losing as few aircraft as possible; secondly, to strike interdiction targets more selectively, by choosing them according to the value they represented to the defender, and the degree to which they would be defended. Thirdly, the rather obvious principle was established that 'group support operations should strike at targets which were worthwhile in terms of the likely costs of mounting such missions'.[120] One of the prime choices of targets was hydroelectric power stations, which supplied power not only to munitions factories in North Korea but also to Manchuria. This proved to be more successful than the previous principles of operation.

Under Robert McNamara in the 1960s, the Pentagon took up the idea that one could influence the enemy's morale through the use of air power. Even after the Second World War, the US Strategic Bombing Survey noted: 'Civilian morale was a vital weapon in the German arsenal. The people's will to support the war was essential to German victory. German civilian morale, therefore, was an important target for the allies.'[121] By the time the Vietnam War engulfed the United States, it was this idea that came to influence both nuclear and conventional strategy, the latter coming to be dominated by the former in US thinking. The civilian strategists in the Pentagon attempted to apply escalation and signalling thinking developed for a nuclear context to the conflict unfolding in Vietnam.

119. *Ibid.,* p. 150; Basil Collier, *A History of Air Power* (London: Weidenfeld and Nicolson, 1974), pp. 320–2. There were exceptions to this rule also in the German case, e.g. Germany's defensive operations in Italy.

120. Robert O'Neill, *Australia in the Korean War, 1950–53* vol. II *Combat Operations* (Canberra: Australian Government Publishing Service, 1985), p. 379.

121. Morale Division, *The United States Strategic Bombing Survey: The Effects of Strategic Bombing on German Morale* Vol. 1 (May 1946), p. 7.

The obvious difference was that here, air power with conventional ordnance would be used, and not nuclear weapons. As with nuclear weapons in American strategy since 1954, throughout the Vietnam War conventional bombing was seen by key members of consecutive administrations as a 'cheap method of showing the American commitment' – one that would keep US casualties limited, it was hoped, as historian Mark Clodfelter has shown.[122]

While many in the military were highly sceptical of a restricted application of air power modelled on contemporary American thinking about bottom rungs on a nuclear escalation ladder, his civilian advisers persuaded President Lyndon B. Johnson to apply what they referred to as a 'slow squeeze'. The intermittent bombardment of selective industrial and military targets and lines of communications (such as crucial bridges, which, like crucial industries, were the 'panacea targets' of the day[123]) in the North was designed to convey the political signal that unless the North ceased its intervention in the South, the USA would continue to step up, little by little, the air bombardment of the North. Operation *Rolling Thunder* was thus approved and executed during 1965, with three pauses imposed by the civilian defence specialists in the Pentagon, in order to allow for negotiations for an armistice – a vain hope, as it proved. The US administration's express orders to avoid any bombing of the Hanoi-Haiphong area, corresponding to the 'city withhold' concept developed for nuclear contexts – against the demands of the military – and thus the clear designation of areas which would be spared, made US operations both predictable and led the Ho Chi Minh régime to feel it could bear the pain without giving in. Targets chosen instead included military storage areas, power plants, runways and aircraft, supply routes, and ports. Nevertheless, it was mainly civilians who suffered the effects of air bombardment.

Even though the USA dropped 8,000,000 tons of bombs on Vietnam in 1962–73, *Rolling Thunder* was unsuccessful from a US point of view. Only in the final phase of the war was Washington able to impose conditions for an armistice. Both *Linebacker I*, the first phase of this campaign, and *Linebacker II*, following at a quicker pace, targeted a broad set of military installations both in North and

---

122. C.D. Coulthard-Clark, 'The air war in Vietnam: re-evaluating failure', in Stephens (ed.), *The War in the Air*, p. 167; Robert A. Pape, 'Coercive power in the Vietnam War', *International Security* Vol. 15, No. 2 (1990), pp. 103–46; Clodfelter, *The Limits of Air Power*, pp. 55–146.

123. For eye-witness accounts of these operations, see Drew Middleton (ed.), *Air War – Vietnam* (London: Arms and Armour, 1978).

South Vietnam, including again bridges, railway lines, fuel deposits, power stations and pipelines, but not more general civilian and industrial sites. The tenor of *Linebacker* was thus interdiction, and its effects were impressive as the North Vietnamese had turned their armed forces into increasingly regular formations, which were more vulnerable to interdiction bombing than the Communist forces had been previously. *Linebacker II* also included sorties against Hanoi and Haiphong themselves. While this finally made a temporary settlement possible, it was not enough to break the North Vietnamese régime's will to extend its power to South Vietnam, and the US withdrawal *de facto* prepared the way for a Communist victory.

On a tactical level, the Vietnam War saw the development of several uses for air power. The use of helicopters, introduced by the French in their own campaigns in Indochina, was developed further and became a key feature of tactical operations. The use of defoliants, spread by aircraft, and the Americans' use of napalm as previously in the Greek Civil War, and the use of different sorts of ordnance developed non-nuclear employment of aircraft in support of the overall war effort in a variety of different ways. None of them led to decisive US superiority over the irregular forces and later regular but less well armed forces with which they were confronted, as force was applied by the USA according to political calculations which took no account of the essential difference between the enemy's mentality and that of the Washington armchair strategists. Of all the wars in which the Western powers have been involved since 1945, the Vietnam War best fits the criticism made by Armitage and Mason: it was the quintessential case of political power trying to 'compromise by applying political gradualism to a weapon that depends for much of its effectiveness on the characteristics of surprise, concentration and shock action'.[124]

The Vietnam War was still under way when one military correspondent who had covered the war applied the air power lessons of Vietnam in a very practical way. This was General Moshe Dayan, who in 1964–66 had temporarily withdrawn from political life after he had been a minister in the Israeli government. The application of the lessons of Vietnam, and the further development of the targeting priorities of the early phases of the Korean War were embodied in Israel's six-day war against Egypt. Dayan, who had been Chief of Staff until 1958 and had taken part in the Suez campaign, was appointed Defence Minister in 1967 by Prime Minister Eshkol.

124. Air Marshal M.J. Armitage and Air Commodore R.A. Mason, *Air Power in the Nuclear Age, 1945–82: Theory and Practice* (London: Macmillan, 1983), p. 256.

Against the background of a mounting crisis which threatened to lead to an armed conflict unless the Israelis accepted Egypt's territorial demands, Dayan convinced his Cabinet colleagues that any campaign had to begin – in a Douhetian fashion – with achieving complete air dominance, as both air and ground operations could then go forward without undue risk from defensive enemy attacks from the air.

The Arab–Israeli Six-Day War thus began with air strikes against mostly Egyptian, but also Syrian, Jordanian and Iraqi air forces, concentrating air operations mainly on the first two days of the campaign. In a theatre of operations with particularly good visibility (at any rate once the early morning mists of the Nile had cleared), on three successive days, starting on 5 June 1967, the Israelis carried out simultaneous air strikes with all their forces against Egypt's air fields, destroying a very high proportion (300 of Egypt's operational 340) combat aircraft, including all her long-range bombers, most of Egypt's radar stations and her surface-to-air missile sites. This greatly facilitated the ensuing victory on the ground: once the Israelis had achieved air supremacy, their ground forces moved forward to conquer the Sinai peninsula up to the Suez canal, and the Golan heights in Israel's north.

In the following years, Israel tried to prevent Egypt from erecting a more effective air defence system, provided by the USSR in the form of a series of surface-to-air missiles. In October 1973, it was Egypt and its allies that forced war upon Israel. On the morning of 6 October, which was the Jewish holiday of Yom Kippur, Egyptian forces advanced across the Suez Canal with air coverage from helicopters, and Syria attacked the north of Israel through the Golan Heights. By then both Egypt and Syria had become so well equipped with anti-aircraft missiles that it proved impossible for Israel to achieve air superiority, and the Israeli air force suffered heavy losses. In view of the particular strategic importance of the Golan to Israel, it chose to concentrate on the defence of this area first, trading space for time in the Sinai. Most fighting, and the highest Israeli losses were thus incurred in the North, and ultimately, Israel managed to defend the Golan. In the Sinai, however, Israel found itself defeated and forced into a fighting withdrawal. The combination of Egyptian attacks under the shield of missile defences, and the inability of Israeli forces to match numerically the Egyptian and Syrian forces, led to the loss of the peninsula for Israel.[125]

125. Chaim Herzog, *Entscheidung in der Wüste: Lehren des Yom Kippur Krieges* (Frankfurt: Propylaen, 1975).

This operation epitomised the challenge to air warfare which arose from advances made in air defences, both in the form of anti-aircraft shells and missiles. Flak had already caused high attrition rates among attacking aircraft in the Second World War, but on the whole, during that war, fighter aircraft had been the greatest danger to bombers, and the Korean War had seen very substantial losses on the US-led side both through ground-fire and dog-fights in the air. Thereafter the greater threat to attacking aircraft arose from flak and missiles, ground-launched, sea-launched and air-launched. During the Yom Kippur War, Egypt relied heavily on surface-to-air-missiles and flak in its action against Israel. Missiles thus competed with conventional air forces both as alternative means of delivery and as main anti-aircraft weapons, just as long-range missiles had since the late 1950s rivalled aircraft as delivery vehicles of nuclear weapons. In the Yom Kippur War, Israel's vulnerability to air defences was compounded by its lack of strategic space and its need to draw resources away from the Sinai, but to all observers, the war heralded the end of the unlimited ascendancy of the aircraft over air defences.

In another context, both Arab–Israeli wars, like the Korean War before them, stood in a very different tradition of air strategies from that of the massive city bombardment that reached its pinnacle with Tokyo, Dresden, Hiroshima and Nagasaki. The basic concept of Israeli air operations, like Soviet operations during the latter part of the Second World War and most American air operations in Korea, concerned the use of air forces to influence the shape of the theatre of war for the ground forces. By destroying or paralysing enemy air forces, these could be prevented from attacking one's own ground forces. By attacking transport nodes, bridges, supply lines, and by interdicting following echelons of forces, one could further delay ground forces or even prevent them from relieving those encountered by one's own forces in the battle areas. The air forces were used in these wars – in ways more in keeping with the concepts of Wever's German Air Force Doctrine of 1935 or Slessor's thinking of the same time than with the ideals of Trenchard, Goering, Harris, or Curtis Le May – to prepare and support operationally the actions of the ground forces.

The apogee of this development in the twentieth century was the use of air power in the Gulf War of 1990/91 which followed Iraq's invasion of Kuwait. Here, the theatre of war was prepared in an extensive air campaign, which first destroyed Iraqi radar and the missile sites and anything taken to be communication centres of Iraqi anti-aircraft defences. Then, when Iraq was 'blind' to the incoming attacks, coalition air forces destroyed Iraqi aircraft on the ground, on airfields and in shelters, and damaged the runways themselves, basically denying Iraq the ability to fly. Further use was made of aircraft in attacking Iraqi ground forces, including of course tanks and, indeed, forces that had 'dug in', awaiting a frontal assault of the Coalition's own ground forces. Only after air forces – and indeed, missiles launched by the US fleet – had done as much damage as they possibly could, with *conventional*, but highly sophisticated ordnance (precision guided munitions, special cluster bombs developed to destroy runways etc.), were ground forces used with minimal casualties (240 deaths) on the Coalition side to liberate Kuwait and invade Iraq. Contrary to images of the war spread by the media, missiles made up only a small proportion of the ordnance used by the Coalition forces, but specialised missiles were crucial in knocking out Iraqi air defences which might have jeopardised the subsequent bombing campaign.[126]

The six-week air campaign against Iraq in the Gulf War involved 2,800 aircraft of the Coalition forces dropping 85,000 tons of bombs in 110,000 offensive sorties.[127] The objectives of the Air Campaign Plan were summarised by British Air Chief Marshal Sir Patrick Hine as follows:

• The establishment of air superiority
• The isolation and incapacitation of the Iraqi leadership
• The destruction of Iraq's nuclear, biological and chemical warfare capability
• The elimination of Iraq's offensive military capability
• And finally, the ejection of the Iraqi army from Kuwait.

These aims were to be achieved by

• Creating strategic paralysis among the enemy leadership
• Destroying the enemy's will and capacity to fight
• Conducting the campaign over a relatively short time span (weeks not months)
• Targeting the Saddam regime, not the Iraqi people
• Minimising civilian casualties and collateral damage
• Pitting Coalition strengths against Iraqi weaknesses.[128]

---

126. Cf. Eliot A. Cohen *et al.*, *Gulf War Air Power Survey*, vol. 1. (Washington, D.C.: United States Government Printing Office, 1993).
127. G.Waters, *Gulf Lesson One – The Value of Air Power: Doctrinal Lessons for Australia* (Canberra, 1992), quoted in C.D. Coulthard-Clark, 'The air war in Vietnam: re-evaluating failure', in Stephens (ed.), *The War in the Air*, p. 167.
128. Air Chief Marshal Sir Patrick Hine, 'Air operations in the Gulf War', in Stephens (ed.), *The War in the Air*, pp. 304f.

(In this vocabulary, long embedded in British military doctrine, we still find echoes of the Douhetian concern with affecting the enemy's morale – the enemy's will to fight – even though civilians were now specifically *not* targeted.)

In the Gulf War, the targeting of civilians was studiously avoided. Collateral damage was kept small, where it did not occur accidentally. The very small number of losses on the part of Coalition forces also satisfied the desire which, if anything, had grown since the Second World War, to keep one's own casualties to a minimum. The same was true for the airstrikes which in August/September 1995 forced the Serbs to the conference table to bring peace to Bosnia-Hercegovina and for the air-offensive against Yugoslavia in 1999.

For the USA, the haemorrhage of life in the Vietnam War had become a trauma, while France smarted from the losses of the Algerian War, both of which had been fought with conscripts, and both of which to this day have left psychic scars on US and French societies respectively. Coalition operations in the Gulf War were thus deliberately planned to be as different as possible from the Vietnam War: all emphasis was put on shock, initial speed and full impact on the enemy while minimising casualties on the Coalition side. With the Gulf War, *la guerre zéro morts*, the war with zero casualties, became the new buzzword of the post-Cold War era of limited interventions and peacekeeping operations. Here the aircraft seems to have a particularly important rôle. The amount of damage it can inflict at a great distance, with small risks to the pilot if the enemy does not have access to adequate air defence means, seems the pinnacle of superior force and technology. These were the conclusions drawn from the Gulf War by a US Air Force officer:

> The cost in American blood for complete domination of a country of 16 million people and its million-man military was astoundingly low. This significant victory satisfied the legitimate demands of the American people that their wars use technology to keep human losses – on both sides – to an absolute minimum. This victory provides the strategic model for American operations well into the 21st century.[129]

Although belonging to a different tradition of air power strategy, the success of the air campaign in the Gulf War, and the apparent decisiveness of the air strikes in Bosnia, strengthened air enthusiasts' faith in the decisiveness of air power, in itself seen once more

129. Col. John A. Warden, 'Employing air power in the 21st century', in Richard Shultz and Robert Pfaltzgraff (eds.), *The Future of Air Power in the Aftermath of the Gulf War* (Maxwell Air Force Base, AL: Air University Press, 1992), p. 57.

at the end of the century as the panacea weapon which can solve any problem, with minimal casualties on one's own side. In the Gulf War (and less convincingly, in the wars over Bosnia), the faith in air power's quasi omnipotence, expressed by Douhet, Mitchell, and indeed the French strategist and Douhet-follower Pierre-Marie Gallois, who had claimed that one could disband armies because they could be replaced by aircraft delivering nuclear weapons, seemed vindicated by purely 'conventional', not nuclear, air operations.[130] Nevertheless, in the Gulf as in the Balkans, ground forces were still needed, as army leaders had argued defensively since Hiroshima, to occupy and control enemy territory.[131]

What has changed in conventional use of air forces since 1945? The US Air Force still bombed North Korean cities in the Korean War. By the time of the Vietnam War, however, the bombing of enemy cities was avoided or treated as a last option. This was to become a general pattern: since 1954 the air forces of the Western great powers have sought to avoid, at least initially, the direct large-scale air bombardment of enemy cities. Where attacks on cities have been made, they have increasingly been executed with laser-guided bombs or, more recently, *Cruise* missiles, aiming at precision hits of government buildings (e.g. the USA against Tripoli in 1986, Coalition targeting of Iraqi cities in the Gulf War, NATO airstrikes against Yugoslavia in 1999). Western conventional air power strategy increasingly changed to avoid 'collateral damage', and above all, casualties among enemy civilians, as well as casualties on the own side.

This was not a universal change, however. In the early 1990s, Russian forces still indiscriminately bombed the Chechnyan capital, Grozny, albeit mainly with ground-based artillery. In the absence of more sophisticated weapons systems, it was left to Third World powers, such as Iran and Iraq, to re-enact World War II bombing strategies in the late 1980s and early 1990s: missiles with conventional ordnance were used copiously, and specifically against cities, by both sides in the Iran–Iraq war of the early 1980s, in the way Douhet had wanted to see strategic bombers used;[132] Saddam Hussein used them also in air attacks on Tel Aviv in early 1991.

130. Pierre M. Gallois, *L'Adieu aux Armées* (Paris: Albin Michel, 1976).
131. Lawrence Freedman and Efraim Karsh, *The Gulf War* (London: Faber & Faber, 1992).
132. Efraim Karsh, 'Rational ruthlessness: non-conventional and missile warfare in the Iran–Iraq War', in Efraim Karsh, Martin S. Navias and Philip Sabin (eds.), *Non-Conventional Weapons Proliferation in the Middle East* (Oxford: Clarendon Press, 1993), pp. 31–48.

Both in effect and imprecision, these bombing raids were reminiscent of the German V2 rockets of the Second World War.

Just as Western powers have not been involved in wars on the scale and with the war aims of the First and Second World Wars since 1945, the overall tendency of air power doctrine in the West, particularly where put into practice, outside planning for an all-out war with the Warsaw Pact, has been towards ever greater emphasis on precision (achieved only gradually, beginning in the 1970s, through 'smart' or precision-guided missiles or laser-guided bombs which can home in on their target) and the avoidance of collateral damage affecting civilians. Aircraft still complement missiles in this trend, as in general the rule holds that the shorter the range from which a missile (or guided bomb) is fired, the more accurately it can be targeted. Guided bombs dropped from aircraft are cheaper than missiles, and less complex in their navigation technology. Moreover, an aircraft can be deployed flexibly and can be recalled, while a missile with a range comparable to that of an aircraft, once fired, can only be aborted for a short period of time, if at all. In Western strategy – but only there – Hiroshima and Nagasaki have been the high-water mark of deliberate city bombing, even though the Korean War still saw instances of it. But technology is a factor as important as anything in this context, as the option of pursuing other targets, which William Mitchell and John Slessor would have wished for even in the 1920s and 1930s, only became available in the last decades of the twentieth century. What Hiroshima and Nagasaki, and the Gulf War did have in common was that bombing was used to force the enemy to comply with one's own demands.

IMPOSING ONE'S WILL ON THE ENEMY

The ideal of 'imposing one's will on the enemy' (as Clausewitz had defined the aim of war), which had been associated closely with Hiroshima and Nagasaki, at the end of the century lived on both in conventional and nuclear strategy (we have seen Sir Patrick Hine referring to it as a key element of the Coalition forces' conventional strategy in the Gulf War). In the context of air strategy, it was the belief that one could impose one's will upon the enemy more easily through air bombardment (particularly of the civilian population) than by overwhelming the enemy's ground forces, an idea which we have traced back to British and German military thinking during the First World War and to Douhet's early reflections on air power. One might call this bombing a form of 'coercion' (or what the American academic Thomas Schelling calls 'compellence'[133]) – a subject about which a large body of literature exists, making ever more refined calculations on the basis of ever greater unknowns about the enemy. The crux of these arguments is the question as to whether conventional or nuclear air bombardment (or the threat thereof) can force an enemy to do one's will, as Clausewitz would have put it more simply. This idea, related to air attacks, was developed prior to the nuclear age. Richard Overy in his seminal article on the pre-1939 origins of deterrence has concluded that 'it was widely assumed that major war between the powers would not only be a war of nation against nation, but also a war in which air attack would so undermine and demoralise the war willingness of enemy populations that air strikes might procure surrender on their own'.[134]

During the Second World War the Germans did initially try to use this instrument in the form of reprisals for Allied bombing raids, in order to discourage raids against cities. Because of an accidental bombing of London by the *Luftwaffe* in 1940,[135] this intended political signal was largely lost on the British, and the result was a mutual degradation of principles, resulting in all-out city bombing by both sides. Later the Americans tried to use bombing to send political signals to the Vietnamese government, but this did not produce the intended results. One of the few cases where one might be able to say that airstrikes had the intended political effect was the US raid on Libya in 1986: while the technical execution fell short of the expected result – Colonel Ghaddafi survived unscathed, a small child in his family was killed, and the French Embassy was reduced to rubble – there was, after this event, a noticeable decline in Libyan governmental support for international terrorism. Other than that, however, the use of air power to transmit political signals of a finer sort (and thus to impose a certain reaction on the enemy) has rarely shown positive results.

The bombing of Hiroshima and Nagasaki was of course political signalling of a special sort: not only was it assumed that one could signal to the enemy government, but also to the enemy nation, forcing it to surrender. The question whether Douhet and his colleagues in other countries were right about the ability to break the

133. Thomas C. Schelling, *Arms and Influence* (New Haven, Ct.: Yale University Press, 1966).

134. R.J. Overy, 'Air power and the origins of deterrence theory', p. 76.

135. Horst Boog, 'The Luftwaffe and indiscriminate bombing to 1942', in Horst Boog (ed.), *The Conduct of the Air War in the Second World War: An International Comparison* (Oxford: Berg, 1992), pp. 389f.

enemy's will to resist by bombing his urban populations from the
air must be tested against the results of the US Strategic Bombing
Survey conducted after the Second World War. We have already
seen that the survey did not estimate that Hiroshima and Nagasaki
were necessary. It also concluded that in Japan, through mere 'conventional' strategic bombing,

> morale did fall and deterioration of the social fabric became gen-
> eral. People became critical of their leaders and lost confidence in
> one another. Even though the unity of the nation was falling apart,
> people were not able to organize for revolt; they simply became
> more and more obsessed with finding individual solutions to their
> own severe and urgent personal problems.[136]

The Japanese population did not think it had the authority or the
right to urge surrender: they were used to leaving such decisions
to the government, and in the last instance it was of course the
Emperor who took the decision to surrender. While the Japanese
government's war was doggedly supported by the population, the
Japanese themselves were not the ultimate sovereign in the country, nor did they think of seizing power fom the government when
things went badly for their country. Ultimately, America was at war
not with an enemy nation, but with an enemy government which
drew on the strength of its subservient and hard-working population and industry.

David Chuter in a trenchant article on the political aims of air
bombardment has observed that, since the First World War, there
has been in Britain but also in the USA the Douhetian expectation
that enemy populations, once under air attack, will urge their governments to accept an armistice. He has shown also that generally, and
not only in the case of the Japanese population, this expectation
has not been fulfilled, because it was and remains ill-founded.[137]
We have already seen that Tirpitz's advocacy of air attacks on London did not bring forth the expected result of pressure to surrender in the First World War, nor did German bombardment of
London in the Second World War result in an uprising of the
British population against its government (even if Whitehall officials lived in some dread of public responses to bombardment).
The German population in the Second World War was no more

---

136. Morale Division, *The United States Strategic Bombing Survey: The Effects of Strategic Bombing on Japanese Morale* (June 1947), p. 1.
137. David Chuter, 'Triumph of the will? Or, why surrender is not always inevitable', *Review of International Studies* Vol. 23 (1997).

willing to rise up to overthrow its government than the Japanese had been. Although the two cultures responded differently to aerial attack – Japanese felt strongly affected by the bombardment of Japanese cities even if they had not themselves experienced it, while German morale only plunged when bombing had been experienced personally – neither produced large groups of people willing to risk confrontation with their own government.[138]

Significantly, the belief that air bombardment will somehow affect the population's will and translate itself into a popular insurgence against the government has lived on into the Cold War and beyond. This belief has not been linked to air power alone, and has been applied to other measures which could affect the civilian populations, such as economic blockades or terrorism, both still very relevant today. In connection with naval blockades, it is a concept which predates the invention of aircraft. It influenced American and British thinking in the Gulf War of 1990/91. It has been the consistent theme of US policies towards Cuba from the early 1960s, and of UN policies towards Iraq and the warring factions in former Yugoslavia. In none of these cases has it been shown to be justified by subsequent reactions on the part of enemy populations.

Robert Pape, in one of his seminal works on air power, has argued that it is here that the difference between nuclear weapons used to target civilian populations, and conventional weapons used in the same manner, is fundamental: 'coercion based on punishing civilians [with conventional ordnance] rarely succeeds' because 'governments are often willing to countenance considerable civilian punishment' to achieve important war aims.[139] Admittedly, past instances of the conventional bombing of cities with the aim of imposing one's will on the enemy support Pape's argument (and even there, the 28 or 32 cases he notes hardly amount to hard statistical data). But the only two cases of nuclear use in war in world history can hardly be elevated to evidence confirming a rule, particularly as we have seen that the US Strategic Bombing Survey concluded that Japan was close to surrender anyway and would have done so even without the use of atomic bombs.[140] One can thus only underline his scepticism

---

138. *The Effects of Strategic Bombing on Japanese Morale*, p. 2; *The Effects of Strategic Bombing on German Morale* Vol. I (May 1946), p. 1.

139. Robert A. Pape, 'Coercion and military strategy: Why denial works and punishment doesn't', *Journal of Strategic Studies*, Vol. 15, No. 4 (December 1992), pp. 423–75.

140. See Chapter 1.

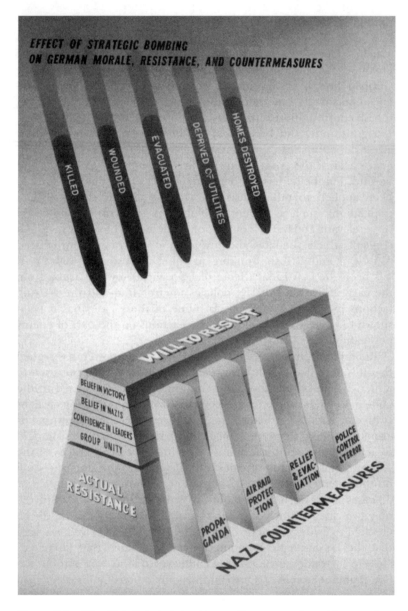

Figure 2.1 *The effect of strategic bombing on German morale, resistance and countermeasures*

Source: Morale Division: *The United States Strategic Bombing Survey: The Effects of Strategic Bombing on German Morale* Vol. I (May 1946), p. 6.

about the utility of inflicting pain on enemy civilians in order to impose one's will upon an enemy government. As Robert Pape has concluded: 'Modern . . . states have extremely high pain thresholds when important interests are at stake, which conventional munitions cannot overcome. Low or moderate levels of punishment inspire more anger than fear; heavy bombardment produces apathy, not rebellion.'[141]

Nevertheless, the assumption that one can send unmistakable signals to the enemy through air strikes is with us still, as is the notion that one can impose one's will on the *enemy population* through military means, which did not in fact occur in the cases either of Japan or Germany in the Second World War. Both assumptions have proved erroneous in most contexts, even though the Japanese surrender after the atom bombs were used against Japan is taken as evidence for the correctness of both.

Nuclear strategies

In the final section of this chapter, we will look at the evolution of nuclear strategy. Since 1945, there have been several nuclear strategies. That of the USA has undergone the most dramatic developments; in addition to this there have – separately – been the nuclear strategies of Britain (which over time also underwent significant changes), France, and collectively, NATO. We have already given a brief overview of the USSR's nuclear strategies, deeply integrated as they were with its conventional strategies. Finally, there is the nuclear strategy of China, about which very little is known, and the strategies of the smallest nuclear powers, Israel, India, and most recently, Pakistan.

There is not the space here to deal in detail with the histories and development of each of these states' nuclear strategies, [142] even where they are not deliberately shrouded in ambiguity, as in the

---

141. Robert A. Pape, *Bombing to Win: Air Power and Coercion in War* (Ithaca: Cornell University Press, 1996), p. 316.

142. For the development of NATO, British and French nuclear strategies, see Heuser, *Nuclear Strategies and Forces*; for US nuclear strategy, see Desmond Ball and Jeffrey Richelson (eds.), *Strategic Nuclear Targeting* (Ithaca: Cornell University Press, 1984); for Chinese nuclear strategy, see Georges Tan Eng Bok, 'Strategic doctrine', in Gerald Segal and William Tow (eds.), *Chinese Defence Policy* (London: Macmillan, 1984), pp. 3–17 and Litai Xue, 'The evolution of China's nuclear strategy', in John Hopkins and Weixing Hu, *Strategic Views from the Second Tier: the Nuclear Weapons Policies of France, Britain and China* (San Diego: IGCC, 1994), pp. 167–92.

case of Israel.[143] It seems more useful to deal with them themati-
cally. Three themes stand out, two of which can be seen to have
commonalities with the nuclear use of 1945: city targeting, and the
political war termination rationale of nuclear strategy. As we shall
see, the third, which is the war-fighting or military rationale, follows
a quite different logic, particularly if applied to an adversary who is
also a nuclear power.

HIROSHIMA AND NAGASAKI: THE CONTINUATION OF CITY TARGETING

The destruction of Hiroshima and Nagasaki was strategic targeting
in its crudest form: while both contained industry related to the
war effort, the choice of the 'ground zero' for dropping the respective atomic bombs was made so as to have the maximum effect
on the population and general built-up area, not with a view to
destroying these industries in particular or sparing the civilians (or
describing their destruction as a collateral effect of the bombing,
as opposed to the main, intended effect).[144] Cities targeted in this
way, for the value they represented to the enemy (as opposed to
the contribution they made to the enemy's war effort), would later
be called 'value' targets (as opposed to 'military' targets). Because
of technical problems with hitting targets that were smaller, of un-
certain location because mobile or well disguised or protected by
secrecy, but also because of a desire to retain an ultimate deterrent
threat ('if you do not desist from your attack, we will ultimately
destroy your cities') cities remained on the target lists of all the
nuclear powers, as far as we can tell from evidence that is in the
public domain.

To give just a few examples, two key US contingency plans for
countering major aggression by the Soviet Union and its satellites,
TROJAN and OFFTACKLE of 1949, assigned 147 and 220 atomic bombs
respectively against 70 and 104 enemy cities.[145] OFFTACKLE noted
that American strategic air forces would be 'aimed at vital elements
of the Soviet warmaking capacity and at the retardation of Soviet

143. Seymour Hersh, *The Samson Option: Israel, America and the Bomb* (2nd rev. edn.
London: Faber & Faber, 1993); Uri Bar-Joseph, 'The hidden debate: the formation of
nuclear doctrines in the Middle East', *Journal of Strategic Studies* Vol. 5, No. 2 (June
1982), pp. 205–27; Edwin S. Cochran, 'Deliberate ambiguity: an analysis of Israel's
nuclear strategy', *Journal of Strategic Studies* Vol. 19, No. 3 (Sept. 1996), pp. 321–42.
144. See Chapter 1.
145. Peter J. Roman, 'Curtis Le May and the origins of NATO atomic targeting',
Journal of Strategic Studies Vol. 16, No. 1 (March 1993), p. 51.

advances in western Eurasia'.[146] Even during the 1960s, when the USA was keenest to signal that it would spare such 'value' targets until pushed to extremes by the enemy, US planners insisted that strikes against such ultimate targets had to remain options, if only to convince the enemy that he must turn back as there was worse punishment in store for him if he did not.

The United Kingdom, while long preferring targeting of military installations (especially installations needed by the enemy to use nuclear weapons against Britain), consciously developed the credible option of striking at Soviet cities, particularly Moscow. This 'Moscow criterion' meant that successive British governments felt compelled to develop their own missile technology further, when an anti-ballistic missile defence system was set up around Moscow in the early 1970s, so as to ensure that British missiles still had a chance of penetrating these defences.

British governments early on allowed themselves to be convinced that deterrence was in the eye of the beholder, and that Britain's supreme values might not be shared by the Soviet leaders, who might value power more greatly than their cities. British governments henceforth veiled their strategic targeting choices in calculated ambiguity: the Defence White Paper of 1958 explained that 'the strategy of N.A.T.O. is based on the frank recognition that a full-scale Soviet attack could not be repelled without resort to a massive nuclear bombardment of the *sources of power in Russia*'.[147] This was also the ultimate set of targets for Britain, as we see in an official document of 1980, which explained that the British 'concept of deterrence is concerned essentially with posing a potential threat to *key aspects of Soviet state power*'.[148] This ambiguity allows speculation as to whether such targets might have included Soviet leadership bunkers rather than cities (where the two did not coincide), reflecting the observation often made that that Soviet leaders did not necessarily balk at great losses of human lives to further their political aims.[149]

French nuclear strategy took many cues from British strategy of the late 1950s. Thus French official publications described the

146. Quoted in Roman, 'Curtis Le May', p. 52.
147. HMG, 'Report on Defence: Britain's Contribution to Peace and Security', Cmnd. 363 (London: HMSO, Feb. 1958), § 12, my italics.
148. 'Defence Open Government Document 80/23' (July 1980), my italics.
149. E.g. Albert Wohlstetter, 'Bishops, statesmen, and other strategists on the bombing of innocents', *Commentary* (June 1983), pp. 15–35, quoted in Colin S. Gray, 'War-fighting for deterrence', *Journal of Strategic Studies* Vol. 7, No. 1 (March 1984), p. 18.

strategic targets for France's nuclear weapons as the 'vital targets' (*objectifs vitaux*)[150] or the 'vitals' (*oeuvres vives*)[151] of Soviet society. Again, there is calculated ambiguity here. Operationally, French strategic targets were principal Soviet cities from the time France first had an independent bomber force (1964/65). One French Prime Minister, Raymond Barre, explicitly noted in 1980 that French deterrence hinged on the threat of 'the assured destruction of a significant part of [the enemy's] cities and of his economy'.[152] Official French estimates have stated enemy casualties as a consequence of the execution of France's strategic nuclear strikes at 14 to 20 million deaths;[153] an alternative figure that has often been quoted is that of 40–50 million, or the equivalent of the French population. French Cold War nuclear strategy was based on an argument of proportionality, namely on the idea that the ability to inflict pain on the USSR proportionate to the gains it would derive from conquering France (hence the linking of the casualty figure to the population of France) would suffice as a deterrent.[154] (This was done in a narrow application of American ideas of operational analysis, of which the French became inordinately fond in the 1960s and 1970s.)

It is important to note in this context that the weapons which were designed for such city targeting soon differed greatly from those used over Hiroshima and Nagasaki. Where these are estimated to have had the force of 14 and 21 kt respectively, the hydrogen bomb as developed by the USA, the Soviet Union and Britain in the 1950s and by France in the 1960s often had fifty to sixty times – and in the case of one Soviet test of 1961, five hundred times – the destructive energy of these earliest atomic bombs. With this in mind, over time, it was this city-targeting option that was most vehemently criticised, particularly in Britain and the USA, and in non-nuclear allied countries such as the Netherlands and

150. 4th defence procurement law of May 1976, quoted in Marcel Duval and Yves Le Baut: *L'arme nucléaire française: Pourquoi et comment?* (Paris: Kronos, 1992), p. 57.
151. First used by Pierre M. Gallois, 'Défense et sécurité dans un monde "multipolaire"', *Forces aériennes françaises* Vol. 18, No. 206 (Aug./Sept. 1964), p. 222. Cf also David Yost, 'French nuclear targeting', in Desmond Ball and Jeffrey Richelson (eds.), *Strategic Nuclear Targeting* (Ithaca: Cornell University Press, 1986), pp. 132–3.
152. Raymond Barre, 'La politique de défense de la France', *Revue Défense Nationale* Vol. 36, No. 10 (Nov. 1980), p. 12; see also speeches by Prime Minister Pierre Mauroy at the IHEDN in Sept. 1981, and General Jeannou Lacaze at the CHEAR in the same month.
153. Yost, 'French nuclear targeting', p. 131.
154. An argument that can be traced back to Pierre-Marie Gallois writing in 1961, quoted in Lucien Poirier, *Des Stratégies nucléaires* (Paris: Hachette, 1977), p. 307.

the FRG. Moreover, a city-targeting strategy was of doubtful credibility once one was dealing not with a non-nuclear power like Japan as adversary, but with the nuclear superpower USSR, that could avenge the destruction of its major cities with strategic nuclear retaliation against Western cities. Once one had entered the era of 'mutually assured destruction' ('MAD'), how could anybody credibly threaten to use nuclear weapons to destroy enemy cities? If they could not *realistically* threaten nuclear use, however, then their nuclear weapons might not play any part in deterring a less than all-out enemy onslaught. As one British strategist wrote,

> To regard nuclear war entirely as something too horrible to contemplate and to evolve no strategies more subtle than all-out mutual annihilation would lead towards paralysis in crisis and vulnerability to nuclear blackmail by more stout-hearted or reckless opponents.[155]

This realisation urged all three Western powers to think about how to develop realistic scenarios for nuclear use, in order to make nuclear deterrence more realistic, or, to use the favourite British term which became part of NATO's *credo*, 'credible'. (The Soviet Union did not have this problem because of (a) the prevalently military rationale of its nuclear strategy, and (b) the ideological argument that Lenin *had* to be right in his analysis that no technological innovation could change the nature of war – see above.) How, then, could one make the use of nuclear weapons credible? There were two approaches: one emphasising their military utility, another, their political function.

NUCLEAR WAR FIGHTING, OR HOW TO RATIONALISE THE MILITARY USE OF NUCLEAR WEAPONS

The military utility of nuclear weapons was indeed briefly contemplated by several military men and the physicists who developed the first atomic bombs in the USA at the same time as the decision was taken to use these bombs against Hiroshima and Nagasaki.[156] It was first studied systematically in the early 1950s by American scientists and military planners tasked by the US government to develop alternatives to the very large conventional forces needed

155. Laurence Martin, 'Limited nuclear war', in Michael Howard (ed.), *Restraints on War: Studies in the Limitation of Armed Conflict* (Oxford: Oxford University Press, 1979), p. 119.

156. Barton J. Bernstein, 'Eclipsed by Hiroshima and Nagasaki', *International Security* Vol. 15, No. 4 (Spring 1991), pp. 149–73.

for America's strategy of repelling Communist aggression on the level on which it occurred (conventional attack – conventional defence; nuclear attack – nuclear defence). As the Korean War was taking place, smaller nuclear weapons were developed, which meant that they could be attached to short-range missiles, or dropped at fairly close range from aircraft. The idea was to use them 'tactically', i.e. against enemy armed forces, in support of ground operations, not far from the battlefield. Unprecedented concentrations of fire-power could now theoretically be used against enemy forces. Short-range ground-to-ground nuclear missiles such as *Honest John*, and later *Lance*, but also air-launched bombs, and atomic demolition munitions (ADM) were developed, while for use at sea, nuclear depth charges, and for use in the air, nuclear-tipped anti-aircraft missiles such as *Nike-Hercules* were built. Training in their use in support of conventional forces was carried out jointly with allies.

The great advantage which a number of strategists and indeed a number of governments (mainly the US and British governments from the late 1950s) saw in such 'tactical' nuclear weapons was that their large-scale effects could compensate for reductions in US and UK conventional forces. For example, a large-scale invasion of NATO territory by forces of the Warsaw Treaty Organisation (WTO) presumed that the latter had to concentrate before breaking through NATO defences. In order to offset such a concentrated mass of enemy forces, NATO either needed even more conventional forces than the enemy, or it could plan to target those troop concentrations with tactical nuclear weapons, or to create additional obstacles through exploding ADM on NATO territory. In a later context, to catch a Soviet submarine carrying nuclear missiles aimed at NATO territory, NATO either needed a large number of hunter submarines (even then with only a small chance of hitting and sinking the dangerous enemy), or it could seek to destroy it with a nuclear depth charge, in which case a fairly approximate target could be hit with a great degree of certainty. Oncoming Soviet aircraft carrying nuclear weapons might collectively be brought down in one big nuclear explosion caused by a *Nike-Hercules*, which again produced a higher likelihood of success than conventional air-defence systems, which could not be guaranteed to strike all their targets, and might even be outnumbered or 'saturated'. There were thus ways in which the use of nuclear weapons could be contemplated for military reasons.

In the 1970s such plans for the use of nuclear weapons with the aim of military effectiveness underwent some modification with the development of precision-guided weapons and the satellite intelligence necessary to guide them to targets far beyond the 'forward edge of battle'. Moreover, with the advent of greater accuracy, missile warhead yields could be reduced, again rendering it more practicable to use such weapons (given that one wanted to reduce the effects of the explosion of one's own weapons on one's own forces or populations). The technology was in place in the early 1980s with *Cruise* and *Pershing II* missiles and air-launched missiles which could strike forces and military installations in the enemy's rear, forming one component of NATO's doctrine of *Follow-On Forces Attack*, adopted in 1985.

The argument for the need for selective nuclear strikes that could be executed on a level below strategic strikes was accepted throughout NATO. But it was exclusively the USA which moved to a doctrine with National Security Decision Memorandum 242, Presidential Directive 59 and National Security Decision Directive 13 which made it the American aim to 'prevail' in a war, even a longer nuclear war, by developing nuclear use options which would progressively incapacitate the enemy's war effort.[157] This 'war fighting' nuclear doctrine was only abandoned by the USA in November 1997, when it adopted its first post-Cold War nuclear strategy in the form of a new Presidential Decision Directive.[158]

In many respects one could argue that with this war-fighting doctrine the USA took a leaf out of the Soviet strategy book. In the USSR, all attempts to question Lenin's dictum about the eternal validity of Clausewitz's dictum that war was a (rational) tool of politics were quashed – questioning Lenin would have been tantamount to bringing down the 'objective' truth of Marxist-Leninist teaching. Therefore, as we have seen, Soviet strategists tended to argue that all war, even nuclear war, had to be 'winnable', and it had to be the USSR that prevailed. The USSR therefore developed a strategy which maximised the military use of nuclear weapons, in order to speed up Soviet operations, to break through enemy defences and, above all, to eliminate pre-emptively the enemy's own nuclear forces before they could destroy the USSR. [159] The latter

157. Peter Pringle and William Arkin, *SIOP: The Secret U.S. Plan for Nuclear War* (London: New York: W.W. Norton, 1983), pp. 189ff.

158. R. Jeffrey Smith, 'Clinton directive changes strategy on nuclear arms', *The Washington Post* (7 December 1997); Steven Lee Myers, 'U.S. "updates" nuclear war guidelines', *New York Times* (8 December 1997).

159. Sokolovskij, *Military Strategy*, p. 293; A.A. Sidorenko, *The Offensive* (early 1970s?), quoted in Joseph D. Douglass, *Soviet Military Strategy in Europe* (New York, Oxford: Pergamon Press, 1980), p. 89.

was obviously a growing problem with the growth of the arsenal of the USA. In this context, the Soviet leadership expected its own military to be ready to incur certain death through irradiation and almost certain death in particularly high-risk operations, appealing to its forces' sense of self-sacrifice.[160]

It was only in 1987 that the Soviet Union ceased to regard nuclear weapons as just another form of weapon, which had to be subject to Lenin's dicta.[161] Indeed, the doctrine adopted by post-Communist Russia in 1993 seemed inspired by Western nuclear use doctrine, one rationalised politically as defensive. At the end of 1997, however, there was some concern that, with the new National Security Concept, Russia might be resurrecting pre-1987 Soviet thinking, by emphasising nuclear weapons particularly in a 'tactical' or 'operational' context – just as nuclear weapons were becoming increasingly taboo in the West.[162]

As a postscript it needs to be said that counter-force targeting in its most blatant form, namely that of a pre-emptive strike, was indeed contemplated also on the Western side. When the Soviet Union first developed nuclear weapons, the American Strategic Air Command was sorely tempted by the idea of a pre-emptive counter-force strategy. Its chief from 1948 until 1952, General Curtis Le May, opined in 1949 that 'It would appear economical and logical to adopt the objective of completely avoiding enemy attack against our strategic force by destroying his atomic force before it can attack ours.'[163] Le May wanted to receive for himself the right to authorise nuclear air strikes,[164] a right which was temporarily bestowed upon the SACEUR (Supreme Allied Commander Europe), when General Lauris Norstad held this post.[165] Fortunately, Le May's ideas – and any subsequent American ideas of nuclear use in actual wars – were nipped in the bud by America's Presidents.

The concentration by military planners on the military utility of nuclear weapons both in the Soviet and in the US case can be explained also in bureaucratic terms, by looking at the demands that were made of these planners. In both cases, planners were tasked to study the utility of nuclear weapons, and procedural logic

---

160. A.S. Milovidov, *The Philosophical Heritage of V.I. Lenin and Problems of Contemporary War* (Moscow: 1972), quoted in Douglass, *Soviet Military Strategy in Europe*, pp. 83f.

161. Cf. Heuser, 'Warsaw Pact nuclear doctrines'.

162. *Krasnaya Zvesda* (27 Dec. 1997).

163. Quoted in Peter J. Roman, 'Curtis Le May', p. 49.   164. *Ibid.*, p. 54.

165. Stephen Twigge and Alan Macmillan, 'Britain, the United States, and the development of NATO strategy, 1950–1964', *Journal of Strategic Studies* Vol. 19, No. 2 (June 1996), p. 275.

turned the resulting plans into the basis for operational strategy. Military planners, when asked to study an option, have the duty to do so. In NATO, where the emphasis was placed on the *deterrence* of war, and later, in addition, the need for a *credible* (i.e. technically implementable) nuclear strategy, which would enhance deterrence, planners could tell themselves that their work was done *pro forma*, with some confidence that it would never be translated into practice.[166] Soviet planners in turn were driven by the imperative of finding ways of defending Soviet society against NATO in a nuclear war, so that Socialism would survive, and the obvious way of doing so was by doing everything – including using nuclear weapons – to wipe out NATO's nuclear forces before these could destroy the USSR. A third structural factor leading to the planning for nuclear war fighting lay in the task given to engineers to take weapons developments further – and the results time and again encouraged the consideration of new ways in which nuclear weapons could be *used*. Both the secret cities in the Soviet Union and the nuclear weapons laboratories in the American desert were under pressure to produce value for the resources which were being pumped into them, and if value – or new nuclear weapons systems – was produced, they would want to prove it by suggesting military ways of exploiting the new developments (whether these were smaller missiles, more accurate missiles, lower flying missiles, or whatever). Along with developing ever greater hydrogen bombs, scientists were thus encouraged to develop smaller, more limited, more 'usable' nuclear weapons, and thus to bring them closer to conventional weapons. This began, as we have seen, in the mid-1950s with the miniaturisation of nuclear weapons; even in 1956 early 'clean' bombs (early models for the enhanced radiation weapon of the late 1970s, the 'neutron bomb') were developed, with reduced nuclear fall-out.[167] The pursuit of planning for nuclear war fighting, and the development of weapons that seemingly opened up new options is thus not entirely surprising, given research, development, planning and procurement structures, notwithstanding the enormity which the implementation of such plans would have entailed. And yet, plans for nuclear war fighting were a departure from the anti-city use of the first two atomic bombs, which had aimed at catalysing the political decision to surrender, not to defeat an enemy in a nuclear battle.

---

166. For Western assessments of the Soviet threat and the likelihood of war, see Heuser, *Nuclear Strategies and Forces for Europe*, ch. 1.

167. Max Freedman, 'U.S. reduces H-bomb hazards', *Manchester Guardian* (21 July 1956); Henry Lowrie, 'America has "clean" bomb', *Daily Express* (22 May 1957).

DETERRENCE AND WAR-TERMINATION, OR HOW TO
RATIONALISE THE POLITICAL USE OF NUCLEAR WEAPONS

In the same way as the military, diplomats and defence civil servants tried to squeeze some political utility out of existing nuclear weapons. Again, the basic premise is not unintelligible: civil servants in NATO countries, particularly in Europe, were above all concerned to make any further major war unthinkable. They put all their money on and their effort into deterrence, but, as noted above, they accepted to a greater or lesser degree that deterrence was a function of the credibility of the threat inherent in deterrence being implemented.

Deterrence as a concept existed a long time before nuclear weapons, of course. But, as George Quester has shown so brilliantly, the very direct ways in which the threat of nuclear weapons was used to convey a deterrence message, and much of the planning for nuclear strategy, had their roots in air strategy prior to the Second World War. In the 1930s it was hoped vainly, particularly in Britain, that the existence of a British bomber force would frighten Germany off any bombing campaigns against British cities, for fear of retaliation.[168] The air bombardment was 'regarded as a menace, a withheld thunderbolt, an impending calamity. All nations fear it. For that very reason it should be a deterrent influence against war' as the British strategist J.M. Spaight wrote in 1938.[169] Much French and British deterrence thinking dating from the First World War and after was resurrected in Britain and France in particular. Through nuclear deterrence, small nuclear powers could be as strong as large nuclear powers, argued Admiral Raoul Castex even in 1945.[170] French governments were attracted by this line of argument, putting much of their hope in the deterrent quality of nuclear weapons, even vis-à-vis an aggressor 'who is much stronger'. The French thus became determined to acquire them for their own country.[171] A committee within the British government produced a report on 16 June 1945 which noted: 'the only answer that we can see to the atomic bomb is to be prepared to use it ourselves in

168. George H. Quester, *Deterrence before Hiroshima: The Airpower Background of Modern Strategy* (New York: John Wiley, 1966).

169. J.M. Spaight, *Air Power in the Next War* (London: Geoffrey Bles, 1938), p. 126, quoted in Quester, *Deterrence before Hiroshima*, p. 102.

170. Admiral Castex, 'Aperçus sur la bombe atomique', *Revue Défense nationale* Vol. 2 (Oct. 1945).

171. Quoted in Georges-Henri Soutou, 'La politique nucléaire de Pierre Mendès France', *Relations Internationales* No. 59 (Autumn 1989), p. 326, emphasis added.

retaliation. A knowledge that we were prepared, in the last resort, to do this might well deter an aggressive nation.'[172] Nor was such deterrent thinking unknown to Americans. The US academic strategist Bernard Brodie commented on the first use of the atomic bomb: 'Thus far the chief purpose of our military establishment has been to win wars. From now on its chief purpose must be to avoid them. It can have no other purpose.'[173]

Once Moscow had the bomb, optimism about the banishment of all war through nuclear weapons waned. Britons reasoned (here in the words of the First Sea Lord, Lord Mountbatten, some years later), that once there was a 'nuclear equipoise' between East and West,

> this deterrent will no longer deter war, as it does now. It will only deter *thermonuclear* war. Once again we shall have to face the possibility of war being fought with conventional forces ... because thermonuclear action by two power blocs, each with the maximum destruction in its possession, would mean world suicide.[174]

Convinced that the Soviets must share this view, it was British civil servants who took the lead in developing a refined argument for nuclear use as part of nuclear deterrence. Lord Mountbatten's reasoning, as exemplified above, was that while nuclear war might be banned through mutual deterrence, conventional war, on a lower level, might well not be. This meant that major *conventional* war, but nevertheless major war on the scale of the First and Second World Wars, might be possible again in Europe, and that was a nightmare in its own right to Europeans. How could nuclear deterrence be extended to ban major conventional war?

Credibility was at the heart of this question. How could NATO (or any individual nuclear power) threaten to use nuclear weapons in reaction to a merely conventional attack if it was itself blatantly afraid of nuclear retaliation? A complicated answer was found, which hinged on the assumption that the USSR was as afraid of nuclear war as were NATO members: it was to signal to the Soviets that they should not underestimate NATO's determination to defend itself against *any* attack, as it might well resort to nuclear use, even

172. COS(45)402(0), quoted in Julian Lewis, *Changing Direction: British Military Planning for Post-War Strategic Defence, 1942–1947* (London: The Sherwood Press, 1988), p. 187.

173. Bernard Brodie ed., *The Absolute Weapon* (New York: Harcourt Brace, 1946), p. 76.

174. Quoted in Twigge and Macmillan, 'Britain, the United States', p. 264.

against a purely conventional assault, but in a way that would *not* immediately drive the USSR to full, massive retaliation. The 'political signalling' function of a first nuclear use by NATO in response to a purely conventional attack by the Warsaw Treaty Organisation was invented, with a deliberate emphasis on its political purpose (getting the adversary to rethink, and to stop his aggression), rather than on any military gains to be made by such use. This reasoning, developed by Britain and presented to NATO in 1961, became the basis of NATO's doctrine for its own first use of nuclear weapons.[175] Here again, a way was found to rationalise the use of nuclear weapons – but in a strictly limited fashion, expressly avoiding collateral damage, where possible, and avoiding the enemy's 'high value targets', in particular his cities. (While French operational strategy embraced a similar concept of first use – as an ultimate test of the enemy's intention – France otherwise remained committed to a massive retaliation strategy, which, French strategists courageously maintained, would banish major conventional as well as nuclear war from French soil.)

British and, under British influence, NATO strategy thus hinged on the ability to convey to the adversary through the use of nuclear weapons a complex political message or 'signal' (which would have been expressed simultaneously through a communiqué): namely, that NATO was willing to use nuclear weapons, but also to give the adversary a last chance to back off before resorting to all-out nuclear war. This would have to be done without making the adversary so desperate that he would react to initial NATO nuclear use by resorting to all-out retaliation. British planners assumed that this meant NATO's first use should steer clear of targeting cities, as we have noted.

Related developments can be identified in the US strategic thinking of the late 1950s and early 1960s. Analysts in think tanks in the late 1950s called for more differentiated options than the supposed all-or-nothing of 'massive retaliation'. In 1962, when John F. Kennedy brought some of these analysts into the Pentagon, which was headed by Robert McNamara, they had an influence on policy-making. Seeing nuclear weapons as so awesome that, surely, the enemy would be willing to negotiate rather than risk their use, the American analysts talked about gradual escalation of military operations against the enemy, who should perpetually be kept in awe of the next,

---

175. Beatrice Heuser: 'Containing uncertainty: Options for British nuclear strategy', *Review of International Studies* Vol. 19, No. 3 (July 1993), pp. 245–67; Twigge and Macmillan, 'Britain, the United States'; Heuser, *Nuclear Strategies and Forces for Europe*, chs. 2, 3.

more horrible step the USA might take. The obvious hope was that the enemy, being rational, would weigh up the cost of submission against the actual pain inflicted on him at present and the potential pain still held in store; depending on his tolerance for such pain, he would then surrender sooner or later. In their parlance, cities should initially be 'withhold targets' or sanctuaries in the early stages of such a nuclearised war. This in itself was not a total innovation – sanctuaries in warfare had been recognised by many different cultures, and had indeed played a rôle even in the First World War.[176]

Many related concepts of nuclear targeting also predated the development of nuclear weapons. Counterforce and countervalue strategies had been developed, as had deterrence. Signalling (reprisals) and the concept of 'withhold targets' had been developed, but did not work well (the accidental German bombing of London in the Second World War has already been referred to, which falsely signalled that Berlin had now decided to escalate to city bombardment). We thus find that there were few, if any, completely new ideas in the political use of nuclear weapons, if taken on their own. The novelty of these concepts consisted more in the mix in which they were presented, and the scale on which they would have been implemented, had nuclear war broken out between NATO and WTO. What many of these ideas about the *political* purposes of nuclear use had in common with the thinking underlying the use of atomic weapons against Hiroshima and Nagasaki was the aim of *terminating* a war (had a Third World War broken out) at the least possible cost to one's own side. Outside the Soviet Union, few strategists in the nuclear age wholeheartedly espoused the idea that a nuclear war could lead to a victory in the sense in which 15 August 1945 was a victory for the USA.

IS VICTORY POSSIBLE IN NUCLEAR WAR?

In considering the novelty or continuity of nuclear strategy, compared with previous, non-nuclear strategies, let us finally turn to the question of victory. Is victory possible in nuclear war, or can we see here a turning point in which nuclear weapons are irreconcilable with the concept of victory? The use of atom bombs in the Far East in 1945 was clearly still subject to the old logic: the bombs used here seemed to be decisive weapons, and played a part in bringing

176. Quester, *Deterrence before Hiroshima*, p. 73.

about clear victory, in the sense of unconditional surrender on the part of the enemy. We have seen that Marxism-Leninism postulated that the victory of the Socialist system in a cataclysmic war would be a historical inevitability that could not be affected by technological innovation. It was the very doubts cast on this view by Mikhail Gorbachëv himself which contributed crucially to the erosion of the Marxist-Leninist belief system and its final collapse.

In the early Cold War, US and then also NATO strategy aimed at victory in the same sense as in World War II. But gradually, with the development of Soviet nuclear weapons, the concept of victory in this sense retreated. Indeed, NATO strategy from the end of the 1950s stopped using the term, and increasingly, terms such as 'termination of hostilities', and, at best, the hope for the return to the *status quo ante* (i.e. Soviet withdrawal from the territory the WTO would have invaded during such a war) delineated the war aims.[177]

After the Vietnam War, a ground swell of feeling among sections of the American 'strategic community' rose to protest against having been denied 'victory' by the constraints of political considerations, and against the drop in morale in the US military. Some US defence experts looked on with envy when the Israelis carried the day in 1967 and the British won the Falklands War in 1982, and called for a return of the belief in 'victory' as opposed to the 'debellicization' of the USA.[178] They were open to persuasion when Colin Gray, a British academic strategist of the 'robust' persuasion, in 1979 made 'the case for a theory of victory', arguing that the USA, like the Soviet Union, should adopt a 'nuclear war-fighting' strategy, think of ways in which nuclear weapons might profitably be used if it came to war, including targeting military installations, and striking at targets that would be important for the Soviet recovery after such a war, such as Soviet industry and the leadership.[179] Gray's campaign for rehabilitating the concept of 'victory' in the nuclear era met with pronounced misgivings in Europe in particular, including from some of the greatest establishment figures among defence academics.[180] In view of this reaction among America's

177. Beatrice Heuser, 'Victory in a nuclear war? A comparison of NATO and WTO war aims and strategies', *Contemporary European History* (expected April 1999).

178. Edward N. Luttwak, 'On the meaning of victory', *The Washington Quarterly* Vol. 5, No. 4 (Autumn 1982), pp. 17–24.

179. Colin S. Gray, 'Nuclear strategy: the case for a theory of victory', *International Security* Vol. 4, No. 1 (Summer 1979), pp. 67f., 77; Colin Gray and Keith Payne, 'Victory is possible', *Foreign Policy* No. 39 (Summer 1980).

180. Michael E. Howard, 'On fighting a nuclear war', *International Security* Vol. 5, No. 4 (Spring 1981), pp. 3–17.

allies, US Secretary of Defense Caspar Weinberger felt obliged to note in 1983, 'We, for our part, are under no illusion about the dangers of a nuclear war between the major powers; we believe that neither side could win such a war.'[181] Nevertheless, there was also much support for 'victory' thinking, particularly in US government circles, and Gray rode on the crest of a tide of thinking in the late Carter and first Reagan administrations. Gray belatedly explained that what he meant by victory was 'no more and certainly no less than that the United States achieves its political objectives (whatever they may be – and they may be quite modest)'.[182] In any case, Gray pleaded for formulating Western targeting in accordance with what the Soviet Union feared most, not with what the West feared most. In his view, 'The Soviet state, if it is capable of being "provoked", would be provoked by the reality of anticipation of damage to its essential instruments of coercive control, not by collateral damage to civilian society.'[183] Perhaps he was not aware just how right he was – the Soviet leadership was certainly 'provoked' and greatly agitated in the period of 1979–84 by Western talk about war-winning nuclear strategies, and the deployment of the *Cruise* and *Pershing II* missiles by NATO from late 1983 was seen in the light of this threat.[184]

This attempt to resurrect the concept of victory arguably contributed crucially to the last big East–West crisis. Fortunately, moderate thinking prevailed over military hysteria in the Kremlin, and as a direct consequence, the Cold War drew to a close. Since then, victory has been sought and – militarily – found in the *conventional* field of the Gulf War. It is striking that nuclear powers have since 1945 been relatively chary of threatening nuclear use against non-nuclear powers;[185] indeed, in the late 1970s and early 1980s, the five declared nuclear powers undertook not to do so.[186] In nuclear terms, despite arguments to the contrary, Hiroshima and Nagasaki may

181. Quoted in Colin S. Gray, 'War-fighting for deterrence', *Journal for Strategic Studies* Vol. 7, No. 1 (March 1984), p. 7.

182. Gray, 'War-fighting for Deterrence', p. 6.   183. *Ibid.*, p. 16.

184. Christopher Andrew and Oleg Gordievsky, *KGB: the Story of its Inside Operations from Lenin to Gorbachev* (New York: HarperCollins, 1990).

185. Examples include the nuclear 'brinkmanship' and implied threats against China over Korea in 1954 and in the Quemoy Matsu crisis of 1958.

186. In the late 1970s, and early 1980s, the declared nuclear powers provided 'negative security assurances' to all non-nuclear states (attaching certain conditions) in declarations to the United Nations' General Assembly. The US commitment, however, is arguably invalidated by a recent shift to extending nuclear deterrence to any enemy intention of using chemical or biological weapons, see Tom Rhodes, 'US to aim missiles at "rogue nations"', *The Times* (8 Dec. 1997).

well have been the first and last time that nuclear weapons could bring about an undisputed victory that could be meaningfully enjoyed by the victorious power. In that sense, August 1945 was very much a turning point in strategy.

CONCLUSIONS: IS NUCLEAR STRATEGY VERY DIFFERENT FROM AIR POWER STRATEGY?

We have noted that, except for the explosive (and radiation) yield of the atomic bombs used, Hiroshima and Nagasaki were in all respects merely the application of World War II conventional city bombing practice, and the application of strategic thinking that had been developed since 1914 with conventional ordnance in mind. Richard Overy has rightly observed: 'While it is certainly true that nuclear weaponry has seen a radical qualitative jump in the air threat, there is a danger of exaggerating the change in 1945. Air power theory and force structure before 1939 show strong lines of continuity with the post-war world.' In his view, the difference made by 1945 was that theory, which had 'run ahead of the technology', was once more in line with technology.[187]

In conventional strategy (and particularly in air power tactics), the nuclear age saw developments which had little to do with the invention of nuclear weapons, even if one important war – America's war in Vietnam – was fought under the shadow of evolving American nuclear strategy. Conventional air power has been used in many different ways since 1945 – from purely tactical, in support of battle, to ways of which Douhet would have approved. Bernard Brodie noted that Douhet's optimism about the invulnerability of bombers was vindicated once the nuclear bomb was invented as ordnance.[188] At the time of the Gulf War, however, Douhet's belief in aircraft as decisive weapon seemed to have been vindicated even by advanced *conventional* ordnance.[189] The introduction of the nuclear bomb led to the culmination of city bombing, eventually catalysing Western societies' distaste for the massive killing of civilians through air bombardment, and ushered in a new age of more discriminate use of air power.

187. R.J. Overy, 'Air power and the origins of deterrence theory before 1939', *Journal of Strategic Studies* Vol. 15, No. 1 (March 1992), p. 74.
188. Bernard Brodie, *Strategy in the Missile Age* (Princeton, NJ: Princeton UP, 1959), p. 73.
189. Claudio G. Segre, 'Giulio Douhet: strategist, theorist, prophet?, *Journal of Strategic Studies* Vol. 15, No. 3 (Sept. 1992), pp. 351–66.

At the end of the twentieth century, we can say with relief that since their invention, nuclear weapons have been used in war only in 1945. While cities have remained on the targeting lists of all nuclear powers, as far as we can tell, there has also been growing revulsion against the idea of applying such a targeting plan. Whether, however, this revulsion is shared by all cultures who at the beginning of the twenty-first century have nuclear weapons within their reach remains to be seen; this is a question we will discuss further in Chapter 5. Before studying the genesis of this rejection of warfare with massive, and particularly, massive civilian, casualties by Western societies, we shall now turn to the epitome of immoral thinking about war: the advocacy and glorification of 'total war', and the relationship between that and nuclear war.

CHAPTER THREE

A Turning Point in the Development of 'Total War'?

For a morally strong people, the war decision lies solely in the victory on the battlefield *and in the annihilation* of the enemy army *and of the enemy nation*, though they [themselves] remain morally strong and psychically united.

(Erich von Ludendorff: *Der Totale Krieg*)[1]

This chapter deals mainly with concepts and with attempts to categorise wars, in themselves very complex historical events, in terms of such concepts. This involves a high degree of abstraction, and any such conceptualisation is therefore controversial. The attempt to identify suitable definitions for the concept of 'total war', and to apply them to real wars and events, does not primarily serve a moral aim. Instead, it is designed to serve as an analytical tool enabling us to compare and contrast different war aims and manifestations of war which can be the basis of any objective judgement about them – as far as phenomena inflicting so much suffering and pain, which for each person experiencing it is a highly personal tragedy, can ever be objectivised. It is only by clarifying such concepts that we can judge whether, according to our definition, nuclear bombing is an act of 'total war', and if so in what sense.

In the following, then, we will start with some definitions of 'total war', and the connection of this concept with that of totalitarianism. We will then apply this definition to wars throughout history, to see whether it fits any wars prior to that which culminated in the first atomic bombardment. Looking particularly at the Second World War, we will compare and contrast the war aims of

---

1. Erich Ludendorff, *Der Totale Krieg* (Munich: Ludendorffs Verlag GmbH, 1935), translated by Dr A.S. Rappoport as *The Nation at War* (London: Hutchinson & Co., 1936), p. 168, italics mine.

the major protagonists, trying to establish whether, by our definition, they were 'total', and what the implications are for the first ever use of atomic bombs. Finally, we will apply the definitions to wars both before and since the Second World War.

LIMITED WAR, ABSOLUTE WAR, TOTAL WAR AND THE WAR MACHINE – DEFINITIONS

Before homing in on definitions of 'total war', it will be useful to acquire a further tool-box of terms and definitions to facilitate the differentiation between 'total wars' and other forms of warfare. These are:

- **Limited wars**, i.e. wars limited in aim (e.g. the seizure of limited territory, access to sea-routes or natural resources, without seeking the destruction of the enemy's government or state or the replacement of a ruler), or wars limited in the way they were fought (e.g. only 'men of military age' would be treated as enemies, or only soldiers on the battlefield but not civilians), or wars limited in time, space or quantity of people and resources involved. This concept goes back to Clausewitz's categorisation of wars.[2]
- **'Absolute' wars**, to use the Clausewitzian terminology, by which he meant wars aiming at the complete defeat of the enemy's armed forces in battle with the consequence of bringing down the state (or other system of government). Absolute wars, in terms of war aims, would include all wars of colonial expansion, although the battles involved could often be limited in scope.[3]
- **The 'War Machine'**,[4] or what Arthur Koestler has called the 'destructive organisational engine of war'.[5] The term will be used here to refer to the industrial and technical factors, as well as the centralised administrative and operational structures of states which transformed warfare between the time of Napoleon and that of the First World War: these include enhanced, industrialised production of coal and other fuels, steel, and thus armaments and arms systems; the major technological innovations (the railway, the telegraph, the steamship, new and more deadly guns);

2. Carl von Clausewitz, *On War* (Berlin: Dümmler, 1832), beginning of Book VIII.

3. Clausewitz's model of the 'absolute' war, Napoleonic warfare, aimed at the destruction of the enemy's system of government or state, and indeed at the replacement of his political ideology by another: *On War*, Book VIII Ch. 2.

4. This term is used, in a somewhat looser sense, by Daniel Pick, *War Machine: The Rationalisation of Slaughter in the Modern Age* (New Haven: Yale University Press, 1993).

5. Arthur Koestler, *Janus: A Summing Up* (London: Hutchinson, 1978), p. 90.

enhanced state control over populations, with the involvement of these populations in warfare through conscription, propaganda (including through universal primary school education), but also taxation; a reshaping of the workforce to suit the needs of a war industry; and finally, the change in the conduct of warfare which led to ever more lethal firepower and ever 'emptier' battlefields, with an ever wider dispersal of operations in growing theatres of war. The War Machine we will take to mean all the factors *other than ideology and political aims* which came together to transform war in scale and effectiveness. In other words, the fully developed War Machine is a system, a state, an industrial society geared up for the waging of war, minus the ideology. This phenomenon of the ever more machine-like and anonymous war, which was only identified gradually by a few intellectuals like Carl von Clausewitz, Richard Cobden or John Ruskin, became more widely understood only with the mass slaughter of the American Civil War of 1861–65, of the Franco–German war of 1870/71, and then, finally, of the First World War.[6]

- **Genocide**, as defined by the convention adopted by the UN General Assembly in 1948:

  any of the following acts committed with intent to destroy, in whole or in part, a national, ethnical, racial or religions group, as such:
  (a) Killing members of the group;
  (b) Causing serious bodily or mental harm to members of the group;
  (c) Deliberately inflicting on the group conditions of life calculated to bring about its physical destruction in whole or in part;
  (d) Imposing measures intended to prevent births within the group;
  (e) Forcibly transferring children of the group to another group.[7]

With these terms to help us, let us now turn to definitions of 'total war'.

Definitions of 'total war' and the link with totalitarianism

DEFINITIONS OF 'TOTAL WAR'

In Anglo-American and even in French literature, we often encounter the term 'total war', used very loosely (and often without the

6. Pick, *War Machine*.
7. 'Convention on the Prevention and Punishment of the Crime of Genocide', 78 U.N.T.S. 277.

slightest attempt to define the term), usually meaning 'total mobilization of national resources'.[8] In 1915, Alphonse Seché wrote about the 'totalisation of the national strength' in war by a harnessing of the economy to the war effort.[9] The French member of parliament Léon Daudet prided himself on having invented the expression 'total war', and his definition concerned primarily the way in which the Germans were waging the First World War, with a clear focus on the comprehensive mobilisation of the country's resources for war:

> What is total war? It is the extension of the fight, in its climaxes as well as in its phases of residual violence, to the political, economic, commercial, industrial, intellectual and financial domains. It is not only armies that fight, but also traditions, institutions, customs, rules of conduct, spirits, and above all the banks. Germany is mobilised on all those levels, in all those ways . . . She has constantly sought, beyond the military front, to disorganise materially and morally the people she has been attacking.[10]

It is in this sense that Anglo-American historians often use the expression, and they use it for a variety of wars, most frequently, to describe the Second, but also the First World War. Occasionally, writers use it to describe the American Civil War, or even the French Revolutionary and Napoleonic Wars. It is quite wrongly attributed to Clausewitz.[11]

There is more to the idea of 'total war', however, than the total mobilisation of the economy and the population in the war effort. The additional dimension which the term 'total war' was to acquire hinges on its link with totalitarianism. The word 'totalitarian' was first used, it seems, by Mussolini's adversaries in Italy in the early 1920s, before it was appropriated by Mussolini himself with considerable pride. The East German historian Gerhard Foerster has studied the link between total war and totalitarian society: Ernst Jünger in 1930 published an article entitled 'Total Mobilisation', in which he advocated that there should 'not be anything that cannot be understood as a function of the State', i.e. all aspects of society, of

---

8. Berenice Carroll, *Design for Total War: Arms and Economics in the Third Reich* (The Hague: Mouton, 1968), p. 9.

9. Alphonse Seché, *Les Guerres d'Enfer* (Paris: E. Sansot, 1915), p. 124.

10. Léon Daudet, *La Guerre Totale* (Paris: Nouvelle Librairie Nationale, 1918), pp. 8f.

11. Clausewitz never used the term, and more importantly, in his analysis of Napoleonic War (or indeed any other campaigns) never blurred the line between combatants and non-combatants, which, as we shall see, is crucial to the definition of Total War.

the life of a people, should become the business of the state, should be *'erfaßt'* (controlled) by the state.[12] Indeed, the rôle of the state is central to earliest German writing about 'total war', and in time for Hitler's *Machtergreifung* (seizure of power), right-wingers advocated the creation of a 'total state', 'total' clearly being used synonymously with 'totalitarian'.[13] The actual expression 'total war', according to Longerich,[14] is first found in Germany in historian-sociologist Carl Schmitt's book on the end of the Second German Empire, in which he claimed that the German General Staff had prepared Germany for a 'total war' even in the First World War.[15]

The most important work on the subject, however, is Erich Ludendorff's book of 1935, bearing the actual title, *Total War*.[16] Earlier writers had advocated similar concepts of war, which should encompass the entire society, but without using the expression 'total war', and without going quite to the lengths of Ludendorff and his followers.[17] Ludendorff's was only the tip of the iceberg of publications of this sort in Germany, but it is the use of the term and the concept as elaborated so forcefully by Ludendorff that spread rapidly from 1935, and for decades it became the point of reference of writing on the subject.[18] The comprehensiveness and extreme logic of Ludendorff's development of the subject, and its total application by National Socialist Germany, make it the benchmark that will be used here for the totality of any war.

Let us therefore focus on Ludendorff and his notion of Total War (used with capitals, we shall henceforth take the term to mean what Ludendorff described). General Erich Ludendorff, a Prussian

---

12. Ernst Jünger, 'Die totale Mobilmachung', *Krieg und Krieger* (Berlin, 1930), pp. 11–30, quoted in Gerhard Foerster, *Totaler Krieg und Blitzkrieg: Die Theorie des totalen Krieges und des Blitzkrieges in der Militärdoktrin des faschistischen Deutschland am Vorabend des 2. Weltkrieges* (East Berlin: Militärverlag der DDR, 1967).
13. Ernst Forsthoff, *Der totale Staat* (Hamburg: Hanseatische Verlagsanstalt, 1933).
14. Peter Longerich, 'Joseph Goebbels und der totale Krieg', *Vierteljahreshefte für Zeitgeschichte* Vol. 35 (1987), pp. 289–314.
15. Carl Schmitt, *Staatsgefüge und Zusammenbruch des 2. Reiches* (Hamburg: 1934), p. 31, quoted in Longerich, 'Joseph Goebbels'.
16. Ludendorff, *Der Totale Krieg*. On the importance of Ludendorff's book, see also the seminal article by Hans-Ulrich Wehler, ' "Absoluter" und "totaler" Krieg: von Clausewitz zu Ludendorff', in *Politische Vierteljahresschrift* Vol. 10 (1969), pp. 220–48.
17. This arguably included the writings of Friedrich von Bernhardi, *Vom Krieg der Zukunft* (Berlin: Ernst Siegfried Mittler & Sohn, 1920) and Hans Reitter, *Der Zukunftskrieg und seine Waffen* (Leipzig, 1924), etc.
18. Further examples quoted by Foerster include: J.W. Ludowici, *Totale Landesverteidigung* (Berlin: Oldenbourg, 1936); Hans-Heinrich Ambrosius, 'Zur Totalität des Zukunftskriegs', in *Wissen und Wehr* Vol. 18 (1937), pp. 187–98; Guido Fischer, *Wehrwirtschaft: Ihre Grundlagen und Theorien* (Munich 1936); Hermann Franke (ed.), *Handbuch der Neuzeitlichen Wehrwissenschaften* vol. I (Berlin/Leipzig, 1936), entry 'Krieg'.

by birth, ranked only after Field Marshal von Hindenburg in terms of importance and success in the German operations on the Eastern Front during the First World War, and eventually commanded the entire conduct of German land warfare. Even then, he wanted to settle ethnic German populations in the East to ensure German control of conquered areas, and he advocated unlimited submarine warfare, not sparing commercial or passenger shipping.

After the German defeat, Ludendorff joined the National Socialist movement in its very infancy, participated in the Hitler-led putsch of November 1923, and was a member of the German parliament (*Reichstag*) from 1924 until 1928. In 1925 the National Socialists put him forward as their candidate in the elections for the German presidency. He founded an association to fight against the 'supra-state powers' (whom he identified as Freemasons, Jews, Jesuits and Marxists), called after the battle of Tannenberg, the major success of Germany on the Eastern Front during the First World War. That victory had made Hindenburg and Ludendorff popular heroes. This Tannenberg Federation was dissolved by Hitler, whose competitor Ludendorff was; his ideas, however, differed little from those of Hitler himself, and can be described as the epitome of National Socialist thinking about war.

In his book of 1935 on *Total War*, Ludendorff dismissed Clausewitz's ideas of war as far too restricted, as nations were not really involved in the wars Clausewitz described. Ludendorff thought that 'von Clausewitz's book belongs to a past development in history which has now been entirely superseded', as 'Clausewitz only thinks of the annihilation of the hostile armies in battle'. Indeed, he thought Clausewitzian thinking had shackled the creativity of German strategists up to the twentieth century.

Of quite another character, different from that of the wars waged during the last 150 years, was the [First] World War. The War of 1914 has not been waged solely by the armed forces of the belligerent nations, which strove to destroy and annihilate themselves mutually. The nations themselves enlisted in the service of warfare, and the War being directed against the nations themselves, involved the latter very deeply . . . not only between the armed forces did the combat rage along those huge fronts and on distant oceans. The moral[e] and vital forces of the hostile populations were assailed for the purpose of corrupting and paralysing them . . . total war . . . , far from being the concern of the military forces alone, directly touches the life and soul of every single member of the belligerent nations . . . Not only the armies, but the populations themselves are

now indirectly subjected to the operations of war, although in varying degrees . . . Nations are now directly involved in a war through
blockades and propaganda . . . *Total warfare is thus directed not only
against the fighting forces, but indirectly also against the nations themselves*
. . . The nature of a total war postulates that it can be waged only
when the existence of the entire nation is actually being threatened,
and the latter is really determined to wage such a war.[19]

Crucial to Ludendorff's definition is thus the involvement of the
population in the war effort, and the effects that the war has on the
populations themselves. 'Nations', incidentally (and not surprisingly,
given his National Socialist mindset), were seen in racial terms, as
groups that were conscious of their race and therefore motivated to
fight against the supra- and international powers such as the Jewish
people and the Roman Church.[20] He drew a direct connection
between the will to victory, the religious commitment to a German
'god' he wished the nation to worship, and the 'observation of
psychical and racial laws' (and abstention from alcohol and nico-
tine) in the procreation of healthy German children. German men
and women should feel responsible 'for the increase of the nation':
indeed it should be impressed on women

> that the performance of the noble task of motherhood is a national
> duty. Thus only will be surmounted the infinite danger of decreasing
> births the painful effects of which must be deeply felt in the Army;
> thus only will healthy increasing generations arise which will supply
> the Army with numerous vigorous men and enable it to wage war
> and bear the burden of a total war.[21]

Ludendorff's involvement of the nation as a whole in warfare thus
encompassed procreation in order to produce more soldiers, but
also all aspects of macro-economics, the shape and functioning of
society (in peacetime, which was seen as a preparatory period for
war, as much as in war itself), its government, and of course, above
all, its armed forces and strategy in war.

The future war he yearned for, and the principles of Total War
that he developed, were inspired by his experience of the First
World War. He envisaged a far greater involvement of the civilian

---

19. Ludendorff, *Der Totale Krieg*, trans. by Rappoport as *The Nation at War*, pp. 14–
16. Rappoport's translation uses 'totalitarian' for the German term '*total*', and I have
replaced it with 'total', to be more faithful to the German original.
20. Ludendorff, *The Nation at War*, p. 24. Ludendorff's views of the European
Union would have been close to those of many Britons in the early and mid-1990s.
21. *Ibid.*, p. 45.

populations than in the previous war. 'Casualties brought about by aircraft far beyond the front' were one of the 'hardships . . . inflicted on the people by the fighting, in which the inhabitants are directly involved.' In a future war, 'bombing air squadrons must inexorably and without pity be sent' against 'the people in the enemy country'.[22] Indeed, for Ludendorff a future war should be different from the First World War in one decisive way: a future war's aim should be 'the *annihilation* of the enemy Army *and of the enemy nation*'.[23]

We can thus say that Ludendorff's war aims of 1935 went beyond those of any war that had taken place in Europe at least since 1648: they did not merely consist of the victory over the enemy army of the battlefield, nor even the annihilation of the enemy's armed forces, but it included the annihilation of the enemy population. This might sound absurd if the National Socialists had not put precisely this plan into practice, with the persecution of the very people singled out by Ludendorff as arch enemies of his own racial group: the Jews.

In using the term Total War in this chapter, Ludendorff's criteria will be applied. Total War thus encompasses both:

- the total application of the War Machine, which of course includes the total mobilisation of one's population for the war effort;
- genocide, or the explicit 'annihilation of . . . the enemy nation', deliberately not distinguishing between combatants and non-combatants, for the purpose of which he advocated population bombing from the air.

Ludendorff's thinking about Total War has indeed cast the mould for any subsequent definition of the term. The expression 'totalitarian or total war' was first used in English literature in 1940s, referring to a war in which not only the enemy's armed forces, but his nation, was the direct adversary in war.[24] This definition clearly stands in the tradition of Ludendorff's. In 1941 we find a useful summary given by Cyril Falls, Chichele Professor of the History of War in Oxford and thus the doyen of all British academics studying war, who took Ludendorff's work as the starting point of his on book *The Nature of Modern Warfare*. He wrote that Total War was

22. *Ibid.*, p. 165.   23. *Ibid.*, p. 168, italics mine.
24. *Hutchinson's Pictorial History of the War* (2 Oct.–26 Nov. 1940), p. 183, quoted in *Oxford English Dictionary*, Supplement vol. IV (1986) p. 922.

a reversion to barbarism on the part of men who are no less barbarians – perhaps more so – because they are scientific barbarians. It destroys all the painful work of jurists, statesmen, and soldiers who strove to prevent needless suffering. It spurns formal declarations of war, distinctions between combatants and non-combatants, respect for neutrality... Above all it advocates, one might almost say that it is based upon, indiscriminate attack, especially from the air, directed against the civilian population.[25]

Finally, let us add two German encyclopaedia definitions of Total War:

- A war of annihilation, waged with most extreme means (weapons and propaganda). 'Total Mobilisation' (Ernst Jünger) of all military, economic and spiritual forces necessarily leads to the elimination of the difference between combatants and non-combatants. Total war thus breaks out of the principles of the *jus in bello* and the limits of classical international law. The adversary becomes an absolute enemy who is to be annihilated. While both world wars were on the brink between classical war and total war, modern weapons technology [post-1945] contains the danger of a total, absolute war...[26]

- Expression for a war, in which all human, material and moral reserves of a people are comprehensively drawn upon and put in the service of an annihilation strategy, which does away with traditional differentiations between combatants and non-combatants, uses modern technology for mass extermination (terror-war) as much as using economic, psychological and ideological war. Developed during and after the First World War by military men and military theoreticians such as E. Ludendorff and G. Douhet, total war was first comprehensively realised during the Second World War in Germany. Essential phases were those of 'total mobilisation' of the male and female work forces within the 'Empire' and in the occupied territories since 1942/43, and the appointment of J. Goebbels as 'Chargé General for the Total War Effort' in 1944.[27]

Any other usage of the term, signifying merely the application of the War Machine in any form, is too loose for the purposes of our analysis here. As we shall see, the distinction between Ludendorff's use of the term, and the looser usage that has crept into British and American writing, is crucial to any judgement of the atomic

25. Cyril Falls, *The Nature of Modern Warfare* (London: Methuen, 1941), p. 6.
26. *Brockhaus Enzyclopädie* (Wiesbaden: F.A. Brockhaus, 1973) vol. 18 p. 775.
27. *Meyers Enzyklopädisches Lexikon* (Mannheim/Zürich: Lexikonverlag, Bibliographisches Institut, 1978), p. 605.

bombing of Hiroshima and Nagasaki on the one hand and genocide on the other.

'TOTAL WAR' AND TOTALITARIANISM

Ludendorff's translator, Dr A.S. Rappoport, writing in 1936, translated 'total war' (*Totaler Krieg*) as 'totalitarian' throughout. Here we must explore the links between these two concepts. The term 'totalitarian' was clearly in use at the time of Ludendorff's writing. But the main analyst of the concept of totalitarianism was Hannah Arendt. As she saw it, totalitarianism comprises several elements: an all-encompassing bureaucracy which 'intrude[s] upon the private individual and his inner life with equal brutality';[28] a doctrine which goes beyond any common sense or 'utilitarianism', that imposes certain policies which by the standards of other belief-systems harm those it claims to defend;[29] disregard or even negation of individuality, proclaiming that the individual human being is nothing, while the group is everything; a long-term mobilisation of society and its economy, putting it on a war footing even in times of peace:

> Totalitarianism in power uses the state administration for its long-range goal of world conquest and for the direction of the branches of the movement; it establishes the secret police as the executors and guardians of its domestic experiment in constantly transforming reality into fiction; and it finally erects concentration camps as special laboratories to carry through its experiment in total domination.[30]

The distant aim of global rule is used to make ever new demands for ever more sacrifices, 'great initial successes are consciously ruined or neglected for the sake of the ultimate, ideologically defined goal'.[31] There is a '[s]upreme disregard for immediate consequences' while 'ruthlessness' is extolled as a virtue; ' "idealism", i.e. the unwavering faith in an ideological fictitious world' is more important 'than [mere] lust for power'. These traits 'have all introduced into international politics a new and more disturbing factor than mere aggressiveness would have been able to do'.[32] For these traits are so incomprehensible to pragmatic (particularly Anglo-Saxon) *real-politicians* that those are constantly baffled by such a totalitarian

---

28. Hannah Arendt, *The Origins of Totalitarianism* (New York: Harcourt, Brace, 1949?), p. 245.
29. *Ibid.*, pp. 338f.
30. *Ibid.*, p. 378; on the goal of global conquest, see also pp. 394f.
31. *Ibid.*, p. 429.   32. *Ibid.*, pp. 396f.

régime's moves and policies, because it is totally driven and dominated by the exclusive logic of its ideology,[33] its 'ideological superstition' (or what Raymond Aron has called their 'quasi-religious
doctrine'.)[34] Hannah Arendt made it very clear: these *totalitarian
systems are by no means illogical*; Hitler and Stalin were no madmen,
but applied with merciless logic to the very last consequence their
own ideologies and their own interpretations of the world. At the
same time, their claim to have the only true interpretation of the
world and of the forces of History/Nature, and to have the only
programme for changing the world in accordance with the forces
of History/Nature, tolerated no rival systems, no rival interpretations, and certainly no dissidents, no doubts, no questions. Concentration camps designed to eliminate the enemy within were thus as
logical a consequence of their beliefs as war against any rival external systems: internal persecutions were part of the same war. As
Lucy Davidowicz has put it, Hitler's war was a 'war against the Jews'[35]
(and Slavs), and Auschwitz was its ultimate battle of annihilation.
In the same sense, Stalin's wars were wars against the 'class enemy',
whether incarnated in the *kulaks* or Tartar and Ukrainian peasants
he deported or starved at home, or embodied in Germany's 'fascist-
imperialist monopoly capitalism' or the 'imperialism of Britain and
the USA'.

Raymond Aron in his *Century of Total War* (a literal translation of
the original French title would be: 'The Chain of Wars', and the
book is thus less concerned with definitions of 'total war' than one
might suspect from the English title)[36] added some further ideas to
Arendt's interpretations. He tried to bring some valuable clarity
to the question of where the line is to be drawn between the total
mobilisation of society which Britain and to some extent the USA
experienced in the First and Second World Wars, and a totalitarian

33. Arendt on ideologies and on all 'isms' (*ibid.*, pp. 431f.): 'Ideologies are harmless,
uncritical, and arbitrary opinions only as long as they are not believed in seriously.
Once their claim to total validity is taken literally they become the nuclei of logical
systems in which, as in the system of paranoiacs, everything follows comprehensibly
and even compulsorily once the first premise is accepted. The insanity of such
systems lies not only in their first premise and in the very logicality with which they
are constructed. The curious logicality of all isms, their simple-minded trust in the
salvation value of stubborn devotion without regard for specific, varying factors,
already harbors the first germs of totalitarian contempt for reality and factuality.'

34. Raymond Aron, *The Century of Total War*, trans. E.W. Dickes and O.S. Griffiths
(London: Derek Verschoyle, 1954), p. 89.

35. Lucy Davidowicz, *The War against the Jews, 1933–1945* (Harmondsworth: Penguin, 1977).

36. *Les Guerres en Chaîne* (Paris: Gallimard, 1951).

system. 'Such is the similarity of style between the two', wrote Aron, 'that some historians have seen in the totalitarian regime, simply a prolongation of total mobilisation, an attempt to make permanent what was necessary in wartime.' But Aron saw a difference in the 'state monopoly of publicity and ideology' which were essential to the USSR and the Hitler's Third Empire (*Reich*).

> The example of the Western democracies shows that mobilisation implies perhaps a total state, not a totalitarian state. The parliaments continued to function in Britain and France from 1914 to 1918, and in Britain and the United States from 1939 to 1945. Planned economy does not necessarily outlive victory.[37]

In totalitarian systems, however, the aspiration to total domination of society outlives any specific war, because the notion of being engaged in a perpetual struggle against its adversaries forms an essential part of the 'quasi-religious doctrine' on which the system is based. War is part of the system's very essence.

> The National Socialist regime was . . . strongly marked by memories of the war or by the anticipation of another one. Ludendorff, immediately after the defeat, had drawn up a plan for the total organisation of the nation . . . The National Socialist ideology was intended by some of its prophets to become the equivalent of Shintoism, the 'national religion' which Ludendorff admired and considered indispensable to the power of collectivities struggling for their existence. Administrative centralisation, economic planning, and ideological propaganda, necessary for mobilisation or for preparation for war, were regarded by the Hitlerites as the normal state of things. The *garrison state*, the military state, belongs to the age of wars, but it results from wars not directly but through the intermediary of the totalitarian parties and doctrines.

And Aron concluded:

> In spite of similarities of style and institutions, there remains inherent difference between total mobilisation for war and totalitarianism. In the former case, all that is demanded is a temporary unanimity, limited to a single object; in the latter, the objective is a permanent unanimity expanded into a system of values and of thought. In the former case there is a temporary suspension of certain liberties and an organisation of the integral effort of the country; in the latter, the masses are taught that the service of the collectivity is at every moment their supreme value, has sovereign rights over men and property.[38]

37. Aron, *The Century of Total War*, p. 89.   38. *Ibid.*, pp. 89f.

What this does, however, mean, is that during times of war, the 'democracies are in danger of being contaminated by the enemy'.[39] In times of war, a democracy fighting against a totalitarian system might become, if temporarily, similar to it.

Let us recapitulate: Total War is waged by an entire population against not only the armed forces of a designated enemy group, but against every one of its members, man, woman or child, explicitly denying any distinction between combatants and non-combatants. It is thus 'universalised violence' (Raymond Aron).[40] The aim is to achieve the complete domination of an enemy group (as defined by a particular ideology) by one's own group (equally defined by that ideology), to the point where the enemy group is exterminated or at least quite literally enslaved. Total War is the enacting of the struggle between these two groups which according to the constituent doctrine of totalitarian régimes is an essential part of their destinies, according to the laws of history, nature or providence, a struggle which goes on even in times of formal peace. The entire totalitarian society is prepared for the Total War effort, its War Machine dominates its militarised society in peacetime almost as much as in war – as Lenin put it, 'peace is the continuation of the class struggle by other means'. At all times, the totalitarian régime holds the monopoly for truth and propaganda. Dissidents are enemies, and thus the enemy within is as dangerous as the enemy without, or even more so.

Have any wars prior to World War II been Total Wars?

Applying these definitions, then, we can make a brief and very superficial categorisation of wars in Europe until the Second World War. Any war that deliberately aimed to annihilate large numbers of defenceless enemy non-combatants, contains the genocidal, ideological element of a Total War. The wars of Rome and Carthage were clearly not limited wars, and did indeed have a touch of the Total War (minus the War Machine, which presupposes technology and industrialisation), as the Romans finally and deliberately deleted Carthage from the map. Many of the barbarian incursions into the Roman Empire from the third century, including finally

39. *Ibid.*, p. 91.   40. *Ibid.*, p. 41.

the raids of Attila across Europe, may qualify, although it cannot be established to what extent the killing of the citizens of towns and villages which were raided, looted and burnt by them was ideologically motivated and premeditated in the way it was by the National Socialists. Many persecutions carried out by the medieval Church have a strong touch of the Total War: there was the doctrine, there was the claim to hold the only truth, there was the stated aim of eradicating heretics who through their doubts and alternative ways of interpreting the Bible were a dangerous enemy within, and there was the organisation – the Church itself – which largely monopolised propaganda. The Albigensian Crusades[41] aimed deliberately at the destruction of the Cathar heretics, men, women and children, as did the persecutions of Jews throughout the Middle Ages and beyond, in the tradition which Ludendorff's anti-Semitism stands. Much of the killing that went on in the wars of religion in the fifteenth to seventeenth centuries had such a bent, and the Thirty Years' War, in which friend and foe were generally separated by religion (instead of Ludendorff's race) and which reduced the population of most of Europe by a third, was closer to a Total War than the limited wars of the eighteenth century. Medieval concepts of justice, which lived on well into the twentieth century, made it permissible to put the population of any besieged town or city 'to the sword' if they had refused to surrender and if their town was eventually taken – in classical antiquity the male population would have been slain and the women and children sold off into slavery, as in the cases of Troy or Carthage. Late examples of such deliberate massacres, sparing neither women, children, nor the old and infirm, and containing an element of reprisal, included the sack of Magdeburg by the Swedes in the Thirty Years' War, or even, in the Second World War, the deliberate extermination of the populations of Lidice in Czechoslovakia and Oradour in France by German armed forces.

By contrast, the leaders of the French Revolution and Napoleon deliberately did not wish any harm upon the populations of other states: indeed, these wars were seen by the French as wars of liberation, in which they would free the oppressed peoples of Europe from the régimes under which they were languishing.[42] Yet there was a foreshadowing of the totalitarian in the determination of the

---

41. See Chapter 4.
42. Frank Attar, *La Révolution Française déclare la guerre à l'Europe* including documents (Brussels: Eds. Complexe, 1992), see particularly *décret du 20 avril 1792*, p. 165.

French revolutionaries to exterminate their entire aristocracy, and the *Terreur* as much as the ideology inspiring them, in the brilliant analysis of Talmon, contained the germs of future totalitarian régimes.[43]

Between 1815 and 1861, war moved 'from its military to its industrial phase', in the words of historian Richard Challener.[44] The War Machine was taking shape, coming fully into being with industrialisation, universal schooling, and crucial technical innovations which contributed to both state control of the population, propaganda and mobility, and the increasing power of ever expanding bureaucracies, unquestioning tools of their political masters, self-serving and organised to preserve their own power and existence. H.G. Wells and Alphonse Seché were profoundly inspired by this development, and are among the first to have articulated the World War I experience of the mechanisation and ever more comprehensive bureaucratisation of the war effort.[45]

This War Machine began to dominate European warfare increasingly from the mid-1860s onwards, and the wars between Prussia and Denmark, Prussia and Austria, and finally the Franco–Prussian War resulted in growing casualty figures (which came as a shock to many particularly after the 'long peace' that had reigned in most of Europe since the Napoleonic wars) and an increasing economic involvement of the populations of these countries in the war effort. There was not yet any notion of wanting to *annihilate* all Prussians, Danes, Austrians, or French. Nor did Northerners and Southerners in the USA hate each other to the point where they wished to exterminate each other – and yet the American Civil War (1861–65) resulted in 622,000 battlefield deaths. There was no conscious attempt to massacre civilians on the British, French, and German sides in the First World War, and yet the way in which just such civilians – men and boys at ever younger ages – were conscripted into their armies has led the historian Richard L. Rubenstein to come to the controversial conclusion that with the mass casualties in battle in that war, 'a giant step was taken towards the death camps

43. J.L. Talmon, *The Origins of Totalitarian Democracy* (London: Martin Secker & Warburg, 1952).
44. Richard Challener, *The French Theory of the Nation in Arms, 1866–1939* (New York: Columbia University Press, 1955), p. 91.
45. Eric Markusen and David Kopf, *The Holocaust and Strategic Bombing* (Boulder, Co.: Westview Press, 1995), pp. 81–4; 210–37; Alphonse Seché, *Les Guerres d'Enfer* (Paris: E. Sansot, 1915), p. 276; H.G. Wells, *Anticipations of the Reaction of Mechanical and Scientific Progress upon Human Life and Thought* (London: Chapman & Hall, 1901).

of World War II'.[46] The growth of the War Machine, like genocide, went hand in hand with the spread of nationalism, which, glorifying one's own group (arbitrarily defined as nation), branded all others as inferior, less important, even inimical, while giving governments all the arguments for taking warfare to extremes, brushing aside all restraints on warfare. This was done in the interest of the 'nation' – even if far less than half of the population of that very nation was respected enough by the ruling élite to be trusted with the vote.[47]

Nationalism was also the breeding ground of racial totalitarianism, inspired by Social Darwinism of the sort we have seen Douhet, Trenchard and Knauss quote in the 1920s and 1930s.[48] This was a strong factor by the end of the nineteenth century, and it was this ideology that gave the War Machine its devastating totalitarian character. There were early glimpses of both the technical and its ideological side of Total War in the First World War, and there are points where we can say that it was technical limitations, rather than ethical restraints, which prevented it from fully blossoming into Total War. German air raids against Britain and their civilian casualties, one could say, were limited on technical grounds rather than due to moral restraints; there were strong racist touches in German plans for the resettlement of populations both on the Belgian border and in the East; rhetoric on all sides was nationalist verging on racist (all protagonists at some stage claimed to be the salt of the earth, ready to test their mettle against what they thought of as genetically, morally and socially inferior antagonists).[49] Nevertheless, there was also a strong strand of liberal propaganda which stressed the defence of freedom and ethnic self-determination, keeping the aims of this war, at least on the Allied side, untainted by

46. Richard L. Rubenstein, *The Cunning of History: The Holocaust and the American Future* (New York: Harper Colophon Books, originally 1975, repr. 1978), p. 8.

47. It is worth recalling that universal adult suffrage was only established in Britain in 1928, in the USA in 1920 and in France in 1945, while Germany adopted it in 1918 and Communist Russia in 1917. Prior to this time, not even all adult males were enfranchised in some of these countries – thus in Britain many of those who fought in the First World War did not have the vote. All powers entering into the First World War thus did not involve at least half their adult population in their election processes, and can therefore not be called full democracies or 'nation-states', in the sense of a nation being sovereign within those states.

On genocide and nationalism, see Helen Fein, *Accounting for Genocide: National Responses and Jewish Victimization during the Holocaust* (New York: Free Press, 1979), pp. 90–2.

48. See Chapter 2.

49. Paul Fussell, *The Great War and Modern Memory* (Oxford: Oxford University Press, 1975), pp. 75–90; J.M. Roberts: *Europe 1880–1945* (2nd edn., London: Longman, 1970), pp. 65–8.

Total War aims of the sort that Ludendorff was already developing during the First World War. Overall, the First World War by and large upheld the distinction between combatants and non-combatants, and was thus not a Total War.

Much of the inter-war thinking about air power, even in the Western countries, fell under the spell of Social Darwinism. Sir Frederick Sykes wrote in his 1918 paper 'Air Power Requirements for the Empire':

> Future wars between civilised nations will be struggles for life in which entire populations, together with their industrial resources, will be thrown into the scale. Evolution has brought about the creation of air fleets to meet the demands of such warfare.[50]

And we have seen in Chapter 2 how enamoured Trenchard was of chauvinistic comparisons of British morale and the morale of the French, the Germans and the Italians. Meanwhile, totalitarian rhetoric was thriving in Italy, as one might have guessed from Douhet's writing, although he himself did not use the term. We have already seen that the term 'totalitarian' was first used in Italy, and became a word with positive connotations, associated with Fascism.[51] It is thus not entirely surprising that several of the armed conflicts of the inter-war period already clearly had the aims of Total Wars, namely the complete enslavement or extermination of the enemy population, the integration of its territory into one's own Empire, and all this as a step towards further expansion. These conflicts include the Soviet Union's wars against neighbouring states (with the concomitant extermination of 'the class enemy', wherever he could be found), and Italy's campaign against Abyssinia. None of these fully brought the War Machine into operation, but they fully applied totalitarian, genocidal ideologies.

In short, as far as the term can be used anachronistically (i.e. before Ludendorff defined it), there have been wars in history which made the total destruction of civilians their aim, rejecting distinctions between combatants and non-combatants. Before the end of the nineteenth century, they lacked the War Machine which turned a political (or religious) programme into a thorough Holocaust. But even with lesser technical means at their disposal, fanatics in previous centuries managed deliberately to organise wholesale massacres which in spirit and effect were Total Wars.

50. Sykes, *From Many Angles* (London: Harrap, 1942), p. 561.
51. R.J.B. Bosworth, *Explaining Auschwitz and Hiroshima: History Writing and the Second World War, 1945–1990* (London: Routledge, 1993), p. 20.

Let us turn, then, to the Second World War itself, in which we will subsume Japan's campaigns against Manchuria and China.

The war aims of the major powers in World War II

GERMANY

The sociologist Leo Kuper wrote in his work on genocide:

> The changing nature of warfare, with a movement to total warfare, and the technological means for the instantaneous annihilation of large populations, creates a situation conducive to genocidal conflict. This potential was realized in the Second World War, when Germany employed genocide in its war for domination . . .[52]

The clearest case of a Total War as conducted by a totalitarian system is of course the war in Europe, as unleashed by National Socialist Germany. Hitler's own ideology, although tolerant of fellow Aryan peoples whom he saw as natural (indeed, genetic!) allies, was very close indeed to Ludendorff's, as noted above. In his speeches, but also in *Mein Kampf* (1924) and his later *Secret Book* (dictated in 1928, but not published until after the war), Hitler identified France as Germany's eternal and traditional enemy.[53] Hitler's ideal constellation would have been to ally with Italy and Britain, each country colonising a different part of the world, against France and Russia, and above all, against the Jewish and Slav peoples.

There is no indication in any of Hitler's writing or actions until his declaration of war against the USA in 1941 that Hitler wanted to 'rule the world', as Geoffrey Stoakes has demonstrated convincingly.[54] But at the same time, Hitler's obsession with a global Jewish conspiracy led him to a paranoid concern about almost all parts of the world, bar Japan, which he liked – not least because the Japanese population prided itself on its racial purity.[55]

The Jews stood at the centre of all his preoccupations, as much as did the German people or the Aryan race. 'All the events of

52. Leo Kuper, *Genocide: Its political use in the 20th century* (New Haven, Ct.: Yale University Press, 1981), p. 46.

53. *Hitler's Secret Book* (trans. Salvator Attanasio, New York: Crove Press, 1961), pp. 128.

54. Geoffrey Stoakes, *Hitler and the Quest for World Dominion* (Leamington Spa: Berg, 1986), pp. 222f.

55. John Fox, *Germany and the Far Eastern Crisis, 1931–1938: a Study in Diplomacy and Ideology* (Oxford: Clarendon, 1982).

world history are but the expression of the racial instinct for self-preservation', wrote Hitler in *Mein Kampf*; this racial struggle, for Hitler, was the 'key to world history'. Jäckel commented rightly, 'for Hitler, the bearers and the elements of history are peoples and races, not – as in other views of history, individuals, classes, cultures or anything else'.[56] Hitler's aims flowed logically from the belief that he was to lead the Aryan race to the domination of the European continent, to give it 'living space' for it to increase numerically and prosper. Hitler's political and thus war aims were not merely the political domination of continental Europe. It was the elimination from that area of all Jews, and the enslavement of all other non-Aryans as an inferior workforce.

Hitler's overall strategy flowed relatively logically from his beliefs: Aryans had to thrive and increase in numbers, which, Hitler was convinced, meant the need for more 'living space', which in turn meant that other peoples, notably the supposedly inferior Slavs, had to be deprived of theirs. Jews, whom he described as particularly dangerous because of their ability to assimilate so easily to the Aryan race, had to be kept out of this territory, indeed, as Hitler defined them as the eternal enemy of the Germanic race, he wanted to see them expelled or exterminated.

Disappointed and indeed somewhat surprised that Aryan Britain would not back Germany in this endeavour, and that Britain actually declared war on Germany, Hitler convinced himself that Britain's was in fact a weak society, undermined by Jews and general decadence, and called upon the Germans to support air warfare against the United Kingdom. The German population was increasingly mobilised psychologically for the war effort through propaganda, and central to this campaign was Hitler's close associate Joseph Goebbels. In a famous speech in the sport-palace in Berlin of 18 February 1943, he asked the audience:

> The English claim that the German people has lost its faith in victory. I ask you: do you believe, with the Leader (*Führer*) and with us, in the final, total victory of the German people?
>
> ... the English claim that the German people is no longer eager to shoulder the war effort ... I ask you: are you and is the German people prepared, if the Leader orders it, to work ten, twelve or, if necessary, fourteen and sixteen hours a day ... for the victory?

---

56. Eberhard Jäckel, *Hitler's Weltanschauung* (trans. Herbert Arnold; Middletown, Conn.: Wesleyan University Press, 1972), p. 88.

. . . the English claim that the German people is resisting the total war measures of the government. [They claim the German people] does not want total war, but capitulation (Interjections: Never, never, never!). I ask you: Do you want total war? Do you want it more total and radical than we can even imagine it today?[57]

The hysterically enthusiastic response of his audience was one single, massive shout of 'Yes', followed by prolonged applause and '*Sieg Heils*'.

There is no doubt, by the criteria discussed above, that the German way of war in the Second World War was a Total one. Indeed, as Hannah Arendt so rightly noted, Hitler took his own doctrine to its logical conclusion. Auschwitz was the logical culmination of Total War, its apogee and perfection. Consequently, when Germany could no longer win the war, this logic of destruction logically had to be turned on the Germans themselves: Albert Speer recalled that towards the end of the war, when the Russians were clearly winning, Hitler concluded that the German people had 'lost' this Darwinian struggle for predominance, and had shown themselves unfit to survive: 'Because the [German] people had proved to be the weaker one, . . . the future belonged exclusively to the stronger Eastpeople [the Slavs]. Those [Germans] surviving the war would in any case be the less valuable, as the good ones had been killed in the war.' On 19 March 1945, Hitler practically ordered the self-destruction of the German state and its resources, and he himself committed suicide soon after.[58] Indeed, he encouraged other Germans to follow him; Goebbels, who had enlisted the public's support for Total War, killed not only himself and his wife, but also their young children, fully applying the logic of his ideology until the very end, and taking it to its extreme.

JAPAN

Let us turn now to Germany's ally Japan, the victim of the atomic bombing which is at the centre of this reflection. Since the adoption of the Meiji constitution in 1889, and despite the adoption of universal adult manhood suffrage in 1925, Japanese society had developed a form of Emperor-worship which grew to quasi-religious proportions in the 1930s. Fearful of Communism, riding on a wave of anti-Western feelings and increasing romantic nostalgia for what

---

57. Text in Lothar Gruchmann, *Totaler Krieg* (Munich: dtv, 1991), pp. 247ff.
58. Text *ibid.*, p. 253.

were seen as original Japanese values, including the sense of self-sacrifice and popular solidarity, a great majority of Japanese, it seems, favoured a more authoritarian system of government that dispensed with parliamentary trappings. The military, recruiting officers from all social classes and aspiring to represent a nation which had universal male military service, saw itself as the agent of a renewal of the polity that would modernise by 'returning' to Japan's past, putting loyalty to the Emperor as embodiment of both nation and state at the centre of a state religion. This was the Shintoism Ludendorff so admired, an uncritical worship of Japaneseness through worship of the Emperor and his mythical divine ancestry, focusing on a wide network of shrines devoted to this cult that had been revived in the 1880s to further identification with the Emperor and the new constitution. It went along with pronounced intolerance of alternative views, and, as in Germany under the National Socialists, anti-war writing in literature and newspapers was censored and dissidents, particularly Communists, were imprisoned, albeit in much smaller numbers.[59]

From the beginning of the twentieth century, conformity of thinking and unquestioning obedience based on Shintoism and racist nationalism were enforced though universal primary school education, where contempt of the Koreans and Taiwanese whose territories Japan colonised was inculcated into Japanese children. Military instruction in all middle schools was made compulsory for boys from the mid-1920s. Disdain for international law and particularly the League of Nations was spread through schools. Offensive jingles about the cowardice and inferiority of the Chinese were as rife in Japanese schools as anti-Jewish jokes and caricatures were in National Socialist Germany, and prepared the generation of young men who would be sent to fight on the Asian mainland from 1937 for the atrocities they would commit there.[60] Meanwhile the political and personal rights of Koreans and Taiwanese were almost non-existent, compared with the constitutional rights of the Japanese, and even these were not great – freedom of expression, for example, was severely circumscribed.[61] According to historian Saburo Ienaga, the Japanese attitude 'was identical with the European and American conviction that control of colonies in Asia, the Pacific, and Africa was "manifest destiny"'.[62] Just as in Germany, Japanese

59. Saburo Ienaga: *Japan's Last War: World War II and the Japanese, 1931–1945* (Oxford: Basil Blackwell, 1979), pp. 14–18.
60. Ienaga: *Japan's Last War*, pp. 6f., 26–9.
61. *Ibid.*, pp. 7–12, 19f.   62. *Ibid.*, p. 9.

thinkers believed that their population needed an outlet – 'living space' – abroad, and that for this reason Japan needed to colonise territories in China, Manchuria and Korea.[63]

In the early 1930s, there was a substantial movement within Japanese society, focusing not least on young military officers, that sought to bring about a new revolution within the existing imperial system, which would have served to increase the Emperor's standing still further (if that was possible) and do away with any remnants of democracy. The aim was described as the *Showa Restoration*, again with the fiction of returning to a more wholesome, holy past. Japanese society was increasingly militarised, fanaticised and mobilised for the war effort. Saburo Ienaga argued that 'In the sense that the Right [in Japan] as a political movement resembled Nazism and Italian fascism, the term fascism has a certain validity for Japan also.'[64] And the rise and preponderance of the Japanese Right went along with the decline of parliamentary democracy. By mid-1941, the population in general was organised politically into neighbourhood groups (*tonarigumi*), committees for small towns, parts of large towns, subordinated to centralised town committees, prefectures and committees at a national level. These were designed to raise money for the war effort, distribute rationed commodities (which from 1940 included clothing, sugar, flour, rice, vegetables, and all sorts of fuel), and to harmonise public opinion in support of the sacrifices needed for the imperial war. What little diversity of opinion, criticism of the Emperor or the state existed, was suppressed and punished.[65] There were thus many features reminiscent of the totalitarian systems of Europe.

Meanwhile the Japanese army moved steadily into China, at once exploiting the pressure from the Communists on the Chinese Nationalist régime under Chiang Kai Shek, and furthering the eviction of the foreign powers from China. But in the process, it was the Japanese who imposed themselves as new masters. The war in China to create a Greater East Asia Co-Prosperity Sphere was declared a holy one, based on the 'national mission' of Japan and of the deified Emperor. In late 1943, a Great East Asia Conference, bringing together representatives of collaborating groups from the occupied area, adopted a declaration designed to rival the Atlantic Charter, which stressed the mutual benefit accruing to the countries

63. *Ibid.*, p. 11, quoting Ikezaki Tadakata.   64. *Ibid.*, p. 111.
65. John W. Hall, *Das Japanische Kaiserreich* (Frankfurt/Main: Fischer Bücherei, 1968), pp. 333–5; Paul Akamatsu, 'Japan im Krieg (1937–1945)', in Lucien Bianco (ed.), *Das Moderne Asien* (Frankfurt/Main: Fischer Bücherei, 1969), p. 123.

of 'great East Asia' from co-operation and mutual respect,[66] the reality was a different one: in 1930 Lt. Colonel Ishiwara Kanji, representative of views of the military leaders, wrote, 'The four races of Japan, China, Korea and Manchuria will share a common prosperity through a division of responsibilities: Japanese, political leadership and large industry; Chinese, labour and small industry; Koreans, rice; and Manchus, animal husbandry.'[67] In practice, the local populations in Manchuria and China were treated as second class citizens, indeed as slaves: it is estimated that of the Koreans alone, 370,000 were made to work in one way or another for the Japanese war effort.[68]

An even worse fate was in store for some: the notorious Unit 731 carried out deadly experiments on Manchurians comparable to those which Dr. Joseph Mengele carried out on concentration camp inmates in the German-occupied territories.[69] For Saburo Ienaga, Unit 731 ranks with the 'classic examples of rational atrocities' of Auschwitz and the atomic bombing.[70] As mentioned before,[71] the Japanese conquest of Nanking in December 1937 was accompanied by brutalities which left tens – perhaps hundreds – of thousands of civilians dead, and tens of thousands raped.[72] And throughout Japanese-occupied Asia, 'sexual comfort facilities' were set up, in which local women were forced to prostitute themselves to Japanese soldiers, where these had not gratified themselves by raping (and then usually killing) women in the countries they conquered. The writer Ian Buruma gives an eyewitness account given by a Japanese war veteran, Azuma Shiro:

> Whenever we would take a village [in China, 1937–45], the first thing we'd do was steal food, then we'd take the women and rape them, and finally we'd kill all the men, women, and children to make sure they couldn't slip away and tell the Chinese troops where we were. Otherwise we wouldn't have been able to sleep at night.

Azuma explained that the raping 'wasn't so bad in itself.' But then the Japanese soldiers had to kill them: 'You see, rape was against

66. Akira Iriye: *Power and Culture: The Japanese–American War 1941–1945* (Cambridge, Mass: Harvard University Press, 1981), p. 119.
67. Quoted in Ienaga: *Japan's Last War*, p. 12.   68. *Ibid.*, p. 158.
69. Cf. Phil Williams and D. Wallace, *Unit 731* (London: Hodder & Stoughton, 1989).
70. Ienaga: *Japan's Last War*, pp. 187f.   71. See Chapter 1.
72. Hall, *Das Japanische Kaiserreich*, p. 332, gives the figure as 12,000; R.J. Rummel gives it as 200,000 over four months, from December 1937 until March 1938, with 20,000 women raped – R.J. Rummel, *China's Bloody Century: Genocide and Mass Murder Since 1900* (New Brunswick, N.J.: Transaction Books, 1991), pp. 145f.

the military regulations, so we had to destroy the evidence . . . We felt no shame about it, no guilt. If we had, we couldn't have done it.'[73] Ian Buruma commented:

> Clearly, then, the Nanking Massacre had been the culmination of countless massacres on a smaller scale. But it had been mass murder without a genocidal ideology. It was barbaric, but to Azuma and his comrades, barbarism was part of war.[74]

Ian Buruma gives further views of Japanese who say that Nanking was very different from the extermination of Jews and gypsies by the Germans. One such view quoted is that of Tanaka Masaaki, who in 1984 published a book on *The Fabrication of the 'Nanking Massacre'*:

> Tanaka . . . admits that a few innocent people got killed in the cross fire, but these deaths were incidental. Some soldiers were doubtless a bit tough, but that was due to 'the psychology of war'. In any case, so the argument invariably ends, Hiroshima, having been planned in cold blood, was a far worse crime. 'Unlike in Europe or China', writes Tanaka, 'you won't find one instance of planned, systematic murder in the entire history of Japan.' This is because the Japanese have 'a different sense of values' from the Chinese or the Westerners.[75]

Japanese society was thus largely organised like a totalitarian society, inspired by a fanatical doctrine of Emperor-worship and national self-glorification which it applied to the very last (it is estimated that in Okinawa, about 110,000 Japanese, including civilians, were killed *or committed suicide* rather than surrender to the Americans, who during the invasion lost 12,613 dead and about 40,000 wounded;[76] of the Japanese footsoldiers who had set out to fight in the Pacific War, only 18 per cent returned).[77] Japanese forces between 1937 and 1944 invaded countries around Japan until they dominated all of Asia from Burma to Korea and from the borders of the Soviet Union to Indonesia. Admittedly, there is little evidence that they wanted to establish 'world dominance' (the attack on the USA is seen more as an attempt to force America out of Asia so as to leave Japan a free hand in the conquest of China).

73. Ian Buruma, *The Wages of Guilt: Memories of War in Germany and Japan* (New York: Meridian, 1995), p. 131. For a similar statement that raped women always had to be killed, see Ienaga, *Japan's Last War*, p. 166.
74. Buruma, *Wages of Guilt*, p. 131.   75. Excerpt translated in *ibid.*, pp. 119f.
76. Figures in Dennis D. Wainstock, *The Decision to Drop the Atomic Bomb* (Westport, Ct.: Praeger, 1996), p. 4.
77. Saki Dockrill, 'Hirohito, the Emperor's army and Pearl Harbor', *Review of International Studies* Vol. 18 (1992), p. 323.

Equally, there is no evidence of an ideology which foresaw the systematic extermination of the civilian populations of occupied territories. But with or without advance meditation, atrocities committed among the civilians of these occupied countries were horrendous in quality and quantity, and were accepted as a matter of course, as was the Japanese treatment of prisoners of war.[78] It is difficult not to conclude that Japan was waging a genocidal war in China according to the UN's definition of the term, aiming to enslave if not totally to exterminate the surrounding peoples. They may not have used air power to do so, but they brought to bear the entire Japanese War Machine, plus a murderous, racist ideology, on their largely defenceless victims.

THE USA AND THE UK

It was thus Germany, and arguably Japan, that were waging Total Wars, and it was they who both declared war on the USA. The USA developed atomic bombs – primarily on the assumption that Germany was doing so, and primarily to pre-empt German use. It then used them on Germany's ally Japan, after Germany had been defeated, targeting the civilian populations of Hiroshima and Nagasaki. Was this Total War in the sense of Ludendorff's definition? Or indeed, taking this question one step further, can a state fighting totalitarian (or near-totalitarian perhaps, in the case of Japan) states avoid fighting a Total War?

Leo Kuper, after stating that Germany had clearly realised the potential for Total War with the extermination of the Jews and other minorities (see above), continued: 'but I think the term must also be applied to the atomic bombing of the Japanese cities of Hiroshima and Nagasaki by the U.S.A. and to the pattern bombing by the Allies of such cities as Hamburg and Dresden'.[79] Kuper is not the first to have made such an argument. Judge Randha Binod Pal, an Indian serving on the International Military Tribunal for the Far East, drew a similar analogy between the orders to bomb Hiroshima and Nagasaki, and the war crimes for which Germans were sentenced at the Nuremberg war crimes tribunal.[80] This contention is highly controversial. There are many who think that the crimes

---

78. For which the economic situation is only in part to be blamed, in view of the disdain in which the Japanese held soldiers who surrendered, see Louis Allen: 'The campaigns in Asia and the Pacific', *Journal of Strategic Studies* Vol. 13, No. 1 (March 1990), p. 183.
    79. Kuper, *Genocide*, p. 46.   80. Ienaga: *Japan's Last War*, p. 201.

of Germany cannot be compared with the bombing of enemy cities during war – indeed, many would argue that the Holocaust is in every respect an incomparable, unique event. But there are both American and Japanese scholars who think otherwise, and who would argue that strategic bombing, as carried out in the Second World War, was genocidal.[81]

Let us examine the question from a different angle, that of the theme of our chapter: namely, which fitted the definition of Total War better, the crimes perpetrated by Germany (and Japan), or the strategic bombing carried out by the USA and the United Kingdom? Of course, the American and British War Machines were mobilised. Of course the US and British economies were put on a war footing, populations were mobilised for war, men through conscription, women through factory work. Of course there was war propaganda, controlled by the state, and 'enemy aliens' (including most US citizens of Japanese ethnic origin) were interned in camps, much as refugees from Central Europe were in the United Kingdom.

And yet, the war aims of the USA differed widely from those of Germany or Japan. The USA did not intend to enslave the Japanese population, nor exterminate it. Internment camps in the USA and UK did not serve as slave labour camps, and they were not used for torture or medical experiments. As we have seen,[82] Roosevelt did not want to punish the Japanese population but merely to rid it of its régime and ideology. Nor did President Truman intend to kill Japanese civilians in Hiroshima and Nagasaki in order to exterminate them, but to bring forward the point of surrender, at great cost to the Japanese rather than to the Americans. In other words, the USA was defending itself, without the ideology to make it desire war, or see in it some ultimate, desirable test of its fitness. It built up its own War Machine in self-defence. The economy, technology, level of scientific research in the USA, the refuge of Europe's top nuclear scientists, were the most advanced in the world; America was therefore physically and intellectually able to produce the bomb. The aircraft were there to carry it to a target chosen to hasten the end of the war. In a war that had been imposed upon it, the USA made full use of its own resources. The effect – the killing of a group, without discriminating between combatants and non-combatants, with full military power, particularly with air strikes – came close to Ludendorff's ideal of Total War. The intention,

---

81. Most notably Eric Markusen and David Kopf, *The Holocaust and Strategic Bombing* (Boulder, Co.: Westview Press, 1995), pp. 56–63, 255.
82. See Chapter 1.

however, was otherwise: genocide was not ideologically *intended*, even if the effect has been described as genocide.

Matters are slightly different in the case of the thinking of Trenchard and Harris in the United Kingdom: it actually came close to Ludendorff's and Douhet's, as far as the virtues of targeting civilian populations were concerned. As we have seen, Trenchard was convinced of the superiority of Britons over other peoples, which he thought could be proved by Britain's greater ability to withstand bombing attacks than would their potential enemies.[83] Moreover, we have seen his profession of the belief in his 1928 memorandum that the enemy 'nation' as a whole had to be defeated, and of the crucial rôle played by air attacks in this scheme.[84] Yet both Trenchard and J.F.C. Fuller thought totalitarian régimes would do best in the next great war, because their subjects would do what they were told, unlike democratic peoples.[85] While there was a minority of people in Britain who felt drawn to the law-and-order, virile approach of the blackshirts and the National Socialists, these ideas did not find general acceptance in the UK outside the context of actual war for survival. Even Trenchard cannot be accused of consciously preaching the need for a genocidal war in the way Ludendorff or Ishiwara Kanji did. Perhaps he was constrained by the ethos of his own society. As a Russian general and early air power expert wrote,

> [I]nhuman and brutal use of the air weapon does not appeal to the average Briton, whose moral and cultural level is considerably above Continental standards. Ideas of 'wholesale destruction' strategy . . . can be entertained in peacetime only by the less-civilised or morally inferior nations.[86]

Nor did such ideas appeal to the French in general: even in 1939, the French General Maxime Weygand wrote: 'There is something in these bombardments of defenceless people behind the front that smacks of cowardice which is repugnant to the soldier.'[87]

---

83. Malcolm Smith, *British Air Strategy Between the Wars* (Oxford: Clarendon, 1984), p. 61.

84. Cf. Chapter 2. Text of the memorandum in Charles Webster and Noble Frankland, *The Strategic Air Offensive Against Germany* (London: HMSO, 1961), IV, pp. 74f.

85. Smith, *British Air Strategy*, pp. 61f.

86. Gen. N.N. Golovine and N.N., 'Air strategy' Part III, transl. from Russian, *RAF Quarterly* Vol. 7 (1936), p. 429, also quoted in R.J. Overy, 'Air power and the origins of deterrence theory before 1939', *Journal of Strategic Studies* Vol. 15, No. 1 (March 1992), p. 90.

87. General Maxime Weygand, 'How France is defended', *International Affairs* Vol. 178 (1939), p. 471, quoted in Overy, 'Air power and the origins', p. 92.

In the Second World War, as in the Cold War later, it was the confrontation with opponents who had no such scruples which pushed the liberal democracies to extremes. In 1939 the British strategist J.M. Spaight tried to convince those with moral scruples, particularly the Americans, that the Allies, notwithstanding their ideals, had to adopt a more destructive strategy: '[T]here is no security except armed strength. The golden rule has gone by the board. If the democracies are to survive they must be war-minded, almost bloody-minded – for the time being.'[88] Indeed, they were, and their propaganda machines, working full blast, portrayed the enemy – the Japanese above all, but also the Germans and Italians – as brutish beasts, as animals deserving to be killed in any possible way. In a Gallup poll of 16 August 1945, 85 per cent of Americans asked approved of the recent use of the atom bombs. In a Roper Poll of October 1945, 53.5 per cent of the Americans questioned totally approved of what had been done, 22.7 per cent even went further and thought Japan should have been inundated with nuclear weapons before it had a chance to surrender (by implication, these 22.7 per cent wanted to annihilate as large as possible a proportion of the Japanese civilian population – clearly a Total War aim as Ludendorff defined it).[89]

While anybody can sympathise with the reaction of Bruce Hopper, after visiting Buchenwald in 1945 ('Stench everywhere: piles of human bone remnants at the furnace. Here is the antidote to qualms about strategic bombing'),[90] the problem remains that those killed in the strategic bombing raids were rarely the people who organised the Holocaust or perpetrated the slaughter and rapes of Nanking, the abysmal treatment of prisoners of war, or the human experiments of the concentration camps. Even if a case can be made, that as part of the electorate, the women and the old, making up the highest proportion of the city bombing victims in Germany, were as responsible as any citizen for the crimes their chosen or at least tolerated government was committing, this was not so for the children who were killed.[91] The historian Richard Overy has concluded:

88. J.M. Spaight, *Can America Prevent Frightfulness from the Air?* (London: Sept. 1939), p. 43, quoted in Overy, 'Air power and the origins', p. 87.

89. Sadao Asada, 'The mushroom cloud and national psyches', in Laura Hein and Mark Selden (eds.), *Living with the Bomb* (Armonk, NY: M.E. Sharpe, 1997), p. 177.

90. Quoted in Markusen and Kopf, *The Holocaust and Strategic Bombing*, p. 244.

91. Children made up an even higher proportion in Japan than in Germany or Britain, where many children had been evacuated to the countryside, but still, there were tens of thousands of child victims in total in the raids on Hamburg, Cologne, and Dresden in particular, which was full of civilian refugees.

Perhaps most important of all, wartime strategic bombing, and the fire-bombing of Japan in particular, pushed the Western states across psychological and ethical thresholds that made possible a strategy of mass destruction of civilians from the air, which would never have been countenanced in the 1930s . . .[92]

The problem is, however, that Trenchard and Sykes *did* contemplate such a strategy, and in peacetime. Their intention was defensive, and they did not fantasise about starting a war the way Ludendorff did. But they certainly did countenance such strategic bombing. While Britain and the USA were acting only in self-defence, as Raymond Aron noted, the confrontation with totalitarian enemies rubbed off, and the United Kingdom and America came very close to waging Total War – in *effect*, if not in *spirit*. As Cyril Falls wrote in 1941: 'The very fact that this total war exists in itself threatens the destruction and implies the doom of civilisation . . . civilization and total war cannot long exist together.'[93] Britain and the USA had been fighting monsters, and in the process came close to becoming monsters.[94]

But there is one final test that we can apply in seeking to identify the difference between the USA and the UK on the one hand, and Germany and Japan on the other. It lies in the comparison made by Eric Markusen and David Kopf between the conduct of the Holocaust and the bombing raids. Both Holocaust and bombing raids saw the full application of the War Machine – state, bureaucracy, industry, transport, science and research, propaganda and disinformation, and specialised military.[95] The crucial difference was, however, that true to their original war aims (defensive) and disposition (not hostile to the enemy as 'race' or 'nation'), Americans and Britons ceased all atrocities at the moment of their enemy's surrender, while it was precisely then that Germans and Japanese fully unleashed theirs. Raymond Aron was thus right in concluding from this that the USA and the United Kingdom had

92. Overy, 'Air power and the origins', pp. 94, 96.

93. Cyril Falls, *The Nature of Modern Warfare* (London: Methuen, 1941), pp. 18f.

94. A historical parallel may give an additional explanation for the drift of non-totalitarian powers towards waging Total War. The countries that were overrun by the French in the Revolutionary and Napoleonic Wars turned to copying the French system of waging war in order ultimately to shake off French occupation or to repulse French attacks. In defence against a decisive, superior form of warfare, there is a tendency to copy it, whether or not the war aims are there to go along with it, simply because the alternative is defeat and surrender, options usually abhorred even by pacific societies when confronted with an aggressor.

95. Markusen and Kopf, *The Holocaust and Strategic Bombing*, pp. 183–237; 243.

only *temporarily* become like the monsters they were fighting – they reverted to the essence of their own culture when no longer driven to perversions by the confrontation with totalitarian enemies.

Conclusions: What is the relationship between nuclear war and Total War?

From the atomic bombing in August 1945 until the end of the twentieth century, the world did not see any further nuclear use in war. Indeed, it saw a dwindling number of outright *air* attacks on cities with the express purpose of targeting civilian populations.[96] The air attacks on cities that have occurred – for example in the Korean War or in the Arab-Israeli Wars – usually had the aim of disrupting government control, rather than of specifically killing non-combatants. There have been artillery attacks on cities with the purpose of killing civilians, most recently in the Yugoslav wars, precisely because these were driven by an ideology of genocide, as was Auschwitz. There have also been other, horrendous cases of the active persecution of designated populations, for instance, the estimated millions of victims of Pol Pot's Kampuchea, victims of a civil war, in which one side defined another as eternal enemy much as Stalin defined and treated the *kulaks*, persecuting them relentlessly within their common country. The revenge wreaked by the North Vietnamese against those in the South who held out against them is another horrible example, as is the genocide of the Hutus against the Tutsis in Rwanda in the early 1990s. These did not, on the whole, rely on aircraft, and never on nuclear weapons. Yet in their relentlessness, in their mobilisation of the society for hatred, to the point where most of these killings were done by hand, directly, human being to human being, with guns, bayonets, machetes, is closer to that ultimate struggle of people against people which Ludendorff glorified than was the awful decision to bomb Hiroshima and Nagasaki.

The liberal democracies, by contrast, after the Second World War (and outside a context of actual war) gradually developed more, not fewer, scruples with regard to the waging of Total War. While in 1947 the US Joint Chiefs of Staff asked for 400 atomic bombs, because this was the number required, in their view, for

96. See Chapter 2.

'killing a nation',[97] such language became unacceptable over the following decades. In the early 1980s, US strategy and indeed NATO strategy sought to exploit tensions within the Warsaw Pact which arose from Soviet hegemony. Targeting was designed, particularly in the context of NATO's first use doctrine, to avoid the cities, civilian populations, but also armed forces of Soviet client states (chiefly Poland and Czechoslovakia) and to target mainly Soviet armed forces. The hope was that the USSR's reluctant allies might be persuaded to put down their arms or shake off Soviet oppression, taking advantage of the East–West conflagration to free themselves.[98] But this preference for targeting Soviet (ideally Great Russian?) forces was criticised early on as 'ethnic targeting'. As George Quester has argued

> [A]iming at millions of Great Russians, only because of their ethnicity . . . would rather strike Europeans as behaviour more typical of the defendants than the prosecution at Nuremburg [*sic*]. It is genocide to choose to kill, or not to kill, simply on the basis of the likely language of the victim, rather than hitting him incidentally as part of the general assault on the nation.[99]

Genocide, and anything smacking of Total War, was thus increasingly carefully avoided by the USA and Britain.

Even so, since 1945, in the words again of Richard Overy, Western '[d]eterrent credibility stemmed not from fear of the unknown, but from the evidence of what liberal democracies had done to Hamburg, Dresden and Hiroshima.'[100] It is on the basis of such deterrence that there has not been, since 1945, a major inter-state war comparable to the two world wars or the Thirty Years' or Napoleonic Wars.

What, then, is the essence of the relationship between nuclear war and Total War? As we have seen, some have argued that the bombing of Hiroshima and Nagasaki were acts of Total War. I have argued that it was a reaction to the Total War unleashed by Germany and Japan, and as such a part of the larger phenomenon. In any case, however, it was *reactive*, resulting from the confrontation

97. David Allan Rosenberg, 'American atomic strategy and the hydrogen bomb decision', *Journal of American History* Vol. 66, No. 1 (1979), p. 68, quoted in Overy, 'Air power and the origins', p. 95.

98. General Sir John Hackett *et al.*, *The Third World War* (London: Sidgwick & Jackson, 1978).

99. George H. Quester, 'Ethnic targeting: a bad idea whose time has come', *Journal of Strategic Studies* Vol. 5, No. 2 (June 1982), p. 232.

100. Overy, 'Air power and the origins', pp. 94, 96.

of a non-totalitarian power, desirous only of bringing the war to a close, with two totalitarian enemies, who were willing to fight fanatically, accepting enormous losses of life on their own side, who had to be defeated utterly before they were prepared to surrender. But there was no intention on the part of the US administration to annihilate or enslave *all* the Japanese or the Germans. It is thus that the total number of Japanese dead in the Second World War, enormous though it was, only amounted to about a third of the numbers killed in the Holocaust, and that shortly after the war, both Japanese and Germans were in turn protected by the USA against a common menace emanating, it was thought, from the USSR, and built up economically.

The real culmination of Total War was Auschwitz: that was the extermination of the very population which Ludendorff had arbitrarily defined as *the* enemy in his definition of Total War, taken to its logical extreme. In the evaluation of two experts on genocide, however irrelevant it was for the civilians who lost their lives in air raids on their cities, there is a difference between the victims of Tokyo, Nagasaki, Hiroshima and Dresden on the one hand, and the victims of Auschwitz and Buchenwald on the other: the former were perhaps defenceless as individuals, but they were nonetheless 'part of the group or nation that is at war', whose soldiers were somewhere out there, supposedly defending their interest. The victims of genocide, by contrast, have 'no organized military machinery that might be opposed to that of the perpetrator'.[101]

Unlike the Americans (and the British), the Germans took advantage precisely of the defeat of the states against which they went to war, and of power gained over defenceless non-combatants, to put into action their genocidal masterplan: the rounding-up and extermination of the Jews and Gypsies took place within the territory they controlled and occupied, precisely when those groups were no longer defended by an army.[102] The industrialised structure of the genocide of the German persecution of Jews and other groups has remained unparalleled since, even though in its scope (albeit applied only to the state territory of Kampuchea) and intensity, Pol

101. Frank Chalk and Kurt Jonassohn, *The History and Sociology of Genocide: Analyses and Case Studies* (New Haven: Yale University Press, 1990), pp. 23f., quoted in Markusen and Kopf, *The Holocaust and Strategic Bombing*, p. 67.
102. The failure of Japanese air defences to fight the bombers attacking Tokyo, which has puzzled Americans ever since, was a real, disastrous failure of the Japanese War Machine, but no more than that – even the Japanese military leadership was conscious of its own failure in this respect, see Wainstock, *The Decision to Drop the Atomic Bomb*, p. 99.

Pot's monstrous enterprise has come close. But the events in Kampuchea, as in Rwanda, have demonstrated, if it needs demonstrating, that a régime that is determined to carry out genocide will draw on whatever technology is available to pursue its plan. Ultimately it is not the existence of a War Machine that leads inevitably to Total War, it is the determination to perpetrate genocide that will let the inventive find the tools they need.[103]

What then of the existence of weapons of mass destruction? In a potential future context, would nuclear war amount to genocide? It is difficult to see how the effect of the targeting of cities with several nuclear weapons could be distinguished in effect from genocide, even if the intention were not one born of race or religious hatred. On all sides, the nuclear strategies of the Cold War, in aiming to create deterrence and prevent war, clearly had no genocidal intention, and much of the targeting would have aimed to avoid conurbations as much as possible. But all three Western powers retained city bombing strategies as ultimate fall-back option many decades after Hiroshima and Nagasaki, as advocated by Douhet, Trenchard and Ludendorff in the 1920s and 1930s. Had they ever been applied in war, the effects would have been many times those of Auschwitz, let alone Nanking – and then the question whether or not genocide was *intended* as opposed to *effected* would have been as relevant as medieval debates about the gender of angels.

103. See Chapter 5.

CHAPTER FOUR

A Turning Point in the Thinking about the Morality of War?

The bomb that fell on Hiroshima cut history in two like a knife. Before and after are two different worlds. That cut is more abrupt, decisive, and revolutionary than the cut made by the star over Bethlehem.

(Henry Wieman, writing in 1946)[1]

It is my assertion that the dropping of the atomic bomb on Hiroshima is an event in which the hand of God can be seen. The momentousness of its impact is such that we can now terminate the life functions not only of the human race but of the planet itself. The 'end of time' is now an omnipresent reality.

(Jim Garrison, writing in 1982)[2]

In this chapter we turn to thinking about the morality of war. We shall address the question what difference the invention and the use in 1945 of nuclear weapons (and more generally the existence of weapons of mass destruction) have made to attitudes to war. We shall look at the impact of nuclear weapons on the evolution of 'pacifism', peace- and anti-war movements, of the attitudes of major religions towards war, and of inter-state initiatives to ban certain forms of war and certain forms of weapons, including nuclear weapons. As in all previous chapters, we shall ask what developments were underway anyway, what developments were caused mainly by the growing consciousness of the implications of nuclear weapons, and what developments in thinking about war took a different turn because of them.

1. Henry Wieman, *The Source of Human Good* (London: 1946), p. 37 quoted in Jim Garrison, *The Darkness of God: Theology after Hiroshima* (London: SCM Press, 1982), p. 68.
2. Jim Garrison, *The Darkness of God*, p. 205.

Immorality of war

Before launching into a discussion of the development of anti-war thinking and indeed movements, and the impact of nuclear weapons on them, we need to introduce some precision into the terminology used. There is a difference between pacifism and *pacificism*: the word *pacificism* was employed earlier in both meanings, but we will use it in the definition given by the political scientist Martin Ceadel: *pacificism* 'sees the prevention of war as its main duty and accepts that, however upsetting to the purist's conscience, the controlled use of armed forces may be necessary to achieve this'. Pacifists by contrast think it is wrong to take part in *any* war (and they usually do not believe in the use of force in any way).[3] Conscientious objectors, as Ceadel argues, do not necessarily fall in either category if they merely reject the use of force or participation in war (a particular war or any war) for themselves but do not deduce from this any universal applicability.[4]

Both pacifists and growing numbers of pacificists came to oppose the use of any nuclear weapons. Yet the condemnation of a certain form of weapons is not unique to the nuclear bomb. The use of the crossbow by Christians against Christians was condemned by the Church at the Second Ecumenical Council of the Lateran in 1139; dumdum bullets were banned in the nineteenth century. At the turn from the nineteenth to the twentieth century, many governments agreed to impose upon themselves collectively restrictions designed to lead to more humane conduct of war. Thus the Hague Declaration of 21 July 1899 contained a clause on air warfare prohibiting the release of shells and explosives from balloons.[5]

From the First World War onwards, when they were used copiously, chemical weapons were at the centre of disputes about humanitarian restrictions on warfare. They were not used in the Second World War, but napalm and other chemical weapons were used in the Greek Civil War towards the end of the 1940s, in the Korean War of 1950–53, during the Vietnam War of the 1960s and early 1970s, and in the Iran–Iraq War of the late 1980s. After long campaigning, chemical weapons were banned by treaty in 1993 (it came into force in 1997). Biological weapons were banned by treaty even

3. Martin Ceadel, *Pacifism in Britain, 1914–1943: the Defining of a Faith* (Oxford: Clarendon, 1980), pp. 4f.

4. *Ibid.*, pp. 19–25.

5. Alan Stephens, 'The true believers: air power between the wars', in Alan Stephens (ed.), *The War in the Air 1914–1994* (Fairbairn, Australia: RAAF Base, 1994), p. 57.

earlier, in 1972, but, as it became clear, this convention was ignored by many of its signatories, including the USSR. Land-mines were banned by the Oslo Treaty of 1997. Warnings of genetic weapons (i.e. weapons affecting only individuals with particular genetic dispositions), the dream of many racists, thus far fortunately seem to lack the basis of concrete physiological research, but already there is opposition to the pursuit of research in this direction.[6]

Nuclear weapons are thus not the first nor the only weapons to have provoked opposition to their very existence. But the abolition of nuclear weapons and the internationalisation of all control over nuclear energy (under the UN's authority) became an issue early on. Only a year after the first atomic explosion, the US representative at the UN, Bernard Baruch, proposed a treaty on this matter; the Soviet Union replied by calling for unconditional unilateral nuclear disarmament by the USA, and no agreement was obtained. The two nuclear superpowers only converged in their interest in preventing further nuclear proliferation in the early 1960s, signing a partial nuclear test ban treaty in 1963 and persuading many other governments to sign up to the Nuclear Non-Proliferation Treaty (NPT) in 1968 (and in subsequent years). The NPT was extended indefinitely in 1995, but there is little sign that the five nuclear powers whose existence it acknowledges, the USA, Russia, Britain, France and China, have any firm intention of respecting their engagement in the NPT ultimately to eliminate nuclear weapons altogether. Since the NPT was concluded, the nuclear club had been *de facto* enlarged by Pakistan's nuclear test of May 1998 (India had already conducted a 'peaceful nuclear explosion' in 1974 but tested again, also in 1998).

It is not just nuclear weapons that are controversial. So is the use of all weapons in the bombing of cities. Certain forms of war have been outlawed by international conventions, and these include attacks on towns. Even in 1907, the Hague Convention on land warfare prohibited any 'attack, or bombardment, *by whatever means*, of towns, villages, dwellings, or buildings which are undefended . . .' (Article 25, emphasis mine). Of course it could be argued that this convention applied to land warfare only and not to air warfare. The British Cabinet in the First World War claimed that the convention did not apply to human settlements that were defended by virtue of the fact that they were located in enemy territory and the enemy

6. Hubert Wetzel, 'Alptraum Genwaffe', *Die Zeit* (28 November 1997).

was defending his country.[7] Yet it is clear from the insertion of the clause, 'by whatever means', and by the preamble added at the request of the Russian representative de Martens and named after him, which stressed that general principles of the laws of nations should apply to all cases not explicitly codified in this treaty, that the signatories wanted it to be applied in the broadest possible way.[8]

Similarly, the government representatives attending the Washington Naval Conference of 1921–22 recommended that only military objectives should be legitimate targets for aerial bombardment. From this were derived draft rules on aerial warfare, discussed in The Hague in 1923, but never ratified. They stipulated that only military targets were free to be bombed in war, and then only if this could be done without bombing civilians, i.e. injuring non-combatants (or what would today be called significant collateral damage to civilians). Moreover, they outlawed bombing of civilians with the object of terrorising them (Articles 22 and 24(3) respectively).[9]

Only in 1977 – another world war and many minor wars later – was an international convention drawn up to outlaw city bombing from the air, without specific reference to nuclear weapons. The text of this First Additional Protocol to the Geneva Convention is utterly unambiguous, proscribing attacks on the civilian populations, or threats of violence which are made to terrorise the civilian population (Part IV, Article IV). Nevertheless, in blatant contrast to the language of this protocol, both the USA and the UK made unilateral declarations to the effect that their own nuclear weapons would in no way be affected by it.[10]

Many have continued to press the nuclear powers to go ahead with the nuclear disarmament, uni- or multilateral, to which they committed themselves in the Non-Proliferation Treaty. In the mid-1990s, the abolition of nuclear weapons was proposed by the Canberra Commission, which counts among its members eminent

7. Donald Cameron Watt, 'Restraints on war in the air before 1945', in Michael Howard (ed.), *Restraints on War* (Oxford: Oxford University Press, 1979), pp. 62f.

8. Georg Schwarzenberger, 'Die Legitimität der Atomwaffen', *Europa-Archiv* 13th year, 8th issue (April 1958), pp. 10, 672.

9. Manfred Messerschmidt, 'Strategic air war and international law', in Horst Boog (ed.), *The Conduct of the Air War in the Second World War* (Oxford: Berg, 1992), pp. 298–309.

10. Tony Carty, 'The origins of the doctrine of deterrence and the legal status of nuclear weapons', and 'Legality and nuclear weapons: doctrine of nuclear warfighting', in Howard Davis (ed.), *Ethics and Defence: Power and Responsibility in the Nuclear Age* (Oxford: Blackwell, 1986), pp. 104–54.

individuals such as former French Prime Minister Michel Rocard, the former British Chief of the Defence Staff Field Marshal Lord Carver, and the former director of the International Institute of Strategic Studies (IISS) of London, Professor Robert O'Neill. International pressure for the abolition of nuclear weapons increased with the award of the Nobel Prize to Josef Rotblat who, with the support of both Western and Soviet colleagues, has campaigned against nuclear weapons for decades.[11] In December 1996 an international group of 58 retired high-ranking officers expressed themselves in favour of a total abolition of nuclear weapons. Among the signatories are the former SACEUR General Bernard Rogers, the US commander of the air forces in the Gulf War, General Charles Horner, and General William Odom, former head of the National Security Agency; on the Russian side, we find Alexander Lebed, the former Secretary of the Security Council; General Lev Rokhilin, President of the Defence Committee of the Douma; on the British side, General Sir Hugh Beach, again Field Marshal Lord Carver, Brigadier Michael Harbottle, Air Commodore Alistair Mackie, and on the French side, Admiral Antoine Sanguinetti.[12] These are specific campaigns aiming at the abolition of nuclear weapons, but they can be located in a much older tradition of anti-war movements.

To look at how far such movements owed their rationale to the particularity of nuclear weapons, and at how far they drew their strength from other factors, we will now turn to the development of anti-war reasoning through the ages. We shall do so in order to ascertain to what extent pacifist and pacificist sentiments existed before nuclear weapons, and to what extent present movements aiming to ban war or merely to eliminate nuclear weapons draw on pre-nuclear developments in thinking, and on pre-nuclear institutional or sectarian traditions.

Pacifism before the nineteenth century

Prior to the nineteenth century, the rejection of war tended to be linked to adherence to a particular religion which commanded

11. *Report of the Canberra Commission on the Elimination of Nuclear Weapons* (Canberra: 1996).
12. 'Statement on nuclear weapons', *The Washington Quarterly* Vol. 29, No. 3 (Summer 1997), pp. 125–130; see also General George Lee Butler, former Chief of the Strategic Air Command of the USA, 'The general's bombshell: phasing out the U.S. nuclear arsenal', *The Washington Post* (12 Jan. 1997).

abstention from shedding blood. It was thus perhaps predominantly connected with the wish for personal purity, personal salvation, or an unconditional obedience to religious postulates (irrespective of personal punishment or reward), rather than directly with concern for the abolition of war, or for the safety of oneself and of others. While religious teachers proscribing killing may well have been primarily concerned about the horrors of violence, and only secondarily by the effect of killing somebody else on their disciples' souls, they usually cloaked their teaching in terminology referring strictly to the latter. This is not to deny the impact of the experience of suffering brought about by war on many people's commitment to non-violence. But prior to the nineteenth century, the emphasis tended to be on moral reasons for non-violence deduced from holy scripture and the effects on the potential perpetrator of violence, not primarily on any argument in favour of compassion for the victims of war.[13]

The rejection of the shedding of blood can be traced back very far indeed. The Jewish Torah for one contained within its Mosaic law the clear injunction not to kill, even though war, if authorised by God, is permitted and indeed even a moral obligation. The four Evangelists, recording the teaching of Jesus, provide material which can be interpreted in different ways. Peter Brock has argued that it was early Christians who were probably the first to reject war categorically.[14] Yet Christianity spread not least among the armed forces of the Roman Empire, and in consequence, the early Christians were soon confronted with the question as to how to interpret the Mosaic injunction that 'Thou shalt not kill' and the Sermon on the Mount's 'Blessed are the peacemakers' in connection with military service in defence of the pagan Roman Empire.

The majority of Christians remaining within the teaching of the Church began to accept military service as compatible with their religion. This coincided in the fourth century with the espousal of Christianity by the Emperor Constantine I. He paved the way to making it state religion by first tolerating Christians and then favouring their religion over the other religions present in the Roman Empire. From then on, early Christian teachers fiercely debated the significance of the Old Testament with its many divinely commanded wars: should these be interpreted as metaphorical, as Origen, Tertullian and Lactantius thought, or as guidelines for

---

13. One notable exception is Erasmus of Rotterdam's *Quaerela Pacis* of 1517, in which he specifically underlines the plight of populations involved in war.

14. Peter Brock, *Pacifism in Europe to 1914* (Princeton, NJ: Princeton U.P., 1972), pp. 3–24.

judging whether a war was just and could be supported actively by Christians, as Augustine of Hippo argued at the beginning of the fifth century?[15]

St Augustine came to dominate the teaching of the Roman Catholic Church, which in view of the imperfection of the world recognised war as reconcilable with God's commands if certain criteria were met – those of a just cause, legitimate authority, right intention, real possibility of victory or the proportionality of damage done and benefit reaped; finally, Augustine argued, war had to be the last resort. Thomas Aquinas recodified these rules eight hundred years later, and as we shall see, they have remained the Catholic guidelines for dealing intellectually with the concept of nuclear war. But even the Catholic Church consistently advocated constraints on the use of force, designating non-combatants as people who should be spared in war. Blended with medieval ideas of chivalry, such concepts can be traced back again to St Augustine, and are reflected in early modern times in the writings of Hugo Grotius.[16] As we shall see, perhaps Augustine's most important contribution to Christian thinking about war was the concept of proportionality between the potential damage done through war and the potential benefit it might bring (such as the redressing of wrong). We shall see later how crucial this consideration is in the context of mass warfare, and in particular, of the views of Christians but also of international law on the morality of nuclear war. It has continued to dominate Catholic teaching on war until our day.

HERETICS, PROTESTANTS AND DISSENTERS

From the third century onwards, some Christian splinter groups branded as heretical by successive Church Councils defined abstention from the shedding of any blood (including animal) as their ideal. These included the Manichaeans, Paulicians or Poblicans, Bogomils, Patarins, Cathars or Albigensians, who were vigorously persecuted by the Church. They all had in common that they rejected *all* bloodshed, but that they thought that only a small élite of *perfecti*, perfect human beings, could actually live by the rules of living as vegetarians and not shedding any blood.[17]

---

15. Frederick H. Russell: *The Just War in the Middle Ages* (Cambridge: Cambridge U.P., 1975), pp. 16–26.

16. Donald L. Davidson, *Nuclear Weapons and the American Churches: Ethical Positions and Modern Warfare* (Boulder, Co.: Westview, 1983), pp. 8, 10.

17. A.A. Vasiliev, *History of the Byzantine Empire* vol. II (first Engl. edn. 1928, this edition Milwaukee: University of Wisconsin Press, 1952), p. 383.

Even before the Cathars had been exterminated, a new sect took up the torch of the rejection of killing: from the late twelfth century onwards, the Waldensians rejected all forms of killing. At the end of the fourteenth century, John Wycliff in England introduced similarly revolutionary ideas to those who became known as 'Lollards'. While Wycliff did not reject war, some of his followers did, claiming 'that manslaughter by battle or . . . law . . . without special revelation is express contrarious to the New Testament . . .'.[18]

In Central Europe, the Protestant Reformation was prepared further by the Bohemian Brethren, who were inspired both by Wycliff's teachings and those of the Waldensians. Lollards, Waldensians and the Bohemian reformers (particularly Jan Hus, who was burnt for his beliefs, even though unlike some of his martyred followers, he did not condemn outright the taking of life) were persecuted, and only the Bohemian Brethren survived into the sixteenth century. Under the pressure of persecution by the Catholic Church even the pacifist wing of this group abandoned its earlier beliefs.[19]

The creed of non-violence was next adopted by the Anabaptists, whose movement originated in Zürich. For many, though not all of them, their doctrine of 'defencelessness' meant the rejection of all war. This creed was then taken up by the Mennonites in the sixteenth century, but while they still exist as a sect, particularly in the USA and in the Netherlands, many of them abandoned their pacifist beliefs under the influence of nationalism in the nineteenth century. It has been argued, however, that together with other pacifist movements, they engendered traditions of non-violence in North America which are still alive today.[20] Other groups in the Renaissance shared the Anabaptists' commitment to non-violence, but disappeared in subsequent centuries.

The earliest pacifist movement which can be traced continuously to the present and which directly influenced twentieth-century pacifism originated in England, with the Quakers or the Society of Friends who came into being during the English Civil War, in the middle of the seventeenth century. Towards the end of that century, one of the 'Friends', William Penn, formulated a concept of inter-state order which would obviate war.[21] In the absence of conscription,

---

18. Quoted in Brock, *Pacifism in Europe to 1914*, p. 30.
19. *Ibid.*, pp. 25–58.
20. *Ibid.*, pp. 105–13; 162–254; Peter Brock, *The Roots of War Resistance: Pacifism from the Early Church to Tolstoy* (New York: The Fellowship of Reconciliation, 1981), pp. 36–9.
21. Brock, *Pacifism in Europe to 1914*, pp. 275–7.

Quakers both in England and in North America, where they emigrated in substantial numbers, could mostly choose for themselves to abstain from the use of force; they rarely sought to impose their own conduct upon the rest of the states in which they lived their rather separate existence. Other sects – Scottish Presbyterians and British Baptists and Unitarians – also contributed to pacific leanings both in Britain and in the New World.[22]

The quest for a peaceful inter-state order had not been confined to Quakers, Anabaptists or Mennonites, however. The ravages of the Thirty Years' War on the European mainland persuaded even Richelieu himself that what was needed was an order between the sovereign principalities of Europe which would make the resolution of disputes possible without resorting to war.[23] This quest was renewed in Europe in the era of Enlightenment by those like the Abbé de Saint Pierre and Immanuel Kant who sought ways of bringing about perpetual peace. There are thus old religious roots of pacifism and pacificism, connected mainly with Protestant or Christian sectarian rejections of bloodshed, which in turn formed the basis of secular, humanist arguments that grew in the Age of Enlightenment. Pacifism and pacificism thus clearly antedate the Industrial Revolution and the growth of the War Machine, not to mention weapons of mass destruction.

From the wars of the French Revolution to World War I

At the end of the Age of Reason, the devastation brought upon Europe by the wars of the French Revolution and the Napoleonic Wars had two pronounced effects on Europeans: either to drive them into bellicose nationalism, or to lead them to seek a more stable form of peace under re-established *anciens régimes* (although these were invariably reformed in one way or another). In the new USA, which had been spared the ravages of Bonaparte's campaigns, but had repeatedly been at war with Britain since its independence, a peace society was founded in 1815 by a Presbyterian in New York. In 1816 a similar Society for the Promotion of Permanent and Universal Peace was founded in London with a substantial level of

22. Martin Ceadel, *The Origins of War Prevention* (Oxford: Clarendon, 1996).
23. Anja V. Hartmann, *Rêveurs de Paix? Friedenspläne und Konzeptionen kollektiver Sicherheit bei Crucé, Richelieu and Sully*, Vol. 12, *Beiträge zur deutschen und europäischen Geschichte* (Hamburg: 1995).

support coming particularly from Quakers, but also from members of other Evangelical sects.[24]

While supporters of such peace societies mostly had religious backgrounds which lent themselves to pacifist or pacificist views, arguments had since the eighteenth century been increasingly made in an areligious context. The arguments of those promoting ideas for a more stable peace order moved away from the spiritual salvation of the potential soldier shedding blood and towards compassion for the victims of war, and criticism of war for the suffering it brought rather than for the sin. This concept is found in the writings of Erasmus of Rotterdam, but is otherwise found rarely if at all before the eighteenth century. Such arguments could become a platform for discussion with other Christian sects and indeed with non-Christians, agnostics and atheists. The human misery to which war gave rise was now at the centre of attention, not whether shedding blood was acceptable or unacceptable to God. Pacifism and pacificism became increasingly secular in outlook.

This does not mean that the religious aspect of pacifism disappeared – far from it. Up to the present, pacifism and related movements have been found mostly in Protestant Christian cultures – then as now, pacifism and anti-war initiatives were rarely found in Catholic Christian cultures, and rarely in an organised form in non-Christian cultures.[25] As we shall see, peace movements have tended to mix religious, salvation-oriented arguments with humanist concern for the suffering of the innocent in this world. But more recently, with the secularisation of Western societies, the latter approach (although indubitably rooted at least in part also in religious-moral inspirations) has begun to gain ground, today predominating in the movement directed mainly against nuclear weapons.

Motivated also by faith in the benefits of worldwide commerce, hopes for a general improvement in living conditions and the fear of internal unrest if this did not happen, intellectuals in several countries developed an interest in structurally more pacific interstate orders. While the mechanism of the Concert of Europe was working during the post-Napoleonic 'Long Peace', it was oiled by this quest for peace (both internal and external) and abhorrence of insurrection and war. This inspired faith in the possibility of a system which would promote peace and contain war, ideas which gained support among thinkers throughout the Western world, irrespective of their creed. Thus in the second half of the nineteenth

24. Brock, *Pacifism in Europe to 1914*, pp. 378–81.   25. See below.

century, while the War Machine was being put into place, particularly in Western Europe, a series of movements for a peaceful interstate order came into being in France, Austria, Germany, Denmark, Sweden and elsewhere.

Of importance in its impact on other non-violent movements was the thinking of the great Russian writer and pacifist, Leo Tolstoy, who had many followers in his own country. His influence was still felt when the Russian revolutionaries in overthrowing the Tsar and the government in 1917 opted for peace with Germany. Initially, Tolstoyan pacifism continued to have an influence, but in the late 1920s, it was rooted out by the Communist régime.[26] Tolstoy's ideas and those of a number of other intellectual peace-campaigners throughout Europe contributed to the momentum which led to the conferences in The Hague in 1899 and 1907 respectively, which formulated the limitations on war discussed above.

Pacificism, however, let alone pacifism, remained an elitist or sectarian minority sentiment throughout this century. It was amply offset by the explosive rise of nationalism and Social Darwinism in the last third of the nineteenth century, which culminated in the pro-war hysteria which led to the First World War. Where nationalism dominated, pacifism retreated, as did Christianity as opposed to those using Christianity in the interest of nationalism ('With God for Emperor and Fatherland'). As the British poet Wilfred Owen observed in 1917, as he lay in a military hospital after having been wounded in action, 'pure Christianity will not fit in with pure patriotism'.[27]

Actual pacifism – the rejection of all forms of war even in an imperfect world, as opposed to movements which sought a peaceful and just world order which would obviate war – remained largely confined to the Anglo-Saxon world, and above all to Protestants, while it was almost entirely absent in this period among Catholics and Orthodox.[28]

Socialist opposition to nationalist wars

Besides Christianity and particularly Protestant denominations, a second important root of the peace movements throughout Europe

26. Peter Brock, *Twentieth-Century Pacifism* (New York: Van Nostrand-Reinhold, 1970), p. 104.
27. Quoted in Brock, *Twentieth-Century Pacifism*, p. 40.
28. *Ibid.*, p. 24. On the Orthodox churches, see below.

and beyond lies in Socialism. While the prophets of Socialism, particularly Karl Marx and Friedrich Engels, predicted or indeed advocated the struggle (literally, 'fight') between the classes, they interpreted nationalism as a ploy of the bourgeois capitalist classes to harness the exploited working forces of their own country to their economically profitable fight against other countries. *Proletarier aller Länder, vereinigt euch!*,[29] written on Karl Marx's tombstone in Highgate cemetery, was the appeal of international Socialism both to transcend national boundaries and to rise as an international force to fight the equally international 'class enemy'.

In several countries in the late nineteenth century, however, the Socialist Party and nascent trade union movements opted to abandon a revolutionary approach and to aim for reform through the existing political structures. They were nonetheless deeply torn when their governments went to war, a majority rallying to the nationalist, rather than the internationalist cause. In 1870/71, the Paris *Commune*, strongly Socialist in nature, only gathered momentum when the government of France proved unable to organise an effective defence of the country, but was bloodily crushed by French state forces. The First International, founded in 1864, was dissolved in 1876, partly as a result of the delayed impact of this experience. The Second International, founded in 1889, had internal fault lines along the national divides; debates about the legitimacy of war weakened it considerably from 1900 onwards. As the First World War approached, the deep fissures within French society led many to predict that the Left would undermine the nation's war effort. But the assassination of the most prominent Socialist leader and anti-war agitator, Jean Jaurès, one month after the assassination of the Habsburg heir, cleared the way for the creation of the *'Union Sacrée'*, the sacred union of Left and Right in the face of the German enemy. At the same time his death was symbolic of the demise of the Second International: Jaurès had just returned from a meeting of the Bureau of the Second International in Brussels where he had sought to stem the avalanche of nationalism which, triggered by the shots in Sarajevo, started Europe's race towards war.

Not only in France, but also in Germany, Socialists and Social Democrats proceeded to vote in parliament in favour of funding for the war efforts. Social Democrats in 1914 were split on this issue. Karl Liebknecht and Rosa Luxemburg had been taken to court in 1905 and 1914 respectively for denouncing imperialist warfare. Yet

---

29. 'Workers of the world unite'.

pacificists like Bertha von Suttner, whose novel *Die Waffen Nieder!*[30] of 1905 had deeply influenced the anti-nationalist wing of the German Left, ultimately remained in a minority. In Britain, too, jingoist sentiments won out hands down against Socialist internationalism in 1914.

Pacificism in the inter-war period

For the majority of those participating in it, the First World War was a cataclysmic experience, and it haunts the minds of Europeans to this day as much if not more than the memory of Hiroshima and Nagasaki. The Great War, as it is still called sometimes, led to actual confrontations between pacifists and governments, particularly in the Anglo-Saxon countries, when compulsory military service was introduced. In Britain there were around 16,000 conscientious objectors, in the USA the figure remained under 4,000.[31] If anything, opposition to the war effort grew as the 'War to end all Wars', the '*Der(nier) des Der(nier)s*' dragged on. As a consequence of its mindless carnage, repugnance towards this particular form of mass warfare spread among the military in Britain, France and Germany. All of them called for new forms of warfare. As one of them wrote in 1927, 'if killing is not confined to armed forces then I hold that civilisation is doomed'.[32] Many military men, however, hoped that new forms of military technology, such as air power or armoured warfare, would be more efficient and humane than World War I, which had seen 'morons volunteering to get hung in the wire and shot in the stomach in the mud of Flanders' (Air Marshal Arthur 'Bomber' Harris).[33]

Notably in Britain, the First World War brought a dramatic growth of the awareness among educated middle-class people that war might affect them very directly, carrying them or those closest to them off to the front. From this arose a new interest in foreign affairs, an awareness that *nostra res agitur*. In the past, particularly in Britain in the eighteenth and nineteenth centuries, wars had been fought by the poor, the press-ganged and the adventurous, but generally not by middle-class people (unless they chose careers as officers). In the First World War, by contrast, middle- and upper-class youths

30. 'Lay down your arms!'   31. Brock, *Twentieth-Century Pacifism*, p. 40.
32. 'Squadron Leader', *The Principles of Air Warfare* (1927), p. 69, quoted in Malcolm Smith, *British Air Strategy Between the Wars* (Oxford: Clarendon, 1984), p. 63.
33. Quoted in *ibid.*, p. 64.

had not only volunteered to go and fight, but conscription had forced the more reluctant to follow. The small band of pacifists was mainly middle-class, and it was predominantly the middle classes that were seized by war-weariness, a symptom that spread far beyond the hard core of active proponents of this cause. The general tidal change from admiring war as some gigantic form of sport or romantic contest (which had dominated people's imaginations before the First World War and continued to do so in Germany, Italy and Japan) to one of war-weariness is reflected in some of the literature inspired by World War I. This included the poems of Wilfred Owen and Siegfried Sassoon, Henri Barbusse's *Le Feu*,[34] Roland Dorgelès' *Les Croix de Bois*,[35] Maurice Genevoix's *Ceux de '14*,[36] Arnold Zweig's *Die Erziehung von Verdun*[37] and *Der Streit um den Sergeanten Grischa*,[38] Erich Maria Remarque's *Im Westen Nichts Neues*,[39] Robert Graves's *Goodbye to All That*[40] and Jean Giono's *Le grand troupeau*,[41] works by Britons, Frenchmen and Germans who had fought on opposite sides of the trenches of Flanders. As the historian Keith Robbins has noted, 'On both sides of the Channel, a certain kind of anti-war sentiment seemed more potent than ever before. The generation that had fought did not want to live through that experience again, and the youthful generation had no wish to be caught in the "war trap".'[42]

The tragic losses suffered by so many families in the Great War were difficult to justify either intellectually or emotionally in terms of the propaganda which had been used to kindle the commitment to fight. Retrospectively, the defence of a political system (Britain) which gave the right to vote to 30 per cent of the adult population against a political system (Germany) which accorded this right to half its adult population (i.e. all males, but no women), but was nonetheless dominated by an elite, both countries being monarchies, was difficult to rationalise in terms of a defence of democracy or civilisation. Indeed, the war aims on all sides became increasingly

34. *Under Fire*, originally published 1916.
35. *The Wooden Crosses*, originally published 1919.
36. *Those of 1914*, originally published in five instalments 1916–23.
37. *The Education of Verdun*, originally published 1935.
38. *The Quarrel about Sergeant Grischa*, originally published 1928.
39. *All Quiet on the Western Front*, originally published 1929.
40. Originally published 1929.   41. *The Great Herd*, originally published 1931.
42. Keith Robbins, 'European peace movements and their influence on policy after the First World War', in R. Ahmann, A.M. Birke and Michael Howard (eds.), *The Quest for Stability: Problems of West European Security, 1918–1957* (Oxford: Oxford University Press, 1993), p. 82.

confusing to those who had to bear the consequences of the war, as private soldiers summed it up: 'We're here because we're here because we're here because we're here.'[43]

It was ultimately not only the suffering of the soldiers but also the targeting of civilians, which many of the strategists of this age welcomed,[44] that inspired pacifists to continue their fight against modern forms of war.[45] It is in this opposition that we find a precursor of the views expressed by the anti-nuclear movements which – except in Germany and some of their Scandinavian manifestations – were not so much pacifist but opposed to Total War, war in which civilians were affected as much or more than combatants.

Organised forms of opposition to war, however, continued to be minority movements everywhere. It is crucial to emphasise once again that in the inter-war period, outright pacifism was a small minority phenomenon, even in Britain, although it was larger here than elsewhere.[46] General disappointment with the post-war world gave the pacifists a greater moral standing retrospectively than they had had during the war itself.[47] After the cataclysm of the Great War, pacifist and pacificist movements sprang up in several countries. A war resisters' International was set up in 1921 named *Paco* after the Esperanto for 'peace', with members in Britain, the Netherlands, Germany and Austria.[48] The League of Nations, set up to keep the world safe for democracy (as its founding fathers, the US President Woodrow Wilson and his idealistic adviser Colonel House had hoped) initially inspired faith in many intellectuals who drew on the hopes of the previous century for a peaceful and stable world (or at least European) order. A 'Peace Ballot' in support of the League of Nations was held in Britain in 1935, and societies supporting the League of Nations sprang up, heterogeneous in membership and not always absolutely dedicated to pacifism, but always opposed to war as a means of increasing a state's power.[49]

Support for the League of Nations through membership of the League of Nations Union was one expression of this turn away from national collective egotism and towards the view that an international organisation and international norms could help prevent

---

43. Quoted in Joan Littlewood: *Oh What a Lovely War* (1963).
44. See above, Chapter 2.   45. Brock, *Twentieth-Century Pacifism*, p. 114.
46. Brock, *Twentieth-Century Pacifism*, p. 28.
47. Keith Robbins, *The Abolition of War: The 'Peace Movement' in Britain, 1914–1919* (Cardiff: University of Wales Press, 1976), p. 217.
48. Brock, *Twentieth-Century Pacifism*, p. 110.
49. Robbins, *The Abolition of War*.

or settle conflict peacefully.[50] In 1936, the Peace Pledge Union was founded, an organisation which reflected the public dislike for war in Britain. To join, one had to sign a card on which was printed the sentence 'I renounce war and never again will I support or sanction another', which was more easily said than done. Many of those who joined were then rapidly converted to militant Marxism when in the same year, the Spanish Civil War broke out.[51] In Britain the Independent Labour Party and the No-Conscription Fellowship drew their strength from this, and we find the first personal links of individuals supporting peace movements or movements with pacific inclinations with the anti-nuclear movements after the Second World War, as we shall see.

Pacifism did exist even in the defeated countries of the First World War, albeit on a smaller scale. In Germany, pacifists, and even just pacificists, faced the problem of how to reconcile their own peace-promoting leanings with the danger of being branded traitors by majority opinion within their own country who chafed at the supposed injustice of the Versailles peace settlement.[52] Kurt Hiller, who in 1926 founded the Group of Revolutionary Pacifists, was later imprisoned in a concentration camp before emigrating to the USA. There were tensions between extremists and moderate supporters. The leadership of the German Peace Association became radicalised in 1929. Periodicals of the German peace movement included *Das andere Deutschland* (The Other Germany), edited by Fritz Küster with a circulation of up to 15,000; *Der Friedenskämpfer* (the Peace-Fighter), published by the *Friedensbund der Katholiken* (Catholic Peace League), and *Eiche* (Oaktree), the organ of the Protestant peace movement. Pacifism and pacificism were energetically suppressed by the National Socialist government in Germany from 1933. The German pacifist Carl von Ossietsky, who as editor of the journal *Die Weltbühne* (the World Stage) drew attention to the secret rearmament of Germany, was awarded the Nobel Prize for Peace, but like Hiller was sent to a concentration camp by the German government. Even by 1930, pacifist literature had become profoundly unfashionable in Germany.[53]

In the 1920s, French pacifists also found it difficult to fend off the suspicion that they were in some terrible way acting as agents of the enemy, Germany, which was (rightly) suspected even then of

50. Ceadel, *Pacifism in Britain*, pp. 63f.   51. *Ibid.*, pp. 222–7.
52. Karl Holl and Wolfgang Wette (eds.), *Pazifismus in der Weimarer Republik* (Paderborn: Schöningh, 1981).
53. Wolfram Wette, 'From Kellogg to Hitler (1928–1933)', in Wilhelm Deist (ed.), *The German Military in the Age of Total War* (Oxford: Berg, 1985), pp. 88–93.

working for a revision of the peace settlement of 1919. The will to effect a reconciliation which would break out of the fratricidal pattern of wars between France and Germany had to appeal not to national interests, but to the common, higher interest in peace for Europe, and here were the seeds of European reconciliation and integration which took root only after another bloody war had devastated Europe. Similar views were shared by intellectuals in other states of Europe who had suffered in the First World War. Ideas put forward for European federation in the inter-war years, and particularly the projects of Richard, Count Coudenhove Kalergi and Aristide Briand, tended to aim for structural changes among the states of Europe which would make war among them less likely or even impossible in the future.[54] European integration was thus another attempt to fight against war, an attempt which did not spring directly from any peace movement or Christian tradition, but one which like them was inspired by the horrible experience of the First World War and thus predated the Second.

In the 1930s, however, both political camps in France, the Right and the Left, divided down the middle over defence. A large section of the Left, which had traditionally been opposed at least to nationalist wars, became increasingly militant as the Spanish Civil War was being fought out just across the Pyrenees. Meanwhile an equally important part of the French political Right (and indeed of Flemish Nationalists in Belgium, for example) developed sympathies for many if not all of the aims of National Socialism as it was put into practice across the Rhine. In 1936, when the *Wehrmacht* occupied the Rhineland, there was universal consensus across the French political spectrum that the reversal of this situation was not worth a war, and the desire to avoid war at almost any cost prepared the swift defeat of France in 1940.[55]

Despite the existence of strong anti-war sentiments in most European countries in the 1930s, these hardly merited the name of 'peace movement'; they were not homogeneous, nor were they 'genuinely transnational' in their activities.[56] There was, however, a new International, and it is here that the most coherent opposition to nationalist wars could be found, albeit clearly confined to one end of the political spectrum.

54. Kevin Wilson and Jan van der Dussen (eds.), *The History of the Idea of Europe* (2nd edn. London: Routledge, 1995), pp. 88–146.
55. Jean-Baptiste Duroselle, 'Les précédents historiques: pacifisme des années 30, neutralisme des années 50', in Pierre Lellouche (ed.), *Pacifisme et dissuasion* (Paris: IFRI, 1983), p. 245.
56. Robbins, 'European peace movements', p. 82.

While at the time of the outbreak of the First World War, the
Socialist parties had by and large allowed their nationalism to pre-
dominate over their internationalism, by 1917/18 the Left in the
countries facing defeat (above all Russia) resumed their critical
attitude towards what they were told to be their 'national interest'.
Russia's and Germany's human losses and military defeats once
again tipped the balance in the Leftist camp towards strikes and,
indeed, revolution and against international war. The February and
October Revolutions of 1917 brought about the change of régime
in Russia which made possible the peace agreements of Brest-Litovsk,
which took Russia out of the international war and freed forces for
its large-scale internal wars. When it dawned on them, despite years
of systematic disinformation, that defeat was imminent, many German sailors, soldiers and indeed workers on the 'home front' in
1918 turned to mutinies, strikes and insurrections.

In 1919 – the Paris peace conferences were still underway – the
Third International was founded in Moscow. Significantly, it became known as the 'Komintern', the Communist International.
Throughout the inter-war period, the Komintern showed itself to
be clearly under the leadership of the Soviet Union and was not
supported by the more moderate Socialist elements in Europe. Its
support for peace fluctuated with the narrow self-interest in the
USSR, but in general it adopted the propaganda line of proclaiming itself to be against international war, while denouncing the warmongering of other states (against which it called upon its followers
to stand up and fight). As Peter Brock has commented,[57] from the
1920s, Soviet-led peace movements were almost exclusively destined
for export, and this remained the case until the mid-1980s.

The credibility of the Komintern suffered a serious blow in the
West when Stalin did not follow these proclaimed principles (para-
doxical though they were). He let down the Left-wing Spanish Re-
publicans in the Spanish Civil War (by not matching the clandestine
support given to General Franco by Hitler and Mussolini to the
point of preventing the defeat of the Left), and his Foreign Minister, Molotov, concluded a pact with Hitler's Foreign Minister,
Ribbentrop, in August 1939, carving up Eastern Europe among
them, only to be caught out by Hitler's surprise attack against the
USSR in June 1941. In the inter-war years, then, the Komintern was
not a very convincing inspiration for pacifism.

57. Brock, *Twentieth-Century Pacifism*, p. 106.

More fruitful ideas could be found elsewhere. In India, Mohandas Karamchand Gandhi formed new concepts of non-violent opposition to unjust rule. He drew his concepts from Hindu scripture, although he acknowledged that there was no clear prescription of non-violence in them, combining them with ideas he drew from the Sermon on the Mount, the writings of Ruskin, Emerson, Thoreau and, importantly, Tolstoy.[58] It is worth recalling that although he was not an unconditional opponent of war, Gandhi himself initially favoured non-violent resistance which he urged even on the Jews in National Socialist Germany, and on the Czechoslovaks in 1938.[59] Gandhian views were very popular in Britain in the 1920s and 1930s. But the concept of passive resistance made no sense 'in an age which expected war to be carried on in the future almost exclusively by air bombardment', as the physical confrontation with the enemy who was to be persuaded to stop using force was not possible in such a situation.[60] Gandhi changed his views on the situation in Central Europe, writing later that 'Europe has sold her soul for the sake of a seven days' earthly existence. The peace Europe gained at Munich [a reference to the British and French pressure put on Czechoslovakia to cede territory to Germany] is a triumph of violence.'[61] The thinking Gandhi developed during the inter-war years had an impact on the anti-nuclear movements of the Cold War.

To conclude our survey of the inter-war years by turning our attention to the New World, pacifism remained a very small movement in the USA. A War Resistance League was formed there in 1924 which at its largest had 12,000 members in 1942. While peace wings were created in all major Protestant churches in the USA, they continued to be very small.[62]

A difficult question which is of some concern to us here is the effect pacifism in France but mainly in Britain had on the appeasement of National Socialist Germany in the 1930s. This allegation made by the critics of pacifism was of considerable importance after the Second World War, and anti-nuclear movements were compelled to answer this criticism; on the whole it also discouraged them from priding themselves in the continuity of their pacifist convictions if they had held them in the inter-war years.[63] Indeed, in France the term 'pacifist' became thoroughly discredited, and

58. *Ibid.*, pp. 69–72.   59. *Ibid.*, pp. 93–5.
60. Ceadel, *Pacifism in Britain*, pp. 28f., 88–90.
61. Quoted in Brock, *Twentieth-Century Pacifism*, p. 99.   62. *Ibid.*, p. 108.
63. Christopher Driver, *The Disarmers: A Study in Protest* (London: Hodder & Stoughton, 1964), p. 16.

could not be used without a negative connotation after 1945, while in Scandinavia or indeed Germany, the term retained a positive meaning.[64] As Keith Robbins has noted, many of the most dedicated pacifists abandoned their previous convictions during the course of the 1930s when it became clear that Hitler was deliberately flouting international law, exploiting the war-weariness of other countries to further his own expansionist, racist plans.[65] Famous examples include Albert Einstein, who abandoned his pacifist beliefs virtually overnight.[66] On the other hand many who were not pacifists supported appeasement. Britons were deeply torn in their attitudes towards government policies, and especially the controversial agreements of Munich which aimed to prevent war at all costs.[67] Frenchmen were equally torn: in contrast to the older pattern of Socialist aversion to war and a more nationalist, militant Right, the 1930s saw the very opposite pattern of Left-wingers calling for resistance to Fascism, while important sectors of the French Right were prepared to join forces with National Socialist Germany in its 'crusade' against Communism.[68]

Little wonder then that after the Second World War, some fierce opponents of nuclear weapons denied any previous pacifist leanings, to emphasise their opposition to *nuclear* war, and not war in general. Links tended later to be made by anti-nuclear groups not between the Cold War and developments leading up to the Second World War, but between the Cold War and the pre-World War I period. This symbolism was not lost on the spectators of Joan Littlewood's cynical musical on the waste and carnage of the Great War, entitled *Oh What a Lovely War*. The musical, later turned into a film, was first performed in 1963, towards the end of the first great anti-nuclear campaign in Britain.

Hiroshima and Nagasaki

Thus the Second World War, which unlike the First was so clearly – at any rate retrospectively – a war of Good against Evil, initially served to sap the attraction of absolute pacifism to the point of

64. Pierre Hassner, 'Pacifism et terreur', in Lellouche (ed.), *Pacifisme et dissuasion*, p. 160.
65. Keith Robbins, *Appeasement* (Oxford: Blackwell, 1988, 2nd edn. 1997).
66. Brock, *Twentieth-Century Pacifism*, p. 131.   67. Robbins, *Appeasement*.
68. David Chuter, *Humanity's Soldier: France and International Security, 1919–2001* (Oxford: Berghahn, 1996), pp. 83–172 *passim*; Maurice Vaïsse, 'Le pacifisme français dans les années trente', *Relations internationales* No. 53 (1988), pp. 37–52.

near-extinction. It made a big dent in anti-war thinking in the West, as it was so obviously a just war from the British and American point of view, particularly after the horrors of the National Socialist rule in Germany became fully known.[69] Where the human sacrifices of the First World War had been difficult to justify retrospectively, Hitler ensured that there could be few doubts about the legitimacy of the Second World War on the Allied side. Nevertheless, how could the destruction of two far-away cities compete in Western collective consciousness with the very direct impact of the Great War?

These two events affected neither Hitler nor the people who had brought him to power and had tolerated, aided and executed the horrendous crimes he instigated. Instead, *Little Boy* and *Fat Man* killed, burned and mutilated people who had not been directly involved in the perpetration of atrocities. And the enormity of the atomic explosion resulted in casualty figures conjuring up the possibility of the extermination of humankind.

Initially it was beyond the reach even of the superpower USA, which had dropped its only two assembled atom bombs over Japan, to destroy the world. Only with the advent of the H-bomb and then the arms build-up of the 1960s was a stockpile capable of irradiating the entire globe generated. Nevertheless, the potential for such very extensive destruction was recognised early on. Indeed, as we noted at the beginning of the first chapter, the Japanese Emperor in his declaration of surrender told his subjects of his conviction that continued fighting 'would not only result in an ultimate collapse and obliteration of the Japanese nation, but also it would lead to the total extinction of human civilisation'.[70] The first nuclear bombing could thus be seen as a momentous moral turning point. The power to wipe out human civilisation, indeed perhaps all human life on the planet, was previously seen in the West as an attribute of God alone – man's development of the ability to command life and death seemed to many the ultimate hubris. As one theologian put it:

> If there is any single point which emerges from the . . . discussion of Hiroshima and the advent of the nuclear age, it is that it is now possible to terminate human history completely and irrevocably, a possibility never before conceivable by, much less in the power of, humankind.[71]

69. Ceadel, *Pacifism in Britain*, pp. 313–15.
70. Text in Robert J.C. Buton, *Japan's Decision to Surrender* (Stanford, CA: Stanford University Press, 1954), pp. 1–3.
71. Garrison, *The Darkness of God*, p. 92.

Hitherto, human beings had been able to inflict unspeakable misery upon each other, but they had not come near the possibility of destroying life on earth. The moral dilemma this created was expressed vividly by one British general in a lecture the 1950s:

> The choice of death or dishonour is one which has always faced the professional fighting man . . . He chooses death for himself so that his country may survive, or on a grander scale so that the principles for which he is fighting may survive. Now we are facing a somewhat different situation, when the reply is not to be given by individuals but by countries as a whole. Is it right for the government of a country to choose complete destruction of the population rather than some other alternative, however unpleasant that . . . may be? Should we in any circumstances be morally right to choose not only the termination of our own existence as a nation, but also the existence of future generations of our own countrymen and even of the whole civilised world? To take an example from history, it might well have been that the inhabitants of the Roman Empire, threatened with inevitable conquest by the barbarian hordes, might have considered that the total destruction of humanity would be preferable than [*sic*] the immediate prospects that faced them. How wrong they would have been. The human race can in time recover from almost anything, but it cannot recover from universal death.[72]

This was the new problem that was raised by nuclear weapons and their growing potential for 'overkill': the USA and the USSR were estimated to be able to destroy each other several times over, and the radiation this would unleash, along with the debris it would blow into the atmosphere in the theatres of war alone was early on recognised by physicists to be uncontainable and likely to affect entire continents or even the world as a whole. The fear that mankind would handle irresponsibly its newly acquired ability to exterminate itself became a new, and determining theme in all anti-nuclear and much anti-war literature, whether religiously influenced or not. For both Catholics and non-Catholics, St Augustine's argument of proportionality loomed large: what cause could justify nuclear annihilation? Nuclear war could only be justified if it was assumed that it would in some way remain limited, if, as Soviet strategists argued until the late 1980s, at least the civilisation one was defending could survive, carried on by a substantial number of human beings. In East and West, the greater part of the nuclear strategy debate hinged on the question of how a nuclear war could

72. Lt. Gen. Sir John Cowley, quoted in P.M.S. Blackett, *Studies in War, Nuclear and Conventional* (Edinburgh: Oliver & Boyd, 1962), p. 96.

be prevented, deterred, limited, or won in a meaningful way, without escalation to an all-out level of war. Essentially, nuclear critics doubted that this was possible, while supporters of a nuclear deterrence posture believed that the other side feared escalation as much as oneself and would never let events progress that far. Neither party to the debate in the remotest way wished for such a war.

Hiroshima and Nagasaki were not immediately seen as cataclysmic events, and quotations such as those at the beginning of this chapter are usually found only from the end of the 1950s. While some people involved in the early development of nuclear weapons or planning for their use theorised about these problems early on, awareness of these issues took some time to percolate down to the general public, and anti-nuclear movements took time to spring up in the West. It seemed that the significance of August 1945 had to sink in first, that people were too preoccupied at first with their own survival and their return to normal lives, and that understanding of the implication of nuclear weapons only spread when further countries became nuclear powers. By 1949 the USSR had conducted its first atomic test, by 1953 it had thermonuclear weapons, and in 1957 it beat the USA to the development of intercontinental missiles, challenging the credibility of an American nuclear guarantee in defence of Western Europe's independence. Britain's first atomic test in 1952 and her first thermonuclear test in 1957 could not totally offset her feeling of vulnerability, and the USA was suitably impressed by the Soviet Union's lead in missile technology.

A crucial reason for the development of the peace movement may therefore be found elsewhere than in concern for others. In the words of Herbert Feis:

> The source of restraint lies in fear of consequences; fear of the fact that the enemy will use the same terrible weapon. This was, for example, why neither side used poison gas in the [Second World] war. When humane feeling is allied to such fear, it may command respect . . .

He noted also, significantly, that such a restraint on the use of nuclear weapons had of course been absent in the Second World War (which also goes some way to explain the lack of greater hesitations about using nuclear weapons against Japan).[73] This raises the larger question as to whether human beings in general are

73. Herbert Feis, *The Atomic Bomb and the End of World War II* (Princeton, N.J.: Princeton UP, 1966), p. 192.

likely to feel deeply concerned about suffering they are not immediately confronted with, and which is unlikely to affect them themselves. There is not the space here to pursue this question further,
but the fear of nuclear strikes against the West seems to have made
the crucial difference in some countries between general unease
about nuclear weapons and outright opposition to them. What needs
to be stressed, however, is that from the time when Westerners
began to understand the implications of the existence of nuclear
weapons aimed at them, the great majority became pacificists,
favouring the avoidance of all war if their freedom from Communist domination could be guaranteed otherwise. Deterrence won
very widespread support whereas on the eve of previous wars, particularly the First World War, many in the West had seen war as a
price worth paying to further political aims. The dividing line distinguishing opinion on how the East–West conflict of the Cold War
should be conducted henceforth ran between pacifists and pacificists,
but there was never any sizeable group that advocated deliberate
war against the USSR (or Communist China, for that matter).

In short, the sensitivity of those inclined towards pacificism was
greatly enhanced by their awareness of their own vulnerability, and
this took some years to dawn upon the mass of the populations in
the West. Significantly, peace movements were strongly encouraged
by the USSR – particularly whenever it was lagging behind the West
in the development of nuclear technology – and flourished in Communist circles several years before they gained much support elsewhere in the West.

Peace movements directed by the USSR since 1945: from political tool to political self-destruction

Unlike the demise of the First and Second (Socialist) Internation-
als, the dissolution of the Komintern in May 1943 was not sympto-
matic of the breakdown of an international Communist movement.
Indeed, much of the credibility which Stalin had lost in 1936 in
Spain and in 1939 with the Molotov–Ribbentrop pact was retrieved
by Stalin himself as Generalissimo of the Soviet peoples' long and
lonely campaign of resistance against the *Wehrmacht* in 1941–44.
But the other crucial contribution to restoring the honour of
Communism was made by the Communist or Communist-organised

resistance fighters throughout German- and Italian-occupied territory. Meanwhile important segments of the Right in all occupied countries discredited themselves by collaborating with the German occupation forces.

The *Résistance* was termed anti-Fascist, opposing not only German and Italian occupiers but also 'Quislings' (after the name of a Norwegian politician who accepted collaboration with Hitler) wherever they were. It was pacificist, but certainly not pacifist, and in what was legitimately interpreted by Communists worldwide as a war of self-defence against German National Socialist and Italian Fascist aggression, the rejection of *all* forms of war clearly had no place.

When the war-time alliance disintegrated in 1946/7, a successor to the Komintern was called into being, the Communist Information Bureau (known as 'Kominform'), once again very much under the control of Moscow. In the tradition of the Komintern, it depicted its *raison d'être* as a self-defence against expansionist policies of the West. Its tenor was thus not pacifist, but then initially the conflict with the West was not military, even though military terminology was used abundantly. From early 1948 at the latest, however, Stalin pursued a dual approach: while the USA and Britain had reduced their armed forces radically, Stalin began to build up those of his own country and the other countries he controlled, soon breaching the limits imposed on Bulgaria, Rumania and Hungary by the post-World War II peace treaties. He pushed Soviet scientists to pursue their nuclear programme vigorously while initially campaigning for nuclear disarmament (by the USA), so that the USSR conducted its first nuclear test in August 1949. Almost at once, however, the USSR organised the Stockholm peace conference which issued a peace appeal (1950) to denounce the growing threat of a military clash between the two blocs that were forming in Europe. The danger was depicted as emanating entirely from the West (which had signed the North Atlantic Treaty in April 1949), and the USSR henceforth held the copyright for the brand-name 'Peace Movement'.

The Soviet-led Peace Movement and Soviet propaganda were not directed primarily at nuclear weapons, as the USSR was about to procure them, but against 'imperialist warmongering' in general (or, in the early 1980s, against very specific weapons systems, NATO's *Cruise* and *Pershing II* missiles as symptoms of NATO's bellicose intentions, while passing over in silence similar systems already deployed within the Warsaw Pact). Thus while depicting the Socialist/

Communist world as exclusively reactive and defensive, and NATO (resp. France, Britain and the USA in Asia, the Middle East, Africa and Latin America) as threatening and expansionist, the USSR never opted for pacifism in Martin Ceadel's definition. The option of a just war was not forsworn. The Warsaw Treaty Organisation (WTO), founded in 1955, was not a departure in this sense, nor is it fair to depict, as Soviet and East European historians did during the Cold War, Soviet defensiveness as coming so much later than the North Atlantic Treaty. The WTO merely replaced the bilateral military links that had existed between the Soviet Union and its satellites since the late 1940s and earlier.

Soviet and Kominform support for the peace movements was designed to influence public opinion in the West. From the Eastern Bloc, only the most trusted Communist Party members were sent to attend international rallies. Any such international work was closely controlled by the Soviet Committee for the Defence of Peace, an organ under the control of the Communist Party of the Soviet Union. Indeed, the very concept of 'pacifism' was defined in several versions of the *Great Soviet Encyclopaedia* as a 'bourgeois' phenomenon, while 'Marxist-Leninists distinguish between just and unjust wars, supporting the former and fighting against the latter with determination.' This did not rule out Marxist-Leninists co-operation with pacifists to agitate against unjust or nuclear wars. But pacifism was explicitly rejected as an untenable conviction for any Marxist-Leninist.[74] As the chief of the Soviet armed forces, Marshal Ogarkov, proclaimed in January 1982, it was necessary for the Soviet youth 'always to be ready to defend the motherland, and to prevent the appearance of feelings of complacency, tranquillity and pacifism, as these are dangerous phenomena which could have heavy consequences'.[75]

It was this contradiction that – after working reasonably well for three decades – ultimately contributed to the crumbling of the Soviet system as it was strained to breaking point by the Second Cold War (1979–84). Soviet leaders (and particularly the marshals controlling the Red Army and the Warsaw Treaty Organisation) ranted about the danger of a NATO surprise attack with the Euromissiles deployed from late 1983. At the same time they saw to it that all those within the Eastern Bloc who pointed to the Soviet Union's growing arsenal of nuclear weapons and called for multilateral disarmament were imprisoned.[76] Among these were Nobel

---

74. Michel Tatu, 'L'URSS', in Lellouche (ed.), *Pacifisme et dissuasion*, pp. 309–26.
75. Quoted *ibid.*, p. 320.   76. *Ibid.*, pp. 309–26.

prize-winning physicist Andreij Sakharov and a less famous Soviet citizen, Sergeij Batovrin, who tried to set up a confidence-building initiative in the USSR, and the poet, playwright, philosopher (and later President) Waclaw Havel in Czechoslovakia. Increasingly, this became known to and caused unease among Western peace campaigners (who in the 1980s were often closely connected with human rights groups), until the dual standards applied by the Soviet leadership became understood more widely. Where in earlier Cold War decades, the political dissidents and refugees from Soviet Bloc countries had been studiously ignored by the Left in the West, people like the strongly Socialist political singer Wolf Biermann, who was deported from East Germany because of his subversive but highly popular songs, now became heroes of the Western Left. Henceforth, many religious anti-nuclear groups consciously decided to keep agitators with obvious (Soviet) Communist connections at arm's length.[77]

But Soviet credibility once again seemed saved when the vigorous reformer Mikhail Gorbachëv came to power. In calling for reforms and in alienating the equally reactionary régimes in power in most of the other Communist-ruled countries, Gorbachëv brought many disarmers and anti-nuclear movements in East and West onto his side. Crucially, Gorbachëv himself was wary of nuclear weapons. While the war hysteria among Soviet (and American) leaders and the war scare that affected most of Europe at the beginning of the 1980s had done much to heighten the fear of nuclear war by miscalculation, a single event seems to have tipped the balance in the minds of Gorbachëv and his supporters. On 26 April 1986, the nuclear power station near Chernobyl in Ukraine developed a serious malfunction, and the irradiated material that escaped from the reactor in a huge plume affected not only Ukraine but also its neighbouring states and large swaths of Europe up to Scandinavia and Scotland. Chernobyl brought home to Ukrainians and Russians (and indeed to most other Europeans) the potential effects of even a small tactical nuclear weapon's explosion on their soil, even if it were far from their own cities. Six years later Ukrainian officials claimed that 6,000–8,000 people had been killed by the effects of the accident.[78]

---

77. Pierre Hassner, 'Pacifisme et terreur', in Lellouche (ed.), *Pacifisme et dissuasion*, p. 173.
78. 'Kiev says Chernobyl killed 6,000 to 8,000', *International Herald Tribune* (23 April 1992).

This gave a new impetus to anti-nuclear campaigners. But this time, even critics of nuclear weapons within the USSR were supported from on high: Gorbachëv himself steered East–West relations towards nuclear arms reductions, indeed, he proclaimed total nuclear disarmament as his ultimate goal and was willing even to pay the price of a substantial conventional arms reduction to bring this about.

To conclude, Soviet Communist leaders did not create anti-nuclear or pacifist views in the West in the Cold War. The potential for pacifism or at least for pacificism had long been there, particularly among Protestants and sectarians. At best Soviet-led institutions such as the Kominform added some modest amount of financing and co-ordination to movements which would in all probability have been just as strong and committed without any such support.[79] There was a convergence of interest which led to a certain amount of co-operation, but as we have seen, the roots of anti-nuclear and pacifist movements in the West go back much further than the Russian Revolution.

What can be said, however, is that a belated realisation of how dangerous nuclear weapons were contributed crucially to a change in Soviet military strategy in the late 1980s, and to undermining the entire edifice of Soviet political doctrine on war and peace. By calling into question Lenin's assertion that technological change could not invalidate the Clausewitzian dictum that war was a continuation of politics, and that Socialism had to survive any future war, Soviet strategists put the axe to the roots of the entire tree of Marxist-Leninist teaching. Gorbachëv finally decided to abandon cardinal aspects of this teaching rather than risk nuclear war, and in seeking to avoid war, he finally had to let go peacefully, first of the Soviet empire, and then of Communist rule.

Anti-nuclear movements in Protestant cultures

To emphasise the religious roots of pacifism and anti-nuclear movements in the nuclear era is not to imply that all members of such movements were practising Christians. Many pacifists, pacificists and anti-nuclear demonstrators were not themselves religiously active; many did not even believe in God. But disproportionately often, they did come from active Protestant, Quaker, Methodist,

79. Michael Ploetz, 'Troy besieged: East German perspectives on the Second Cold War', M.S. Ph.D. London, 1997.

Mennonite, or indeed Catholic backgrounds. Indeed, for some, the anti-nuclear 'cause often became a substitute for religion, commanding the same loyalties, exhibiting the same fundamentalism, and arousing the same resentments', as a hagiographer of the British peace movement observed.[80] For many people of Protestant background, who had shaken off the narrow sectarianism of their own families and had come to see religion as a superstition, the anti-nuclear cause seems to have become a substitute for the self-discipline and commitment which religion had inspired in their forefathers, values which they inherited even if they rejected the application to which their parents and grandparents had put them. A puritan family tradition might thus half-consciously be upheld. Indeed, the British anti-nuclear movement has been described as 'a form of witness against the values of the wider society'.[81] This élitist quest for better moral standards for oneself brings to mind some of the factors which led Christian sects through the ages to reject killing.

Among the Christian confessions, various forms of Protestantism were particularly prominent in pacifist and anti-nuclear movements, and with the exception of the USA, countries with predominantly Protestant cultures tended to produce larger and more active movements: this was true for the Netherlands, the FRG, the Scandinavian countries, Britain (and, as an anomaly, the Catholic Flemish part of Belgium). To give just one example, during the Euromissile Crisis, in October 1981, 350,000–400,000 people assembled in Amsterdam to protest against the deployment in Europe of the Euromissiles. In London the anti-nuclear rally of 24 October of the same year is said to have had 150,000 participants, in Bonn 200,000–300,000, in Brussels 100,000–200,000, in Rome 100,000–150,000, while Paris only mustered 50,000.[82]

BRITAIN

Britain, where many of these pacifist sects had enjoyed particularly widespread support in the nineteenth century, was probably the birthplace in the West of movements promoting the abolition of

---

80. Driver, *The Disarmers*, p. vii.
81. Frank Parkin, *Middle Class Radicalism: The Social Bases of the British Campaign for Nuclear Disarmament* (Manchester: Manchester University Press, 1968), p. 39.
82. Helsinki mustered 150,000. Source: Wilfried von Bredow, 'Die Friedens-bewegungen in Frankreich und der Bundesrepublik Deutschland', *Beiträge zur Konfliktforschung* Vol. 12, No. 3 (Autumn 1982), p. 55. For the lower figure for Rome, see Sergio Rossi and Virgilio Ilari, 'Pacifisme à l'Italienne', in Lellouche (ed.), *Pacifisme et dissuasion*, p. 144; for the higher figure for Amsterdam and for Brussels, see Alfred van Staden, 'Pays-Bas et Belgique: la tentation neutraliste', *ibid.*, p. 93.

nuclear weapons. Concern about them, although late in manifest-
ing itself, became focused by the accidental suffering caused to the
Japanese fishermen on the ill-named vessel *Lucky Dragon* in 1954
when the United States conducted thermonuclear tests in the Pacific.
Intellectual opposition grew into a strong populist movement in
the second half of the 1950s, encouraged by the British government's espousal in 1957 of massive retaliation as a national strategy
(thus strongly emphasising nuclear weapons), and by the British–
American agreement to station *Thor* missiles on British soil, which
resulted in public awareness that these missiles might be targets for
Soviet pre-emptive strikes.[83] Opposition against the missile deployment, outside the Labour Party, was organised into various committees, of which the most prominent was to become the Campaign for
Nuclear Disarmament (CND). This was founded in the winter of
1957/58 after an initiative by the Left-wing *New Statesman*'s editor
Kingsley Martin, the philosopher Bertrand Russell (both of whom
had been active in peace campaigns before the Second World War)
and J. Allen Skinner, who had been jailed for his anti-war campaigning in 1916–17.[84] Other founding members included the writer
J.B. Priestley, the physicist Professor P.M.S. Blackett, and the ar-
chaeologist and writer Jacquetta Hawkes.[85] Many trade unions came
out in support of the Campaign, hence the link with the unilateral-
ist anti-nuclear sentiments of the radical Left of the Labour Party.[86]

The most distinctive form of protest organised by CND was its
annual 'Easter marches' to or from the British nuclear research
centre at Aldermaston, which served as the model for similar
marches in Germany and elsewhere in Western Europe (here again,
we find the anti-nuclear demonstration copying Christian patterns!).
The membership of the Campaign grew rapidly between 1958 and
1961, but ran out of steam when *détente* set in 1964.[87] CND gained
popularity again from 1979, when Labour was ousted from office,
the USSR invaded Afghanistan, and the Euromissile crisis dawned.

83. See the press reactions in 1958, e.g. ''Anti-missile storm' gathers over minister', *Daily Telegraph* (25 Feb. 1958), 'Unilateral decision to disarm', *The Times* (7 Mar.
1958), and the Defence Debate in the House of Commons, H. of C. Deb. Vol. 583,
26 Feb., col. 382ff.

84. Driver, *The Disarmers*, p. 14.

85. Richard Taylor, *Against the Bomb: The British Peace Movement, 1958–1965* (Oxford: Clarendon Press, 1988), pp. 5–71.

86. For the links between CND and the Labour Party, see Taylor, *Against the Bomb*,
pp. 275–314; see also Andrew J. Pierre, *Nuclear Politics: The British Experience with
an Independent Strategic Force, 1939–1970* (London: Oxford University Press, 1972),
pp. 201ff.

87. Taylor, *Against the Bomb*, pp. 72–112.

After it had been nearly dormant for almost two decades, its membership rose again steeply, from 3,500 members in 1980 to 50,000 in 1983.[88] The CND-sympathising Left-wing of the Labour Party came to dominate that party's attitude towards nuclear weapons (favouring nuclear disarmament) until the end of the Cold War.

As in the 1950s, CND drew great support from the Protestant churches in Britain, but also from sections of the Catholic Church which gained strength in the early 1980s. A Catholic priest, Mgr Bruce Kent, became Chairman of CND in the early 1980s. But CND was not the only anti-nuclear movement. Two prominent supporters of peace initiatives of the 1920s and 1930s, Lord Noel-Baker (Philip Noel-Baker) and Lord Brockway (Fenner Brockway) launched the World Disarmament Campaign in 1980. A prominent social historian, Professor E.P. Thompson, founded the campaign for European Nuclear Disarmament (END).[89] In defiance of the policies of the British Conservative government, and despite its tradition as the church of the Establishment, the Church of England Synod criticised government policy on nuclear weapons and nuclear strategy. Less surprisingly, the British Council of Churches (where the traditional pacifist tendencies of the 'dissenter' churches were represented) joined in with this criticism.[90]

CND's second peak of activity around 1981–83, reflected a polarisation of British society into supporters and opponents of government policy. Notwithstanding press reports of links between certain trade union leaders whose unions supported the anti-nuclear campaign and Soviet funding, CND was at best marginally influenced by Communist groupings and external machinations. Sentiments found within it, just as its members, were solidly rooted in old British traditions of dissent and popular opposition against governments that were perceived as misguided.

88. For the reasons for its resurgence, see Philip Sabin, *The Third World War Scare in Britain* (London: Macmillan, 1986), pp. 40–49; Hans-Jürgen Rautenberg, 'Friedensbewegungen und Nukleardebatte in westeuropäischen Nato-Staaten', *Beiträge zur Konfliktforschung* Vol. 13, No. 3 (Autumn 1983), p. 139.

89. See e.g. E.P. Thompson, *Protest and Survive* (London: Campaign for Nuclear Disarmament, 1980).

90. British Council of Churches, *Christians and Atomic War: a Discussion of the Moral Aspects of Defence and Disarmament in the Nuclear Age* (London: British Council of Churches, 1959); *idem, The Pattern of Disarmament* (London: British Council of Churches, 1962); *idem, The British Nuclear Deterrent* (London: British Council of Churches, 1963); anti-LRTNF deployment vote by the British Council of Churches, reported in 'Modernization of Nato's long range theatre nuclear weapons', *The Times* (28 Nov. 1979); Bishop of Salisbury (Chairman), *The Church and the Bomb: Nuclear Weapons and Christian Conscience* (London: Hodder & Stoughton, 1982).

It is clear that the issue on which CND focused was that of nuclear war, not just any form of war. No quantitatively comparable opposition to British military intervention with conventional forces in the Falklands War of 1982 could be registered, even though a minority of intellectuals argued that the issue of the 'Malvinas/ Falklands' was not worth the lives of British soldiers. Nor was there much opposition to British involvement in the Gulf War of 1991. The link between the strength of the anti-nuclear movement and perceptions of Britain's own vulnerability are confirmed by the comparative lack of interest shown by Britons in nuclear weapons after the mid-1980s, when the Cold War drew to its close. Once the Soviet threat was removed, the case for nuclear abolition should have grown, had the argument for the retention of nuclear weapons been based on the need to deter the USSR. Instead, no longer fearful of nuclear *retaliation* against Britain in response to British nuclear use, or of a nuclear pre-emptive attack on British nuclear weapons, the disarmers in Britain displayed less interest in the morality of British retention of such weapons. This seems to indicate that a large proportion of Britain's anti-nuclear movement, although inspired by pacifist and religious traditions, was primarily motivated less by a yearning for personal righteousness than by fear of the nuclear devastation of their own country. In Britain it was clearly nuclear weapons which turned a peace movement into a mass movement.

GERMANY

The mix of motivations was different in the Federal Republic of Germany (FRG). Here anti-nuclear protests followed on directly from a very powerful campaign against German (conventional) rearmament, which focused on the Bonn government's acceptance in 1952 of the invitation of the Western powers to reconstitute German armed forces that had not existed in West Germany since 1945.[91] West German opposition to nuclear weapons in 1957/58 was in so many respects a rerun of the earlier anti-rearmament campaign that had been fought under the motto 'Without me' that it was referred to as 'Without me – 2nd edition'.[92]

Opposition towards a national German nuclear programme, still an option at the time, albeit in the framework of European

---

91. Klaus von Schubert, *Wiederbewaffnung und Westintegration* (Stuttgart: DVA, 1970); for the continuity between the anti-rearmament and the anti-nuclear movements, see Wilfried von Bredow, 'The Peace Movement in the Federal Republic of Germany', *Armed Forces and Society* Vol. 9, No. 1 (Autumn 1982), pp. 35–7.
92. 'Ohne mich – in 2. Auflage', *Die Weltwoche* (14 Mar. 1958).

integration,[93] started with German nuclear scientists. Like P.M.S. Blackett in Britain and Andreij Sakharov in the USSR, German nuclear scientists were strongly opposed to the military use of nuclear energy, but there was a particular poignancy in their attitude: most of them had been directly involved in the nuclear programme of the Third Reich, and there is still some debate as to how far their lack of success was deliberate or accidental. Inspired by the international opposition to nuclear weapons forming among nuclear scientists, many prominent West German physicists pledged early on never to contribute to the development of nuclear weapons.[94]

Shortly after the founding of CND in Britain, the FRG saw the foundation of the Campaign *Kampf dem Atomtod* (Battle against Atomic Death). Its members tended to be Left-wingers, and/or Protestants. As in Britain, this campaign lost momentum during the period of détente. Again as in Britain, it revived in the context of the Euromissile crisis in October 1980. The Krefeld appeal was launched to refuse the stationing of further nuclear weapons in Germany.[95] It was led by a 'German Peace Union', the recently formed Green Party and the German Communist Party (DKP),[96] and had soon collected hundreds of thousands of signatures.[97] The Green Party appeared in West German politics at the very end of the 1970s and fully established itself on the political scene from 1980.[98] The movement had the support of up to half the West German population (see Table 4.1 on page 171),[99] and the Greens

93. Cf. Beatrice Heuser, *Nuclear Strategies and Forces in Europe, 1949–2000* (London: Macmillan, 1997), ch. 5.

94. Mark Cioc, *PAX ATOMICA: the Nuclear Defense Debate in West Germany during the Adenauer Era* (New York: Columbia University Press, 1988), pp. 43ff.

95. 'Forum gegen NATO-Atomkriegsplanung in Krefeld, 'Nachrüstungs'-Beschluss muss endlich vom Tisch!', *Unsere Zeit* (17 Nov. 1980); 'Bundesrepublik muss der Vorreiter werden', *Die Neue* (18 Nov. 1980); 'Krefelder Forum: Um unserer Zukunft willen Raketen verhindern', *Unsere Zeit* (21 Nov. 1980); 'Widerstand gegen die Rüstungspolitik der NATO verstärkt sich weiter', *Die Wahrheit* (1 Apr. 1981); 'Aktuelle Kampflosung lautet: "Ächtet die Neutronenwaffe"', *Die Wahrheit* (4 Apr. 1981); see also Ulrich Probst, 'Gegenwärtige Strömungen in der Friedensbewegung', *Europäische Wehrkunde* Vol. 31, No. 2 (Feb. 1982), p. 72.

96. Kurt Fritsch, member of DKP Presidium, 'Gegen US-Atomraketen – im Geiste Lenins, Liebknechts und Luxemburgs für Frieden, gegen Militarismus und Krieg', *Unsere Zeit* (27 Jan. 1981); 'Keine NATO-Atomraketen – alles für den Frieden! Aufruf des 6. Parteitages der DKP in Hannover, Mai 1981', *Unsere Zeit* (2 June 1981).

97. '800,000 Stimmen gegen Nachrüstung', *Die Neue* (15 May 1981).

98. On their political programme, see John Vaughan, 'The Greens' vision of Germany', *Orbis* Vol. 32, No. 1 (Winter 1988), pp. 83–96.

99. According to opinion polls, see Bredow, 'Die Friedensbewegungen', p. 58. Obviously, much depended in each case on the wording of the questions, see Josef Joffe, 'Peace and populism: Why the European anti-nuclear movement failed', *International Security* Vol. 11, No. 4 (Spring 1987), pp. 6–8.

as its leaders proved extremely vocal and well organised, and mobilised the media very effectively.[100] The main demonstrations took place in Bonn in October 1981, in June 1982 in Berlin (during the visit of Ronald Reagan),[101] and again in the autumn of 1983, ebbing fast and suddenly after the actual deployment of the missiles had begun. As early as 1984, actions dwindled in size and number, even though no major developments had changed the international situation and the deployment went ahead steadily.[102] In 1984, the Greens under Joschka Fischer still launched an appeal to the Constitutional Court, to prove that the deployment was unconstitutional (as the FRG had no control over the weapons), but failed.[103] (When Joschka Fischer became Foreign Minister in the SPD–Green coalition government of 1998, one of his first public actions was to question NATO's nuclear 'first use' strategy.)

During this 'Second Cold War', it was not a one-issue movement that dominated the debate, but two political parties: the Greens and, crucially, the SPD. In Germany, as in Britain, it was mainly the Left that opposed nuclear weapons. Drawing on the pacifist traditions of German Social Democracy, the radical wing of the SPD had led the 'Without me' anti-rearmament campaign in the early 1950s, and when it failed to impose its veto in the FRG's parliament, it turned its attention to nuclear weapons.[104] Until the end of the twentieth century, the SPD retained a strongly anti-nuclear wing. During the Euromissile crisis, this included leading politicians such as Erich Ollenhauer, the architect of *Ostpolitik* Egon Bahr, Johannes Rau (a very committed Protestant and future President of the FRG), the later Federal Chancellor Gerhard Schröder, and (Huguenot descendant!) Oskar Lafontaine, who later became Chairman of the SPD and in 1998–99 was Finance Minister under Schröder. Whenever the SPD was in government, the wing of the SPD supporting nuclear weapons prevailed. This was true for the governments of Willy Brandt and Helmut Schmidt as much as for that of Gerhard

100. Bredow, 'Die Friedensbewegungen', p. 58.
101. Variously estimated as having been arranged by 170 to '930 Organisations and Initiatives' – '930 Organisationen und Initiativen rufen zum 10.6. auf', *Unsere Zeit* (11 May 1982); 'Raketenbeschluss der NATO verhindern!', *Die Wahrheit* (26 May 1982).
102. 'Kohl defends missiles as thousands protest', *International Herald Tribune* (22 Nov. 1983); Wilhelm Bifforg, 'Die Habichte sind im Nest', *Der Spiegel* (30 July 1984), pp. 48–55; 'SPD unterstützt Herbstaktionen der "Friedensbewegung"', *Frankfurter Allgemeine Zeitung* (11 Sept. 1984).
103. Anna Tomforde, 'Greens lose appeal on cruise', *Guardian* (19 Dec. 1984).
104. 'Drohungen und ihr Echo', *Aachener Nachrichten* (2 Apr. 1957); 'Streit über die Atomwaffen in Deutschland', *Frankfurter Allgemeine Zeitung* (3 Apr. 1957); 'Ungeschützt wie Hiroshima', *Freie Presse* (Bielefeld, SPD, 10 Apr. 1957).

Schröder, but does not mean that they did not face hard internal opposition. In 1982 an SPD-led government of Helmut Schmidt was brought down by the anti-nuclear wing of the same party, precisely over the issue of the deployment of the Euromissiles, and seventeen years later, Gerhard Schröder was under some pressure from within his own party where nuclear issues were concerned.

On the margins, there were always small Communist parties, which were periodically closed down after being declared unconstitutional by German courts. Here, the Soviet or East German connection was ever present: as the historian Michael Ploetz has shown, there is solid evidence for contacts, payments and other leverage applied by East Germany being brought to bear upon the West German peace movement on many levels.[105] Nevertheless, the emotional involvement of many citizens of the Federal Republic with the fate of those in East Germany was at all times a strong factor in the equation, and many a staunch Christian Democrat NATO-supporter was profoundly troubled by the thought that nuclear weapons stationed in the FRG were aimed at targets in the German Democratic Republic (GDR).

Like every European nuclear debate, the German debate had its philosopher, Karl Jaspers. His writing, groping towards an understanding of the connections between mass-mobilised societies (whether they be totalitarian or not) and weapons of mass destruction, identified a dreadful Hegelian antithesis of the dangers of totalitarianism on the one hand and the dangers of nuclear war on the other, with the only consolation to be found in the hope that the Russian sense of self-preservation might prevail over Soviet ideology.[106] Indeed, the opposition against nuclear weapons had the edge on the *Realpoliticians* culturally. German quality literature of the 1920s and 1930s – as in much as of the post-Second World War period – tended to be anti-militaristic and anti-totalitarian (such as the writings of Erich Maria Remarque: *All Quiet on the Western Front*, already mentioned above). In addition the literature dating from after the Second World War drew attention to the vain sacrifices in support of a diabolical cause which that latter war had demanded, for example in the writing of Heinrich Böll ('Wanderer, kommst du nach Spa . . .'),[107] and Siegfried Lenz: (*Deutschstunde*),[108] or else was Marxist or at least Left-wing Social Democratic (like the writings

105. Michael Ploetz, 'Troy besieged'.
106. Karl Jaspers, *Die Atombombe und die Zukunft der Menschen* (Munich: Piper, 1958, reprint of 1983).
107. 'Thou who passest by, go, tell the Spa . . .'   108. *German Lesson.*

of Bertolt Brecht, Erich Kästner, Günther Grass, Kurt Tucholsky).[109]
The anti-nuclear movement was strongly inspired by writers such as
these. Those of them who were still alive featured regularly at big
rallies, and vocally joined the protesters. There was thus not only
the anti-nuclear element in their campaign, but a more general
anti-militarism, and anti-totalitarianism concerned perhaps as much
with expiating the German crimes of the past as with fending off a
clear and present nuclear danger.

While only a small percentage participated actively in the anti-
nuclear movement, its sentiments were shared very widely (see Table
4.1). An opinion poll conducted by the French Left-wing magazine
Nouvel Observateur on 13 November 1981 found that 58 per cent of
the West Germans asked felt threatened by Soviet missiles, but 33 per
cent felt threatened by the planned deployment of the American
Cruise and *Pershing II* missiles (2 per cent said they felt threatened
by both).[110] The peace movement itself was composed of honest
housewives, bearded pastors and vegetarian ecologists as much as
of knitting feminists (which in Germany is not a contradiction in
terms) and 'Machiavellian realpoliticians'.[111] Although mainly Left-
wing, it was thus a heterogeneous movement if ever there was one.[112]
According to one comparative study of the protest movements, those
in West Germany and the Netherlands had the greatest degree of
'emotionalization' of the issue of nuclear weapons: in the words
of one observer, 'No-where in Western Europe has so much hatred
been accumulated, do the arguments turn so much around friend
and foe thinking as in the German peace movement.'[113]

Much more than in France, and more so even than in Britain,
the two main Christian churches in the FRG took an important
part in public life.[114] Christians in Germany drew their inspiration

---

109. For allusions to their writings, and evidence of their own involvement, in so
far as they were still alive, see 'Pazifismus '81: "Selig sind die Friedfertigen"', *Der
Spiegel* (15 June 1981), pp. 24, 26f., 32; 'Nachrüstung: ohne historische Parallele',
Der Spiegel (14 June 1983), p. 30; 'Die SPD ist nicht die dritte Weltmacht', *Der Spiegel*
(4 July 1983), p. 45; 'Diesmal wollen wir nicht schweigen', *Der Spiegel* (29 Aug. 1983),
p. 24; 'Da ist ein Nerv getroffen worden', *Der Spiegel* (19 Sept. 1983), p. 45.
110. Bredow, 'Die Friedensbewegungen', p. 64.
111. Wilfried von Bredow, 'Sozialer Protest und Friedensbewegung in Westeuropa',
Beiträge zur Konfliktforschung Vol. 15, No. 4 (1985), p. 49.
112. On the very varied ideological background and history of the Green movement, see Anna Bramwell, *Ecology in the Twentieth Century* (New Haven, Ct.: Yale
University Press, 1989); and on their late rise and fall see Anna Bramwell, *The Fading
of the Greens: the Decline in Environmental Politics in the West* (New Haven, Ct.: Yale
University Press, 1994).
113. Rautenberg, 'Friedensbewegungen und Nukleardebatte', p. 155.
114. 'Atomwaffen – was sagt die Kirche?', *Die Welt* (30 Nov. 1957).

TABLE 4.1   *Attitude towards the peace-movement (Emnid-poll of 1981)*

'I oppose it on principle' – 10 %
'I have reservations about it' – 19 %
'I don't have any feelings about it' – 22 %
'I think it's good in principle but I will not take part' – 39 %
'I might participate actively' – 7 %
'I will definitely participate actively' – 1 %
'I am already participating' – 1 %

Source: Der Spiegel (23 Nov. 1981), p. 61

from the (deplorably feeble) Christian resistance to the Third Reich by the committed *Bekennende Christen* (Confessing Christians, with martyrs like the Pastor Dietrich Bonhoeffer and rare survivors like Pastor Martin Niemöller – later a leader of the 'Battle against Nuclear Death' movement – and the Catholic Cardinal Graf Galen). From the early 1950s, opposition to war, German rearmament and nuclear weapons drew heavily on Christian links. Throughout the Cold War, Protestant groups were more prominent than organised Catholic opposition,[115] which initially lacked unanimity,[116] but developed a more pronounced stand against any use of force than Catholic groups in other countries, as we shall see. In 1955 a series of meetings took place, the '*Paulskirche* movement', in the Frankfurt church of St Paul, once the meeting place of the first pan-German parliament, to oppose NATO's nuclear strategies which had become known in the context of the *Carte Blanche* military exercise in 1955.[117]

When the German peace campaign revived around 1980, both Protestants and Catholics organised peace protests.[118] But there was more sympathy for extreme Left anti-nuclear movements among Protestants in Germany, a tendency that became very pronounced

115. See for example Christian Walter (ed.), *Atomwaffen und Ethik: der deutsche Protestantismus und die atomare Aufrüstung, 1954–1961. Dokumente und Kommentare* (Munich: Kaiser, 1981).
116. Anselm Doering-Manteuffel, *Katholizismus und Wiederbewaffnung – die Haltung der deutschen Katholiken gegenüber der Wehrfrage, 1948–1955* (Mainz: Matthias Grünewald Verlag, 1981); Rudolf Fleischmann et al., *Kann der atomare Verteidigungskrieg ein gerechter Krieg sein?* (Munich: Zink, 1960).
117. Cioc, *PAX ATOMICA*, p. 38.
118. 'Bonn soll nicht nachrüsten: Evangelische Akademiker fordern Rücknahme des Beschlusses', *Frankfurter Rundschau* (13 May 1981); 'Viele Sozialdemokraten gegen neue Atomraketen – Pax Christi: 1981 Abrüstungjahr', *Unsere Zeit* (20 Jan. 1981).

during the revival of the Cold War in the early 1980s.[119] The Protestant movement 'Living without arms' with a membership of 15,300 in 1981, proclaimed complete unilateral disarmament as its goal.[120] Again, during this second wave of public protest against nuclear weapons which rose in 1979 and barely subsided after 1983, the Protestant Church took so central a place in the debate that leading politicians had to face the theological challenge this posed.[121]

Protestant, fundamentalist interpretations of the New Testament played an important rôle in the West German peace movement's view of the world. They tended to internalise the danger of nuclear war, seeking within themselves the reasons for their predicament. The following passage, from a book written by the leading SPD politician Oskar Lafontaine, deserves to be quoted at length:

> The bomb unites friend and foe in death. It forces us to rethink, or else we will have no chance of survival. If we are [*sic*] the bomb, the question about our attitude to life arises. If we see in the bomb a material manifestation of our essence, then we have forgotten how to love life, even our own life. Without love, human existence is impossible . . .
>
> He who wants to follow the words of Christ in the Sermon on the Mount must be prepared for the loss of political freedom . . .
>
> Disarmament begins with every one of us. If we have forgotten to let the other be [as he is], with affection and consideration, this attitude can never arise between peoples and states. The eternal attempt to impose one's will upon the other, to use force, is transferred onto inter-state relations. Alliance agreements and arms control agreements cannot change this . . .
>
> We must be aware that we have to start with ourselves, if we want to change things. We will learn to live without violence – that means, to be non-violent.[122]

Crucial to West German attitudes towards war is that they internalised their guilt to such a degree that unlike the Japanese, they rarely if ever articulated any criticism of Allied bombing of Ger-

119. François-Georges Dreyfus, 'Pacifisme et neutralisme en Allemagne Fédérale aujourd'hui', *Revue Défense Nationale* Vol. 38, No. 1 (Jan. 1982), pp. 13–18; *pace* Josef Joffe, 'Peace and populism: Why the European anti-nuclear movement failed', pp. 19f.
120. 'Es gibt eine Explosion von Ängsten', *Der Spiegel* (13 Apr. 1981), p. 18; Patricia Clough, 'Big missile debate by German Protestants', *The Times* (18 June 1981).
121. See e.g. interviews with Dorothee Sölle and Trutz Rendtorff, 'Unsere Gefahr ist das Wischiwaschi', *Der Spiegel* (10 Oct. 1983).
122. Oskar Lafontaine, *Angst vor den Freunden* (Hamburg: Rowohlt. 1983, reprinted 1984), pp. 110–17.

man cities during the Second World War, and never saw it outside the context of their own (inherited) guilt over having started the war.[123]

This was different in the German Democratic Republic (GDR), however, where all responsibility for the war and for the Holocaust was externalised, by blaming it on 'the Fascists', 'the Hitlerites', and never accepting collective responsibilities. Thus in the GDR, there were strong and vocal complaints about the 'capitalist' policies of Britain in particular, which had conducted air raids aimed mainly to hurt, 'dishouse' and ultimately kill workers (thus becoming a textbook example of class warfare).[124] But in the GDR, too, Christian churches (here mainly the Lutherans) were the focus of the grass-roots anti-nuclear movement, which gathered strength during the Euromissile crisis. Moscow's hysteria during those years had the counter-productive effect not of preparing East Europeans for a possible war, but of engendering in many of them the desperate wish to escape this nemesis. And here, the Church became the organising structure. Church-led demonstrations took place in Halle in 1981 and in Dresden in February 1982; a prominent Lutheran pastor, Reiner Eppelmann, launched the 'Berlin appeal' for disarmament soon after, only to have severe difficulties with the GDR's security forces.[125] It was very much the same group, still with a heavy input from the churches, that at the end of the decade brought about the collapse of the GDR and helped cement the end of the Cold War.

OTHER COUNTRIES OF PROTESTANT CULTURE

The smaller Protestant countries of Western Europe each had their own particular mix of attitudes to war, peace and nuclear weapons. Sweden until the end of the century remained firmly committed to the armed neutrality which it espoused at the beginning of the nineteenth century to avoid becoming embroiled in the Napoleonic Wars, and nuclear weapons became as much of a taboo as war or alliances in general. This did not prevent Swedish governments from secretly co-operating quite intensively with the USA and NATO

---

123. Cf. Ian Buruma, *The Wages of Guilt: Memories of War in Germany and Japan* (New York: Meridian, 1994).

124. Olaf Groehler, *Geschichte des Luftkriegs 1910 bis 1980* (East Berlin: Militärverlag der Deutschen Demokratischen Republik, 1981), pp. 377ff.

125. Tatu, 'L'URSS', pp. 309–26.

in their contingency planning for the case of a Soviet attack.[126]
Denmark and Norway were cured of their love of non-alignment by
the German invasion in the Second World War, became founding
members of NATO, and reconciled their domestic pacifists by rejecting the stationing of any nuclear weapons on their territory.
This did not stop their governments from going against public
sentiments by being strong supporters of NATO in every other
respect. The Netherlands were more deeply split internally: its government accepted the stationing of NATO (i.e. US-controlled) nuclear
weapons on their territory, but found that its public in the context
of the Euromissile debate reacted more sharply still than the FRG
or Britain to the imminent deployment. The Netherlands drew on
a long history of reserve about any involvement in inter-state conflicts. In the formative seventeenth century, the Dutch built their
prosperity once they had gained independence from the Habsburgs,
and built it not on territorial acquisition but on trade in peacetime. Unlike Belgium, the Netherlands had managed to preserve
its neutrality in the First World War, and it was only the shock of
the experience of the Second (not unlike that in Norway and Denmark) which led the Dutch to abandon their neutralism. Dutch
anti-nuclear movements did seem to be primarily concerned with
nuclear weapons, while protests against involvement in more limited wars – such as the Gulf War or peacekeeping in Bosnia – was
muted.[127]

We thus find that peace movements, pacifism, and anti-nuclear
movements overlapped, but were not identical in all the Protestant
cultures. For the Germans in particular, after the Second World
War, opposition to nuclear weapons was inseparable from anxieties
about Germany's terrible guilt in the previous war and the decision
to turn away from all war in a quest for collective redemption.[128]
And indeed, these anxieties, unlike in Britain, survived the end of
the Cold War and thus of the first nuclear age. They found a new

126. Ann Sofie Dahl, 'The myth of Swedish neutrality', in Cyril Buffet and Beatrice
Heuser (eds), *Haunted by History: Myths in International Relations* (Oxford: Berghahn,
1998), pp. 28–40; see also Ingemar Dörfer, 'La Scandinavie ou la défense de la
virginité nucléaire', in Pierre Lellouche (ed.), *Pacifisme et dissuasion*, pp. 117–19.
    127. Alfred van Staden, 'Les Pays-Bas et la Belgique: la tentation neutraliste', in
Lellouche (ed.), *Pacifisme et dissuasion*, pp. 89–106; see also Jan Willem Honig, 'Myths
that keep small powers going: Internationalist idealism in the Netherlands', in Buffet and Heuser (eds.), *Haunted by History*, pp. 15–27.
    128. Beatrice Heuser, *Nuclear Mentalities?* (London: Macmillan, 1998), ch. 4.

expression in popular horror evoked by the idea of German participation in the liberation of Kuwait in the Gulf War of 1990/91,
and of reluctance to become involved in peacekeeping in Bosnia-
Hercegovina. The German anti-nuclear movement was a pacifist
movement in that its opposition to war extended to all war until
way into the 1990s. But only very few Germans also rejected the
Atlantic alliance, while the consensus in Sweden made both alliances and nuclear weapons taboo.[129] Norwegians have few difficulties with either alliances or involvement in military missions far from
home, but these should preferably be of a peacekeeping nature;
nuclear weapons are taboo. Britons have no qualms about any form
of involvement in war, other than nuclear war; on the whole, the
majority of the British Left strongly supports NATO, but is deeply
suspicious of any alliance that would not include the USA.[130] In
Protestant cultures, nuclear weapons were thus but one factor among
many in determining popular thinking about the morality of war
and associated issues, such as alliances, or peacekeeping, dissent,
criticism of the government, élitism, pacifism or the desire to atone
for unconnected sins of the past.

War, nuclear weapons and non-Protestant cultures

BUDDHISM, JUDAISM, ORTHODOX CHRISTIANITY, ISLAM

If the anti-nuclear movements were so closely connected with
Protestantism, what were the attitudes of other religions to nuclear
weapons? Buddhism, for example, particularly in its South and
South-East Asian forms, is more uncontroversially pacific than the
Christian Gospels. Yet no organised form of anti-war tradition or
anti-nuclear movement has emerged there: opposition movements
in individual countries such as Burma and China tend to focus on
domestic issues.

Japan is in a very special sense an exception to this rule, as it is
somewhat divorced from religion, and it is almost entirely due to
the experience of Hiroshima and Nagasaki, that the majority of the
Japanese have developed a strong rejection of nuclear war but also
of any involvement in warfare.[131] Article 9 of the (US-imposed)

---

129. Dörfer, 'La Scandinavie ou la défense de la virginité nucléaire', pp. 117–19.
130. *Ibid.*, ch. 2.   131. See also Chapter 1.

Japanese constitution prevented Japan from reconstituting independent armed forces, which were nevertheless then built up, under
close US surveillance. Called Japanese self-defence forces, they have
no mandate to operate in contingencies other than precisely that:
self-defence; concomitantly, the Japanese ministry of defence is called
the Japanese Self-Defence Agency. Like Germany, Japan hesitated
long over the deployment of its forces abroad for peacekeeping
missions. Nevertheless, the commitment to this self-denying ordin-
ance with regard to any future involvement in warfare except in
self-defence, waned somewhat by the end of the twentieth century.
Unlike Germany, Japan on the whole did not squarely assume the
heritage of its responsibility for the suffering it experienced in the
Second World War that it started in the Far East. What seems to
be deeply ingrained into Japanese culture, however, is the 'spirit of
Hiroshima', an unconditional pacifism, to which those supporting
it (particularly the Japanese Left), want to 'convert the world'.[132] It
is in this spirit that the memorial park and museum of Hiroshima
was created.

   Nevertheless, as Ian Buruma notes, there is a very patriotic, self-
righteous undercurrent in this peace movement emanating from
Hiroshima, which has overtones of anti-Americanism both on the
Right and on the Left. Indeed, a growing percentage of Japanese
polled criticised the USA for the bombing of Hiroshima and Nagasaki, rather than the Japanese leadership, who had initiated the
war. Towards the end of 1945, only 19 per cent of the surviving
residents of Hiroshima and Nagasaki (and 12 per cent of all the
Japanese questioned by a US survey) expressed resentment against
the Americans for having used the atomic bomb. 35 per cent thought
it was the fault of Japan, 29 per cent blamed it on war in general. In
1970, 38 per cent of Japanese asked blamed the USA, while only
19 per cent blamed the Japanese leadership. A survey in 1971 resulted in 31 per cent blaming the Americans, only 10 per cent
blamed the Japanese leadership. In 1985, 44 per cent of the Japanese polled said they 'hold it against the United States' that they
had dropped the bombs; in 1991, the figure had risen to 50 per
cent.[133] Meanwhile, there is nothing to suggest that Japan has lost
its aversion to nuclear weapons.

   132. Ian Buruma, *The Wages of Guilt: Memories of War in Germany and Japan* (New
York: Meridian, 1994), pp. 98f.
   133. Sadao Asada, 'The mushroom cloud and national psyches', in Laura Hein
and Mark Selden (eds.), *Living with the Bomb* (Armonk, NY: M.E. Sharpe, 1997),
pp. 174–9.

Moving on to Judaism, we can find here from the beginning both the command 'Thou shalt not kill', and the divine injunction to go to war, when the people of Israel are sent forth to (conquer) the Promised Land, and to fight against Philistines and other tribes in the region. Talmudic scholars have made much effort throughout history to reconcile this apparent paradox; the emerging picture is one of a just war tradition in which the command of God or His chosen representative, a prophet or king, is needed to decree that a war is to be fought. At the same time, it is accepted among Talmudic scholars that Jews must risk death rather than allow others to prevent them from living according to Divine Law. There is, of course, no central Jewish authority comparable to the papacy or the Catholic Church Councils which could determine official dogma in a binding way.[134]

Islam from the beginning held rules derived from Mohammed's pronouncements as recorded in the Koran and *Hadith*, which spelled out the criteria for just wars. Similarly to Judaism (and Augustinian interpretations of Catholicism, see above), the Koran defined war as just and a divine injunction (as the *jihad*) if it was waged defensively, to right injuries, against people trying to prevent Moslems from living according to the Koran. A just war must have these as sole purposes, and must not be fought to gain wealth, glory etc., in which case it would be a sinful war or *harb*. There are also passages in the Koran clearly excluding the harming of non-combatants – children, old people, women, peasants. Aggression is specifically dismissed by Mohammed as contrary to the wishes of God.[135] While deterrence, albeit not under this label, is a concept long familiar to Islam, the indiscriminate destruction of human life on a vast scale, according to Islamic scholars, is outside the remit of what Moslems are allowed to do, even in defence of God's laws in other respects. Only God has the moral right to annihilate a people, if it is clearly wicked.[136] This seems to be a position on which there is agreement among the diverse leaders of the different Islamic denominations, although here again, as in Judaism, there is no sole recognised authority which can fix doctrine for all followers.

134. Grand Rabbi René Gutman, 'Face à l'homicide. Réflexions sur la menace nucléaire à partir de l'expérience et de la tradition juives', in Pierre Viaud (ed.), *Les religions et la guerre* (Paris: Cerf, 1991), pp. 45–59.

135. Dr Wahba Moustapha Zehili, 'Dispositions internationales relatives à la guerre, justifiées au regard de l'islam, et leurs aspects humains caractéristiques', in Viaud (ed.), *Les religions et la guerre*, pp. 389–419.

136. Dr Mohamed Missaoui, 'La dissuasion, les armes nucléaires et les armes nouvelles: une approche islamique', in Viaud (ed.), *Les religions et la guerre*, pp. 423–33.

Orthodox Christianity, both in its Greek and Russian forms, has never accepted that any form of war could be without sin: much to the contrary, for the Eastern Churches, all war springs from man's original sin, and is part of this sin. As one Orthodox scholar has explained, the Orthodox Church 'tends to consider war less as a necessity than as an inevitable consequence of sin'. While priests and monks are excluded from warfare, 'no interdiction is issued against military service, which is an obligation of every citizen of a state, in normal obedience to his prince . . . who would not have any power if it were not given by God . . . Consequently, the Church imposes . . . penances on those who have taken arms, but it prays for them . . .'[137] The Orthodox Church condemns nuclear war as sin just as it condemns conventional war, recognising only a difference of scale.[138]

THE ROMAN CATHOLIC CHURCH

Roman Catholicism, the most centralised of the monotheistic religions and Christian confessions, offers what is perhaps the clearest doctrinal change in reaction to nuclear weapons. In keeping with the Augustinian emphasis on proportionality (war has to be proportionately less of an evil than the evil it is combating), the Catholic Church, despite its particular defensiveness vis-à-vis Communism, felt obliged to concede that all-out nuclear war could not possibly satisfy the Augustinian criterion and thus had to be condemned.

In 1953, Pope Pius XII had told a conference that, given the new forms war could take, self-defence might no longer be the just measure to resort to, as the consequences of war might henceforth exceed the evil of suffering injustice.[139] In 1963, Pope John XXIII in his encyclical *Pacem in Terris* wrote 'in the age which boasts of its atomic power, it no longer makes sense to maintain that war is a fit instrument with which to repair the violation of justice'.[140] This application of the idea of proportionality was taken up by the Second Vatican Council. Assembled in 1965 it agreed in its pastoral constitution *Gaudium et Spes* that the development of new destructive

137. Constantin Andronikof, 'Non la paix mais l'épée', in Viaud (ed.), *Les religions et la guerre*, p. 259.
138. François Thual and Boris Zinovieff, 'Se défendre contre le mal: L'orthodoxie face aux nouvelles formes de guerre', in Viaud (ed.), *Les religions et la guerre*, pp. 282f.
139. Jean-Yves Calvèz, SJ, 'L'Église catholique et la guerre depuis l'apparition des armes de destruction massive', in Viaud (ed.), *Les religions et la guerre*, pp. 127f.
140. Quoted in Donald L. Davidson, *Nuclear Weapons and the American Churches: Ethical Positions on Modern Warfare* (Boulder, Co.: Westview Press, 1983), p. 58.

capabilities had led to the possibility of barbarism worse than anything that had existed before. 'Certainly', it noted,

> war has not been rooted out of human affairs. As long as the danger of war remains and there is not competent and sufficiently powerful authority at the international level, governments cannot be denied the right to legitimate defence once every means of peaceful settlement has been exhausted.

However, the Council went on to interpret Pope Pius XII's words as a condemnation of Total War,[141] and adopted it as a basis for *Gaudium et Spes*. Lagging more than half a century behind the Hague Convention of 1907, the Council added: 'Any act of war aimed indiscriminately at the destruction of entire cities or of extensive areas along with their populations is a crime against God and man himself. It merits unequivocal and unhesitating condemnation.' It conceded that nuclear deterrence might for the time being keep war at bay, but could not be regarded as the path leading to peace in the long term, indeed, it might be 'an utterly treacherous trap for humanity'. Catholic Christians were called upon to work for an alternative which would make it possible that 'all war can be completely outlawed' (a major departure from Catholic Church thinking since Augustine!), by seeking the establishment of 'some universal public authority acknowledged as such by all, and endowed with effective power to safeguard, on behalf of all, security, regard for justice, and respect for rights'. *Gaudium et Spes* specifically noted, however, that in the absence of such a world authority, one could not expect the non-Communist countries to disarm unilaterally.[142]

To what extent were nuclear weapons the cause for this shift in the Roman Catholic Church's position? As one French Jesuit priest has argued, his Church was not merely forced to reconsider its position on war by Hiroshima and Nagasaki, 'but to say the truth about the destruction or quasi-destruction of large cities by bombardment which created hundreds of thousands of victims during the Second World War'.[143] Indeed, the terminology of *Gaudium et Spes* concerned above all air bombardment in general, and Total War, and was not limited to nuclear war. It is significant that the Roman Catholic Church lagged so far behind the thinking that secular governments had developed as long ago as the belligerent days of 1907, or 1923. Until the early 1960s, combat against Communism

---

141. In the way in which we have defined it in Chapter 3.
142. *Gaudium et Spes*, excerpts in Davidson, *Nuclear Weapons*, pp. 58f.
143. Calvèz, 'L'Église catholique et la guerre', p. 123.

was still clearly seen by the Vatican as proportionately the lesser evil and the greater necessity than the explicit condemnation of aerial bombardment of cities or nuclear war.

But in the 1980s, the public debate surrounding nuclear weapons called for still greater precision in the Vatican's teaching. In 1982, at the height of the Euromissile crisis, Pope John Paul II addressed a special United Nations General Assembly session on disarmament on the subject of nuclear war. Here he described as morally acceptable the concept of mutual deterrence on the basis of a balance of forces, not as an end within itself, but only as a step on the way to progressive disarmament. He made the interesting point, which was very much NATO doctrine at the time, that nuclear weapons could not be discussed in isolation, as there was 'a growing interdependence of [different] types of armaments'. He postulated that one therefore also had to look to reducing conventional forces, in view of the great destructive power of some of them.[144]

To sum up, as critics within its own ranks have commented, the Catholic Church thus espoused the paradox of accepting nuclear deterrence, but not accepting that this might hinge on the need for nuclear use, and certainly on credible preparations for nuclear use.[145]

AMERICA

Turning to the impact of Catholic teaching on peace campaigns, one might start with the USA, where Catholics form the largest Christian church. It is here that an active Catholic anti-nuclear movement developed, even though in proportion to the entire population, it remained small. American Catholic pacifism has its roots in the 1930s, when a group called Catholic Worker was founded which was both Catholic and co-operated closely with America's minute Communist movement, and opposed all following wars, from World War II to the Korean and Vietnam Wars, and from the 1950s onwards demonstrated against nuclear weapons. The American branch of the Catholic pacificist movement *Pax Christi*, internationally established in 1945, was founded in 1973. Its statement of purpose read as follows:

144. Quoted in *ibid.*, p. 133.
145. Sir Michael Quinlan, 'The ethics of nuclear deterrence', *Theological Studies* Vol. 48 (1987), pp. 3–25.

Pax Christi U.S.A. intends to contribute to the building of peace and justice by exploring and articulating the ideal of Christian nonviolence and by striving to apply it to personal life and to the structures of society.

The society further committed itself 'to foster both nuclear and general disarmament'.[146] As in other countries, prominent Catholic clergymen took very extreme positions. Archbishop Raymond Hunthausen of Seattle called it a sin merely to build nuclear weapons, and famously called 'Trident . . . the Auschwitz of Puget Sound'.[147] Less radical opponents of nuclear weapons among America's Catholic clergymen included Bishop Leroy Matthiesen of Amarillo, Texas, Archbishop John Quin of San Francisco, and Bishop Roger Mahony, of Stockton, California.

In 1983, feeling that the papal message to the UN of 1982 had not gone far enough, the Catholic bishops of the USA, France and West Germany issued their own pastoral letters on the subject, which tried to make sense of the paradox between the pope's acceptance of deterrence and the condemnation of Total War. The Catholic bishops of the United States postulated that, even though planning needed to underpin nuclear deterrence, it would be impermissible to plan for the use of weapons violating the principle of discrimination between the innocent (civilians) and the guilty (governments), and the Augustinian principle of proportionality. They repeated that deterrence itself was acceptable only as a temporary expedient, justified at best by the determination to move towards disarmament. In no case, the bishops affirmed, echoing *Gaudium et Spes*, was it justifiable to use nuclear weapons against population centres or with the aim of killing predominantly civilians. Retaliatory use of nuclear weapons which in this way would destroy innocent lives they regarded as unacceptable as well. Even planning for nuclear use should be subjected to this criterion:

> Even defensive response to unjust attack can cause destruction which violates the principle of proportionality, going far beyond the limits of legitimate defense. This judgement is particularly important when assessing planned use of nuclear weapons. Any defensive strategy, nuclear or conventional, which exceeds the limits of proportionality is not morally permissible.

Moreover they expressed their conviction that any initiation of nuclear use was unacceptable, and urged NATO to adopt a 'no first use' policy:

146. Quoted in Davidson, *Nuclear Weapons*, p. 71.   147. Quoted in *ibid.*, p. 75.

We do not perceive any situation in which the deliberate initiation of nuclear warfare, on however restricted a scale, can be morally justified. Therefore a serious moral obligation exists to develop non-nuclear defensive strategies as rapidly as possible to preclude any justification for using nuclear weapons in response to nonnuclear attacks.[148]

Protestant churches were also involved in anti-nuclear campaigning in the USA. The non-Catholic Christians of America, represented in the National Council of the Churches of Christ with its 32 Protestant and Orthodox churches, in 1968 called for a cessation of the production, testing and deployment of new nuclear weapons. All of the American Protestant churches called for nuclear disarmament and for the non-violent settlement of international disputes. Four of the American Protestant churches were categorically opposed to any nuclear use, seven to any first use by NATO.[149] In 1981 a selection of Christian organisations, including again the American *Pax Christi* but also representatives of the traditional pacifist churches (Quakers, Mennonites etc.) published a 'New Abolitionist Covenant', in which they noted:

Nuclear war is total war. Unlimited in their violence, indiscriminate in their victims, uncontrollable in their devastation, nuclear weapons have brought humanity to a historical crossroads. More than any previous time in history, the alternatives are peace or destruction. In nuclear war there are no winners. . . . At stake is whether we trust in God or the bomb. We can no longer confess Jesus as Lord and depend on nuclear weapons to save us. Conversion in our day must include turning away from nuclear weapons as we turn to Christ . . . The building and threatened use of nuclear weapons is a sin against God and his creation. We refuse to cooperate any longer with the preparations for total war.[150]

(Here we see the classic pattern of the pacifist stance as it developed before the conversion of Constantine and again since the High Middle Ages among the proto-Protestants and later the Mennonites and Quakers: wars – and here nuclear weapons – are seen as more concerned with the conscience and salvation of the individual and God's will than with the suffering they cause.)

To what extent were such sentiments shared by Americans across the spectrum? In the summer of 1982, the *Christian Science Monitor* conducted an opinion poll, according to which 51 per cent of

148. 'The Challenge of Peace', US Catholic bishops, published in May 1983.
149. Davidson, *Nuclear Weapons*, p. 142.   150. Quoted in *ibid.*, p. 168.

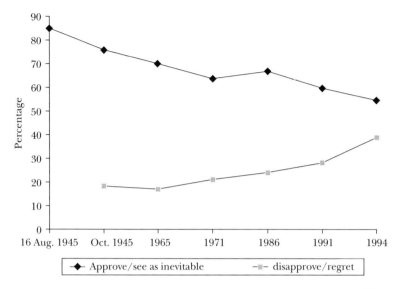

Figure 4.1   *US views on the use of the nuclear weapons on Japan in 1945*[151]

Americans questioned approved 'of possessing nuclear weapons and threatening their use', 43 per cent finding even such a deterrence stance 'morally unacceptable'. Correspondingly, 58 per cent thought America should not divest itself of nuclear weapons unilaterally while 36 per cent thought it should. Yet a mere 25 per cent found 'actual use of nuclear weapons in a war morally acceptable' while 68 per cent did not. 67 per cent did not think the USA should use nuclear weapons if NATO Europe were attacked with conventional forces only (28 per cent thought America should use them).[152] The *Monitor* concluded that according to US opinion in general, 'Nuclear weapons are morally repugnant – but the lesser evil at this point, so long as they are used only . . . to deter rather than to fight.'

American views about the use of the nuclear weapons at Hiroshima and Nagasaki were more conservative. As Figure 4.1 shows, the number of those approving of the bombing diminished over time, and critics of President Truman's decision increased in number.

In the USA, it was on balance less Hiroshima and nuclear weapons than Vietnam and conscription which led to a dramatic increase in pacificist tendencies: here, as in Britain in the 1920s, the

151. Asada, 'The mushroom cloud and national psyches', pp. 177–9.
152. Quoted in Davidson, *Nuclear Weapons*, p. xiv.

realisation that it might affect oneself, one's son, boyfriend or brother, that produced a degree of opposition which neither films like *Dr Strangelove* nor *Failsafe* could ultimately engender. Nevertheless, half a century after the USA became the only power to have used nuclear weapons in war, there is a pronounced unease about the morality of any such use in US society, which is not matched by unease about small, decisive military interventions such as in Panama, Grenada, the Gulf or Haïti, or peacekeeping activities such as in Bosnia, if US casualty figures can be kept low. Unease about the morality of nuclear use finds its echo in the support for a 'no first-use' policy which spread among the US 'defence community'. It was being discussed in the West at least since 1956.[153] In 1982, four former high-ranking US defence officials and diplomats, McGeorge Bundy, Robert McNamara, George Kennan and Gerard Smith made the cause their own,[154] to the horror of those Europeans who, banking on deterrence, believed in the need for a US threat to use nuclear weapons first if required to fend off conventional aggression in Europe.[155] The debate was still going on at the end of the century, when a reconsideration of NATO's strategic concept revived interest in it. But, as noted at the beginning, in the USA, unease about nuclear weapons is paralleled by feelings about other 'weapons of mass destruction', such as chemical and biological weapons, which the USA agreed successively to ban, destroying its own stockpiles.

FRANCE

The situation was quite different again in France. Concerns about peace were rarely connected with nuclear weapons here, but with fear of war in general. Where many Frenchmen had professed pacifism in the 1930s, the tendency after the end of the Second World War was one of neutralism by any other name, coupled with intellectual anti-Americanism. Prominent French supporters of the Stockholm Peace Appeal of 1950 included the Nobel-prize physicist Frédéric Joliot-Curie, the Socialist politician Pierre Cot, the actors/

---

153. Britain, House of Lords Debate, *The Times* (22 March 1956), intervention of Viscount Alexander of Hillsborough. More famous were Robert Tucker *et al.*, *Proposals for No First Use of Nuclear Weapons – Pros and Cons* (Princeton, N.J.: Center for International Studies, 1963).

154. But it had been discussed also nearer the time, see the debate between Samuel T. Cohen and William R. van Cleave, ' "First Use" ou "No First Use"?' *Stratégique* No. 8 (1980), pp. 7–29.

155. McGeorge Bundy, George Kennan, Robert McNamara and Gerard Smith, 'Nuclear weapons and the Atlantic alliance' *Foreign Affairs* Vol. 60, No. 4 (1982).

singers Yves Montand and Simone Signoret, the architect Le Corbusier, the poet Aragon, and Picasso, who painted his famous dove for this occasion. Many who refused to sign up to this Soviet-led initiative, like *Le Monde*'s editor Hubert Beuve-Méry, wanted 'neither Washington, nor Moscow': 'The Americans', he wrote, 'constitute a true danger to France', a view which became and remained widespread in France, albeit mainly in connection with the cultural and economic spheres.[156]

Prior to the development of French nuclear weapons, only the occasional nuclear power station accident would temporarily fuel interest in or even opposition to the French nuclear programme.[157] After the first French test of 1960, however, opposition to French ownership of the bomb began to organise itself, again, as in Britain and West Germany, on the Left. The trade union CGT, dominated by the French Communist Party and the Socialists, staged repeated protests against the French nuclear force throughout the 1960s.[158] In the mid-1960s, around half the French population was sceptical about a French nuclear capability.[159] But this scepticism was in part inspired by uncertainty as to whether France could actually develop independently, without ruining her state economy, a large nuclear force to make deterrence work.

French nuclear strategy, with its explicit counter-value targeting (meaning that the enemy's population centres would be targeted in a reprisal for an attack on France) caused some Catholics concern. In the year when France's first nuclear-armed submarine became operational, the Bishop of Orléans, Mgr Riobé, attacked France's concept of nuclear deterrence on the grounds that its city targeting was unacceptable in view of Vatican II's opposition against indiscriminate targeting of civilians. But Mgr Riobé's protests were drowned in a wave of support from other Catholics for government policy.[160]

156. Jean-Baptiste Duroselle, 'Les précédents historiques', in Lellouche (ed.), *Pacifisme et dissuasion*, pp. 247–9.

157. Pierre de Latil, 'L'explosion souterraine du Hoggar: Deux victimes d'émanations radio-actives hospitalisées', *Le Figaro* (10 May 1952).

158. 'Manifestations dans plusieurs villes', *Le Monde* (19 Nov. 1963); 'Au Parc de Sceau', *Le Monde* (28 Apr. 1964).

159. Cited in Jacques Robert, 'La direction des application militaires du Commissariat à l'Énergie Atomique', *Revue Défense Nationale* Vol. 26, No. 3 (Mar. 1970), p. 374.

160. 'Paix nucléaire et guerre classique', *Le Monde* (12 July 1973); 'La controverse entre l'Amiral de Joybert et le clergé français', *Le Monde* (17 July 1973); Groupe d'officiers chrétiens, 'Réflexions sur la défense', *Revue Défense Nationale* Vol. 29, No. 9 (Oct. 1973), pp. 17–48 which also defended torture and summary executions in times of war; various articles in *Le Monde* (22–23 July 1973).

There were some Christian organisations in France which opposed nuclear weapons, such as the French branch of *Pax Christi*
or the *Commission Justice et Paix*, and later, in the 1980s, a French
section of the Committee for European Nuclear Disarmament that
had been founded in Britain.[161] But these had much less strength
than the Christian movements in Britain, West Germany or even
the USA.

In 1983, the French Catholic bishops, like their American colleagues, followed the Pope's approval of deterrence, but condemned
city targeting. As we have seen, this should have brought them into
conflict with French strategy. And anti-city strategy, as the French
bishops recognised in the document they produced, was 'clearly
condemned by the Council' (Vatican II). Nevertheless, they continued, did the 'immorality of the use' of nuclear weapons against
cities 'render the threat immoral?' Not necessarily, wrote the French
bishops,

> for we cannot 'make an abstraction from the world as it is', as the
> [Vatican] Council said. In the situation of violence and sin which is
> that of this world, the politicians and the military men have the just
> duty to counter the blackmail to which the nation might be submitted
> . . . Confronted with the choice between two evils which are quasi-
> incomparable, capitulation or the counter-threat, . . . one chooses the
> lesser without pretending that one chooses something [inherently]
> good.[162]

Unlike the American branch of *Pax Christi*, the French branch also
came out in support of the French government attitude towards
deterrence.[163] In France, the views of Catholic spokesmen and
governments were thus very close indeed, both clearly rooted in
the same specifically French national culture.

CATHOLICISM IN WEST GERMANY

The West German Catholic bishops agreed with their American
and French colleagues on the postulate that deterrence must be
the aim, not war-fighting. They went further than their colleagues,
however, and stressed that it was the task of the military to work for

161. Forget, 'Le pacifisme en France', pp. 93–109.
162. *Gagner la paix* (1983), quoted in Calvèz, 'L'Église catholique', p. 142.
163. Cardinal Paul Gouyon, President of the French section of *Pax Christi*, 'Pour
une agence nationale du désarmement', *Le Monde* (18 Dec. 1970); see also Forget, 'Le
pacifisme en France', pp. 93–107. See also Pierre Dabezies, 'French political parties
and defense policy', *Armed Forces and Society* Vol. 8, No. 2 (Winter 1982), pp. 244–6.

the prevention of '*all* war', and all military and armaments efforts should be evaluated exclusively from this perspective. The German Catholic bishops postulated, in a position much closer to the German Protestant-inspired peace movement than to the rest of the Catholic Church, that 'The use of force and the threat of its use must be totally excluded from international relations, or at least gradually reduced.' They focused explicitly on the contradiction between the condoning of deterrence and the rejection of any nuclear use:

> To threaten massive extermination, which one never has the right to put into practice – as this is a morally unbearable perspective – is considered to be particularly effective if one aims at war-prevention. This incredible tension cannot be accepted unless the whole of the security policy has as its aim the prevention of war, and unless the military measures remain subordinate to the principal idea of the quest for peace by political means.

They postulated that all military forces must enhance crisis stability, and must in no way convey a political or military advantage if used first.[164] The last point echoed fears frequently expressed in the peace movement at the time and widely propagated by the Soviet Union, that *Cruise* and *Pershing II* missiles were in fact weapons intended for preventive or surprise attacks on Soviet nuclear forces or command centres. The postulate that all military strategy should be subordinated to 'the quest for peace by political means', however, converged with NATO strategy (and thus the Federal Republic's strategy),[165] which contemplated first nuclear use by NATO purely for the purpose of war termination.[166] There was thus a greater degree of convergence between the Catholic thinking on nuclear weapons and the FRG's government's position than between that of many committed Protestants and Bonn's strategy.

BELGIUM, ITALY, SPAIN AND GREECE

Catholic Belgium fell into the two diametrically opposed spheres of cultural influence, Catholic or laicist France on the one hand (with pro-nuclear, but anti-American sentiments) and the Protestant Netherlands on the other. It has been said that according to this division,

164. *Gerechtigkeit schafft Frieden*, pastoral letter of the German bishops (1983), quoted in Calvèz, 'L'Église catholique', pp. 137–41.
165. The FRG was not allowed to have a national strategy independent of that of NATO.
166. Cf. Heuser, *Nuclear Strategies and Forces for Europe*, ch. 2.

the majority of (Francophone) Walloons tended to acquiesce in the existence of nuclear weapons and their deployment, including on Belgian soil, while the (Dutch-speaking) Flemings counted more active anti-nuclear protesters in their ranks. After two German invasions in two world wars, and in view of the bitter memories of (particularly Flemish) appeasement of Germany in the 1930s and collaboration during the Second World War, neutralist tendencies in Belgium were in general lower than among its neighbours.[167]

In Italy, there was little enthusiasm for the anti-nuclear cause. Three waves of peace movements came into being there, each of them clearly Communist-inspired (the Communist party being stronger in Cold-War Italy than in most other West European countries). The first was a reaction against the signing of the North Atlantic Treaty and coincided with the Stockholm Peace Appeal. The second came in the 1960s, and both were anti-American, rather than anti-nuclear or pacifist, in spirit, when all other parts of Italy's establishment saw in the alliance with the USA the sole way to influence, prosperity and security for Italy. The third concerned the Euromissiles, but, despite the large turn-out of the 1981 rally noted above (p. 163), was less pronounced than in the Protestant countries. Again, the movement there was dominated by Communists, but also by the Catholic Left and the small Protestant churches in Italy. On the whole, however, anti-nuclear activists in Italy complained that there was little public interest in the issue in their country.[168]

In Madrid and Athens respectively, the 1981 protests against nuclear weapons rallied the exceptionally high figures of 500,000 and 300,000.[169] This seems incongruous if one tries to relate it merely to Catholicism or Greek Orthodoxy and protests against nuclear weapons. But in both countries, these rallies were symbolic of anti-Americanism rather than of anything else. Spain was in political turmoil, having just emerged from the abortive putsch of the Guardia Civil. The Spanish Left had long considered that America's tacit support for Franco after the Second World War was a betrayal of Republicanism, and was deeply anti-American, and thus also opposed to US nuclear deployment in Europe. Greece felt equally let down by the USA, in this case on the issue of the Turkish invasion of Cyprus in 1975, and PASOK (which under Andreas

167. Alfred van Staden, 'Pays-Bas et Belgique: la tentation neutraliste', in Lellouche (ed.), *Pacifisme et dissuasion*, pp. 89–106.
168. Sergio Rossi and Virgilio Ilari, 'Pacifisme à l'italienne', in Lellouche (ed.), *Pacifisme et dissuasion*, pp. 141–52.
169. Bredow, 'Die Friedensbewegungen', p. 55.

Papandreou formed its first government since the military takeover on 21 October 1981) was probably the most open to suggestion from Moscow among the European Socialist parties of the time. This was less a function of its religion than of the baggage of recent historical memories.

This brief survey has shown that while not inactive, the Roman Catholic Church and its bishops were by and large closer to the agreed positions of the governments of the – then 15 – NATO member states than Protestant church leaders. Looking at individual countries, however, we see that other factors came into play. In each case, specific indigenous experiences, and not just the fear of nuclear weapons, dominated the agenda of the peace protesters and their opponents in all of these countries.

Conclusion

To conclude, much thinking on the morality of war has its roots in religious qualms about killing – found in Buddhism, but also in commandments of Jewish and Christian scripture. In addition we find the more flexible Catholic Church teaching derived from St Augustine, which allows war if it is proportionately a lesser evil than the suffering of injustice. Moreover, limitations on killing in war – concerning the intention and the sparing of non-combatants – can be found both in Christian traditions and in Islam.

Western sensitivity to war seems to have grown and become widely shared since the beginning of the twentieth century, and particularly since the 1950s. Nuclear weapons certainly played a part in this: they provided a focus for peace movements, as they were the extreme weapon of Total War, they came to stand for it, and allowed a *reductio ad absurdum* of the arguments for such war. Yet St Augustine's concept of proportionality, which has become a fundamental principle underlying international norms on the use of force, has never been explicitly linked to nuclear weapons or nuclear use. Moreover, by the end of the twentieth century, the issue of whether the (first) use of nuclear weapons (obviously in what would be claimed to be self-defence) could be outlawed by referring to this principle of proportionality was not settled from a Catholic theological point of view.[170]

170. Bruno Simma (ed.), *The Charter of the United Nations: A Commentary* (Oxford: Oxford University Press, 1995), p. 677.

Moreover, Total War, as we have seen, is not simply a war in which nuclear weapons are used. The gradual and conscious development of Total War culminated in the well-targeted efforts to exterminate entire, arbitrarily defined groups of human beings, all of them non-combatants: this latter point is true for Auschwitz more than it is for Hiroshima and Nagasaki. Revulsion against both has grown in Western societies, along with the rise of an individualism and a further quest for (individual) liberties and the (individual's) pursuit of happiness. Along with declining birth-rates in most European countries, these have led to a change of attitudes towards the sacrifice of human life.

As Western societies have developed the tendency to reject war, particularly Total War, as an instrument of politics (or, in the case of Total War, as excusable for any reason at all), the arguments about this could crystallise around nuclear weapons. Yet Western war-weariness is as much the function of the experience of the First World War, of strategic bombing campaigns in Europe in the Second,[171] and in the case of America, of the American Civil War and then Vietnam, and of the particular cultural developments just described, as of any deeper reflection on nuclear weapons. Indeed, from the point of view of some, nuclear deterrence is precisely the last reinsurance against being conquered by a power that has created Auschwitz, or indeed the Gulag.[172] French intellectuals can thus see in the French nuclear deterrent the ultimate guarantee that their country will not again be overrun, as in 1940, by a totalitarian régime, and that their Jewish fellow-citizens (or any other randomly chosen category of people) will not again be rounded up, deported and murdered – while French society as a whole fails to resist. Compared with the atrocities committed by National Socialist Germany and the Soviet Union under Stalin, Hiroshima and Nagasaki are widely seen as lower in importance.[173]

At the end of the century, Western governments are acting with utmost hesitation even with regard to limited interventions in tiny areas such as Bosnia or Kosovo, even in contexts where nuclear weapons play no rôle at all. Doubts about the morality, but more

---

171. E.g. Berhard E. Trainor, 'Bomber Harris, Bomber Le May: Not the way to wage a war', *International Herald Tribune* (23 Jan. 1992).

172. For examples of this argument, see Claude Simon, 'Lieber Kenzaburo Oe', *Die Zeit* (29 Sept. 1995), and Pierre Hassner, 'Pacifisme et terreur', in Lellouche (ed.), *Pacifisme et dissuasion*.

173. Bertrand Le Gendre, 'Contre l'oubli', in *Le Monde* – special edition to commemorate the 50th anniversary of the bombing of Hiroshima (3 Aug. 1995).

still concerns about the costs of involvement in warfare, which in 1914 were harboured only by small minorities, have become general characteristics of Western societies. Nuclear weapons have certainly played a large part in this, but have not been the only reason for this development.

CHAPTER FIVE

A Turning Point in the History of
Warfare and Inter-societal Relations?

If I were asked to name the most important date in the history of the
human race, I would answer without hesitation, 6th August, 1945.
From the dawn of consciousness until 6th August, 1945, man had
to live with the prospect of his death as an *individual*; since the day
when the first atomic bomb outshone the sun over Hiroshima, he
has had to live with the prospect of his extinction as a *species*.

(Arthur Koestler)[1]

Let all the souls here rest in peace: for we shall not repeat the evil.

(inscription on the cenotaph for the victims of the
Hiroshima bombing)[2]

The previous chapters have focused on the rôle of nuclear weapons
in the Second World War, in the development of strategy, in relation to Total War and to public thinking about war in Western
societies. This chapter addresses the rôle and the effect of nuclear
weapons in relation to human history, which has to such an enormous extent been dominated by the fortunes of war. Hiroshima
and Nagasaki were undoubtedly a watershed in twentieth-century
history in that no Third World War took place between NATO
and the Warsaw Treaty Organisation. Yet, a nuclear war (or indeed
a Total War or any other use of weapons of mass destruction) could
well still take place, as we shall see, with consequences well beyond
the theatre of war. Also, many smaller wars have taken place which
have been very far-reaching in their consequences for the populations of the countries so afflicted. Have nuclear weapons obviated

1. Arthur Koestler, *Janus: A Summing Up* (London: Hutchinson, 1978), p. 1 (emphasis in the original).
2. Quoted in Ian Buruma, *The Wages of Guilt: Memories of War in Germany and Japan*
(New York: Meridian, 1994), p. 93.

major war? Has their invention been a turning point in all inter-societal relations to the point where humans would no longer risk a major war? Have they introduced a permanent change in the behaviour of human societies? How likely is it that the evil of Hiroshima, as the inscription says on the cenotaph in the Peace Park of that city, will not be repeated by us humans again?

To approach these questions, a short excursion suggests itself via the contributions history, anthropology and sociology can make to our understanding of war. We need to address the question of the linearity or reversibility of the development of human abilities to wage war and attitudes to war. We will look at war in the context of human development: we will touch on social factors, and the question why and in what context societies espouse belligerent or pacific values. We will then come to the question whether it is likely that all major war has been banned by the fear of nuclear war, and where, if this is not the case, this leaves nuclear weapons as a technological *acquis* of mankind.

Human history and the history of warfare

Human history, or the history of the *Homo sapiens sapiens*, began more than 60,000 years ago (and in Europe, at least 35,000 years ago). History, in the sense of events documented by written records, has only existed roughly for the past 5,000 years, and even then only in a few exceptionally developed cultures. What archaeological evidence exists prior to ca. 10,000 BC is open to wild speculation, and can barely serve as solid evidence. Even from this date until at least the fifth millennium BC, the evidence is often ambiguous (weapons for war and weapons for hunting are difficult to distinguish, for example) and still open to the sort of speculation that would be unacceptable in the historiography of more recent periods.[3] This means that recorded history has existed, at best, for less than a tenth of the period since the first appearance of human beings like us, and then only covering small segments of humanity. Known history, recorded history, is only a fraction of the actual story of human existence, and one must beware of assuming that

---

3. Cf. Marilyn Keyes Roper, 'A survey of evidence for intrahuman killing in the Pleistocene', *Current Anthropology* Vol. 10 (1969), pp. 427–59; *idem*, 'Evidence of warfare in the Near East from 10,000–4,300 B.C.', in Martin Nettleship, R. Dalegivens and Anderson Nettleship (eds.), *War, its Causes and Correlates* (The Hague: Mouton, 1975), pp. 299–340.

one can generalise about human behaviour from the data provided by recorded history. For example, one cannot say that humanity has *always* known war and conflict, or that war and conflict were never long absent from human lives, as evidence is lacking for the greatest part of the time humankind has existed. Nor do anthropological studies provide enough evidence to fill these glaring holes in our data: each one of them, conducted over a finite period of time, in the absence of historical records, can only provide evidence for that period of time. Had anthropologists visited Britain or the Habsburg lands or the central European principalities in the period 1830–50, in the absence of firm evidence about the past, they might have concluded that these were societies not prone to external aggression. Little, too, about Sweden's behaviour since the Napoleonic Wars and Japan's behaviour since 1949 gives us a clue about the thoroughly aggressive rôle these countries played previously.

What recorded history there is, however, is to a very large extent concerned with war. It is also to a very large extent concerned with government: it is the story of who rules whom, who assumes the leadership of a group or is chosen as leader, who organises a group in agriculture, trade, in hunting, in self-defence or in aggression. Annals of royal or priestly rule are among the earliest forms of historiography, and descriptions of wars constitute the earliest and most formative models of the historiography that was born in the Judaeo-Graeco-Roman cultures. Since the time of the Bible, since the writings of Thucydides and Xenophon, and since the epic poetry of Homer, war and rulers have been at the centre of historiography.

THE HISTORY OF WARFARE PRIOR TO
THE SECOND WORLD WAR

Before running swiftly through European history to look at the place of Hiroshima and Nagasaki in this terrible line of succession of wars and atrocities, it is useful to recall the terms we have introduced in Chapter 3, particularly the Clausewitzian terms of 'limited' and 'absolute' wars, as opposed to the Ludendorffian 'Total War'. Another term often employed is that of 'major war', which will be used loosely here, for want of a narrow definition, in the sense of a war on the scale of the Napoleonic wars, the American Civil War, and the First and Second World Wars.[4]

---

4. John Mueller, *Retreat from Doomsday: On the Obsolescence of Major War* (New York: Basic Books, 1989).

As noted in Chapter 3, bar the absence of an industrialised society, government apparatus, communication etc. in short, the War Machine, there have been wars, at least since classical antiquity, with features of Total War. But war aims have fluctuated over history: the Thirty Years' War with its terrible toll of non-combatant lives was followed by what Clausewitz called cabinet wars with all their limitations (hence, limited wars with limited war aims), which in turn were followed by the wars of the French Revolution and Napoleon with their 'absolute' war aims – the liberation of the peoples of Europe,[5] later the transformation of the inter-state order in Europe, and the subjection of all governments to France's authority. 1815 saw the beginning of a particularly long peace in European history, surpassed only by the long peace since 1945. Yet the wars of the second half of the century with their limited war aims (the annexation or defence of strips of territory, just as in Europe's eighteenth-century wars) employed mass armies in battles hugely wasteful of human lives, as the War Machine was unfolding its effectiveness.

Looking back at the recorded history of warfare, Hiroshima and Nagasaki stand out clearly in one respect: the technological one. Technology is without doubt a crucial factor in the history of warfare. The sheer numeric difference between the numbers of casualties of the Second World War on the one hand, and the numbers killed in Melos or Carthage or in the cities destroyed by the Huns under Attila, particularly in terms of numbers over time, is indisputable. The ability to kill tens of thousands of human beings *within a minute* (and several times that number with the hydrogen bomb, which in the view of nuclear scientists constituted the true turning point in the possibilities of mass extermination)[6] is obviously a factor previously unknown in history.

But let there be no mistake: it takes more than technological innovation to transform technology into a weapon. The often quoted example that the Chinese, having invented gunpowder, never thought of using it in a martial way, finds its parallel in cultures like those of Sweden, Norway, and Canada, which discovered the way to split the atom exclusively in order to extract energy for peaceful

---

5. Frank Attar, *La Révolution Française déclare la guerre à l'Europe* including documents (Brussels: Eds. Complexe, 1992), see particularly *décret du 20 avril 1792*, p. 165.
6. Robert Oppenheimer, American director of the wartime nuclear programme, resigned over President Truman's decision to authorise the development of the 'Super', giving this reason, cf. Herbert York, *The Adviser: Oppenheimer, Teller and the Superbomb* (San Francisco: W.H. Freeman, 1976).

purposes. It took a particular ideology and a particular régime devoted to it, and a particularly efficient government apparatus to hit on the use of diesel engines to kill millions of people through their gases – not what the diesel engine had been invented for. And inversely, the killing of huge numbers of humans, indiscriminately, including non-combatants, has not been limited in history to modern times: there are abundant examples throughout recorded history of the citizens of a town or region being exterminated by conquerors. The difference lies in the numeric toll, the speed, and the thoroughness with which this killing could be carried out, but it is not an invention of the twentieth century. What organised groups of killers can do with rifles or even with machetes has been amply demonstrated in Pol Pot's Kampuchea in the 1970s and in Rwanda in the 1990s, but is not alien to the worlds described by Thucydides or Livy, and was the documented fate of the inhabitants of many besieged towns in the Middle Ages and beyond. The lynching of the citizens of Magdeburg in the Thirty Years' War was a late and particularly horrifying example of this practice; in that war, in the area of the Holy Roman Empire alone, 1,629 towns and 18,310 villages were destroyed, and the population of all towns in this area taken together was reduced by up to 30 per cent of the pre-war figures, with populations in rural areas reduced by up to 50 per cent. The losses of that last Total War of European history before the twentieth century in proportion to the total population of the time exceed by far the losses of the First or Second World Wars, despite the fact that war technology had not progressed much beyond the application of gunpowder through cannon and pistol; the technology that made Verdun and Auschwitz possible, the railway, was absent in the Thirty Years' War just as much as that of aerial bombardment. Indeed, the transport technology of the Thirty Years' War was no different from that of the Roman Empire, which had reached a degree of perfection unsurpassed until the nineteenth century.

The emerging picture of warfare in (recorded) human history is thus one in which several strands interweave to create different forms of warfare:

- the technology available;
- differing forms of co-operation among individuals within a group. This includes the way in which groups are ruled and organised (which from a certain degree of organisation one would call state), which in turn includes the extent to which the productivity of

this group can be exploited for taxation to sustain armed forces, and the extent to which the population itself can be mobilised for the war effort on a purely administrative level;
• beliefs – about the value of life in relation to other values (salvation and afterlife, or the well-being of the family, group, class, race); the importance accorded to suffering; beliefs about one's own group, the issues at stake, and the adversarial group, all of which jointly determine the degree of cruelty one is prepared to undergo or to inflict.

In one sense, technology is perhaps the least among these factors. Technology – particularly transport, but also the technologies of inflicting death upon large numbers of humans from simple fire to gunpowder and missiles to poison gas and nuclear charges – certainly is the great amplifying factor which facilitates and renders efficient operations of mass killing. It is not, however, technology on its own that suggests such operations to humans, even though within an already existing war, technology can offer tempting options, as we have seen in the case of the American administration's use of the atomic bomb in the Second World War. By contrast, all nuclear powers' subsequent abstention from the use of nuclear weapons in other conflicts shows that the mere availability of a weapon does not necessarily lead to its use. Further evidence is provided by the reluctance of all sides, during the Second World War, to use poison gas in combat. Of greater importance, it seems, for the cruelty of a war or the limitations on it, are the other two factors: degree of organisation within groups at war with each other (and closely related, their size, economic strength, ability to silence dissidents and to mobilise the population), and the beliefs held by them.

In another sense, technology in the unique form of weapons of mass destruction, is the greatest factor of them all. Only a war with such weapons might in the extreme case spell the end of human life on earth. Even Hitler's war was limited compared with the potential contained in the nuclear arsenals of East and West in the 1970s and 1980s, and even in the reduced arsenals of the last years of the twentieth century.

TECHNOLOGICAL PROGRESS IN HISTORY: LINEAR OR FLUCTUATING?

Let us look briefly at the evolution of each of these factors in (recorded) history. The Judaeo-Christian heritage has resulted in a

tendency to believe in 'unilinear evolution', an almost linear progress
from sin to redemption, from Adam and Eve's hard toiling struggle
for bare survival to the splendours of Solomon's Jerusalem in the
age of the Temple, from Hobbes's brutal state of nature to a well-
ordered society, from primitive to increasingly sophisticated. Particularly Liberal ('Whig') interpretations of history have sought to
identify some linear pattern of development. Focusing above all on
the development of technology, the idea of 'progress' suggests itself to the superficial observer.

Even where simple technology is concerned, however, there is
no such linearity until the late eighteenth century. Crucial technological inventions made in one corner of the world were often for-
gotten again and not rediscovered until centuries later, or applied
in a limited area or among a limited group of people, leaving other
parts of the world unaffected. The Roman system of roads in Western and Southern Europe had no parallel in sub-Saharan Africa, in
America or large parts of Asia until the twentieth century; the 'black
houses' in northern Scotland, some of them inhabited until the
early twentieth century, are comparable in technology to stone-age
dwellings and furnish evidence that aspects of the stone age continued into the twentieth century not only outside the 'Western world';
bow and arrow are used by isolated tribes in Africa, Latin America
and in the islands of Asia until this day. Different technological
ages have thus coexisted on earth, and even within continents and
countries. Indeed, areas could relapse into less developed technological states after having been technologically more advanced previously, as the history of Dark Age Western and Southern Europe
amply demonstrates. Judging by technological criteria, Lévi-Strauss's
argument of the equivalence of all cultures cannot be applied,
because there are clearly measurable technological differences and
degrees of development. This does not imply a moral judgement,
and it may be that the spiritual life of a Frank in the Dark Ages was
richer than that of a Gallo-Roman in the same area four centuries
earlier, but the Frank's craftsmanship, by comparison with that
of the Roman, was objectively inferior. As far as technology is concerned – to use one fairly objective criterion – there was no linear
progress for tens of thousands of years of human existence, but a
fluctuating development, with setbacks as well as advances.

From the late eighteenth century onward, however, the development of technology changed dramatically, and had an even more
dramatic impact on all other aspects of human life. Since then,
there has been an ever more sharply rising curve of change both in

terms of geometrically increasing innovations and geometrically decreasing time-scale of the spread of these innovations throughout the world. From the invention of the steam-engine to the development of coal-powered industry and to the steam-ship, from the development of the telegraph and radio to the invention of the micro-chip and the ensuing revolution in information technology, the history of technology is one of rapid change, reaching a giddy speed in the late twentieth century. As far as one can tell, this technological revolution is without parallel in the millennia of human existence since the agricultural revolution of the Neolithic, which itself took over 10 millennia to spread throughout the world (with the last nomadic, non-sedentary cultures still existing today). Compared with the technological revolution since the end of the eighteenth century, the construction techniques that erected Stonehenge or the Pyramids, the under-floor heating of Roman villas, the Cartesian wells of the Moorish gardens in Africa and Spain, Roman siege-machines and Leonardo da Vinci's designs of fortresses were all mere blips in human development. While they did not occur in isolation but were produced within cultures which tended to be technologically more developed than others with which they coexisted, they were often without lasting consequence, and they did not engender further innovation in the same geometric multiplication as did discoveries since the age of Enlightenment. Until then, there was no steady technological progress. Since then, however, technological innovations have taken off and multiplied at a breathtaking speed, moving in all directions, seemingly unstoppable and irreversible.

To this extent, nuclear weapons are a function of man's increasing mastery of technology, of a form of inquiry which, while originating in Ancient Greece, only ceased to be blocked by religious taboos when religion began to be squeezed out by rationalism. Ever since, research has pushed back all frontiers of knowledge, barely reined in by painstakingly devised ethical limitations, built on value systems which try to stand up without the threat of divine punishment to support them, devised time and again belatedly, after the new technological breakthrough has already been made. It is crucial to understand that in setting themselves the goal of developing a weapon which can kill masses of people instantly, scientists have explored different directions, and found different solutions: nuclear weapons are *not* the only possible form which the 'ultimate weapon' could have taken. The effects of nuclear weapons overlap with those of biological weapons, and on the lower ends of the spectrum, with

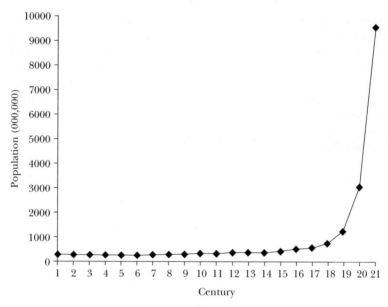

Figure 5.1   *Estimated growth of world population in millions[7]*

those of chemical weapons, or fuel-air explosives. Had nuclear technology not reached the stage where in 1945 atomic fission could be harnessed to deliverable weapons, other innovations would have taken this place sooner or later, as there were many paths for human research to pursue. Moreover, while prior to the eighteenth century, cultures could quite literally forget previous technological achievements, it is widely believed today that in view of the global spread of scientific knowledge through modern communications, technological know-how cannot be kept secret for long, and inventions such as nuclear weapons are within the reach of many scientists, which makes it unlikely that they can be 'disinvented' again.

The technological revolution led to a further revolution of inestimable consequence: the geometric growth of European and later world population since the late eighteenth century, as disease and childhood mortality were progressively fought back. While the

7. Figures taken for the middle of each century. William Eckhardt's statistics from eleventh to mid-twentieth centuries given in Eric Markusen and David Kopf, *The Holocaust and Strategic Bombing: Genocide and Total War in the Twentieth Century* (Boulder, Co.: Westview Press, 1995), p. 33; twenty-first century data estimated by Population Concern, with help of UN Statistical Office (Population Reference Bureau, June 1996).

bubonic plague both in the sixth and the fourteenth centuries and the Thirty Years' War actually significantly reduced European populations, since then, not even the two world wars have resulted in an actual decrease of Europe's, let alone the world's, population. As a result, the sheer number of human beings involved in the First and Second World Wars, fought by populous countries and their dependent colonies, and indeed in the many 'minor' wars of the period since 1945, has exceeded anything previously recorded in history. In the mid-eighteenth century, the entire population of Russia equalled in number Soviet casualties in the Second World War;[8] and yet, due to the birth rate, the total Soviet population was not actually reduced in absolute terms by this 'Great Patriotic War'.

At the end of the second millennium, many feel the need to return to a Malthusian concern about the growth of the world's population in relation to the stagnation of the earth's resources, not only in terms of food production (upon which Malthus focused), but also in terms of energy consumption, and related to that, the availability of *clean* water, and air. At the end of the twentieth century, population growth is taking place mainly in Third World countries, while it has levelled off in the world's technologically most advanced areas (e.g. throughout the European Union), and even gone into negative growth figures in Germany and Italy. But it is precisely the countries with the highest birth rates which are short of vital resources, have cultures in which militant behaviour is admired, and are prone to conflict with neighbours, or indeed to persecutions of minorities within their states. Leo Kuper, who applied the definition of genocide both to German atrocities committed in the Second World War and to Hiroshima and Nagasaki,[9] argued in the early 1980s that, given the working of the international system that is built on the protection of state sovereignty, genocide was in future less likely at the inter-state level than *within* (particularly less developed) states in which different groups might be struggling for domination.[10] After the end of the Cold War, with international readiness to intervene in inter-state conflicts such as the Gulf War, and reluctance to intervene in domestic genocide such as that which occurred within Bosnia-Hercegovina and the remainder of Yugoslavia, Kuper's predictions sound prophetic.

8. Figures in *Der Große Ploetz* (31st edn., Freiburg: Verlag Ploetz, 1991), pp. 495, 598.

9. See Chapter 3.

10. Leo Kuper, *Genocide: Its Political Use in the 20th Century* (New Haven, Ct.: Yale University Press, 1981), p. 46.

Disquietingly, some unstable states are seeking to acquire weapons of mass destruction. And while nuclear weapons, particularly large-yield fission or fusion warheads on inaccurate delivery systems, are not plausible systems for the persecution of intra-state minorities, this might be different for neutron bombs (that exterminate life rather than destroy inanimate objects, and that have reduced long-term effects). Chemical weapons have been used in precisely such contexts (by the Iraqi government against its Kurdish minority).

The effects of rising population figures and density on war-proneness are disputed. Experiments with rats have shown that continual breeding in a limited space can lead the rats to kill each other to the point where the extinction of the total population becomes a possibility.[11] Many different animal species, from lions to baboons, demonstrably react to overcrowding by resorting to intra-species killing (as opposed to usually non-fatal violence designed to establish a 'pecking order'). As with all analogies between animal and human behaviour, one cannot extrapolate that what applies to animals applies also to humans, but many anthropologists see links between population increases and tendencies to go to war. Some speculate that the effective organisation of such dense population centres, with the provision of very good nutrition, hygiene and sewage systems, can alleviate the problems caused to humans by overcrowding, but few if any scientists see no cause for concern in the rapid growth of the world's population.[12]

If ever the idea that wars might serve as biological checks on the growth of populations could be contemplated dispassionately, the existence of the new dimension of weapons of mass destruction changes this: in contemporary circumstances, such a war contains the possibility not only of checking population growth, but of exterminating higher forms of life altogether. What some may see as a self-regulating mechanism of nature, if that is what it is, would now be turned into a self-destruction mechanism, due to the very achievements made by human societies.

---

11. John B. Calhoun, 'Population density and social pathology', *Scientific American* No. 206 (1962), pp. 139–248.

12. Peter A. Corning and Constance Hellyer Corning: 'An evolutionary paradigm for the study of human aggression', in Martin Nettleship, R. Dalegivens and Anderson Nettleship (eds.), *War, its Causes and Collaterals* (The Hague, Mouton, 1975), pp. 359–83; see also Anderson Nettleship's section introduction in the same book, pp. 401–13.

THE DEVELOPMENT OF CO-OPERATION WITHIN GROUPS, OF GOVERNMENT, STATE AND ECONOMY

Like technology, forms of organisation of human society have not developed in a linear way. The ancient civilisations of Mesopotamia and Egypt as much as Greek city-states and their colonies, Rome and her Empire all coexisted in time with and were succeeded in the same areas by less developed forms of group organisation. Sophistication of organisation was not necessarily a guarantee against defeat in war. The highly sophisticated administration of Rome gave birth to a highly sophisticated military system which created the Empire and raised the taxes to support huge centrally controlled armies with soldiers from all parts of the Roman world travelling to and fro within the Empire to defend far-flung frontiers. But under the assault of primitive tribes (who lacked writing, for example), this frontier defence finally collapsed in the West, and with it the Western part of the Empire, unprepared as it was for more primitive forms of collective defence and mobilisation of the civilian population. The Eastern part of the Roman Empire thereafter had a long history of repeated attempts to adapt its social structure to the problems posed by assaults from the outside, as often as not from societies at once more martial and more primitive than the heirs of Rome. And where Rome and Constantinople had once controlled areas as large as, or larger than, the European Union in the year 2000, the political systems (hardly meriting the title of state) which succeeded them had more in common with the tribalism of the indigenous populations in sixteenth-century North America, in seventeenth-century Scotland, or in twentieth-century sub-Saharan Africa, than with the more sophisticated administrations of ancient Egypt, or the Roman, Byzantine or Habsburg Empires. If administrative effectiveness is taken as a yardstick, one can again identify more and less developed forms, following each other helter-skelter, without any steady increase in sophistication until the nineteenth century. Governments and state-like structures, with their ways of organising human groups, thus developed in many directions and forms, with less sophistication often following greater sophistication, and different forms with varying degrees of sophistication existing side by side.

Concomitantly, different forms of warfare, offensive campaigns or defensive campaigns, were supported with differing degrees of success by differing administrative structures and social orders: as Livy recounts, the peasant-farmer of early Roman society was willing to defend the land around Rome with total commitment but reluctant to go far from Italy to fight war elsewhere; the Celts moving south-wards on the Italian peninsula had little to lose and were equally will-ing to fight to the finish, committing mass suicide in case of defeat, which made for very intensive battles for Republican Rome. Profes-sional soldiers alone were easily employed far from the region from which they had come. The European mercenaries of the fifteenth century would fight anywhere, but with less than total commitment, which resulted in limited casualties and often in indecisive cam-paigns in long drawn-out wars which Machiavelli complained about.

When the two sides had different degrees of commitment to war, different tolerance of casualties, and different degrees of in-hibitions about the use of force, as was the case in the wars of the late West Roman Empire, Napoleon's experience in Spain, or in America's war in Vietnam, superior technology and superior state structures would count for little when confronted with greater determination and greater willingness to bear pain. The strength of an inspired, well-organised popular defence made itself felt deci-sively in the defeat of the French knights by armed peasants at Courtrai in Flanders in the battle of spurs of 1302, the defeat of the Duke of Burgundy and his knights by the Swiss pikemen at the battles of Murten (1476) and Nancy (1477), and of the Royalist forces by the riff-raff forming the French Revolutionary forces in the battle of Valmy in 1792. The French Revolutionary Wars consti-tuted a milestone in that they were the first to bring together a sophisticated state with the mobilisation of an exceptionally large proportion of the population in a war effort which the population was led to believe concerned the survival of their chosen way of life – freedom, equality, brotherliness – threatened by repression and a bloody revenge by the Royalists. The confluence of these factors – the state system and the beliefs – made the French wars outstand-ing in their intensity, the model of 'absolute' warfare as analysed by Clausewitz. The extermination of enemy civilians was not the aim of these wars (notwithstanding the bloodiness with which the insurrection in the Vendée was suppressed). And yet, despite the absence of industrialisation, railroads, and centralised war econo-mies, the effectiveness of the mobilisation of the French popula-tion, particularly during the Revolutionary Wars, and the decisiveness of the mass battles of Napoleon were unrivalled until the American Civil War, the Franco-Prussian War and the First World War. The social organisation and control or administration of groups is thus a crucial factor governing the character of war, but it is not on its own the most decisive factor.

THE EVOLUTION OF VALUES AND BELIEFS

It hardly seems accidental that this marriage of state organisation, industrial economy and mobilisation of the population which unfolded in the second half of the nineteenth century coincided with the technological revolution. Both had their roots in the waning of religion: the French Revolution, the first secular revolution that drew its legitimacy not from God but from the people, like natural science, represented a break with all religious-based forms of civilisation the world had hitherto known. Man was now at the centre of the universe, just as God had been in the monotheistic religions before, and as other deities had been for the Greeks and Romans.

This leads us finally to the history of beliefs. The revolution of rationality which had brought forth the technological revolution as much as the French Revolution and democracy, gave birth to a double heritage, one of ever-deepening concern for individual human life and freedom, and another that ranked the well-being of the group above that of the individual. Chapter 4 has chronicled how peace movements turned from concern for one's own salvation in the next world to concern to prevent human suffering in this world under the influence of the Enlightenment. This in part reflected the wish for the greatest possible liberty and the pursuit of happiness for every human being, the insistence on equality before the law, freedom from oppression by others who claimed that the accident of their ancestry entitled them to privileges. At the same time, however, there were the roots of 'totalitarian democracy', in Talmon's famous expression, in the idea of an imposed happiness of the largest number at the expense of the dissenting minority, the conviction that an élite has the right to decide what constitutes happiness, and what constitutes dissent.[13] The systems that have tended towards this totalitarianism, whether under the label of the freeing of the working classes or of the protection of an embattled race, have tended to set these aims high above the value of individual human lives. Totalitarian systems have thus accepted casualties on a scale previously only tolerated by societies firmly believing in God and in an afterlife bringing reward for self-sacrifice in this life, and punishment for cowardice. Totalitarian systems have been prepared to inflict and bear casualties on a scale and in ways only known to societies which saw their enemies as enemies of the gods they worshipped. Technology and state control

13. J.L. Talmon, *The Origins of Totalitarian Democracy* (London: Martin Secker & Warburg, 1952).

helped them make the application of their policies of exterminating the internal enemy more efficient, with more victims in absolute terms and more fatalities over time than any previously recorded mass slaughter. Thus the Albigensian Crusade, the Sicilian Vespers, the St Bartholomew's Day Massacre (3,000–4,000 victims in one night, plus up to 20,000 in subsequent days) and the many pre-twentieth-century persecutions of Jews with all their horrors, or even the German war of annililation against the Hereros (ca. 75,000 victims), numerically pale in comparison with the persecutions of the Armenians in the Ottoman Empire (estimated figures are between half a million and one-and-a-half million victims), not to mention the Holocaust and the Stalinist atrocities.

Mass extermination on the *absolute* scale seen in the early twentieth century and in the Second World War thus presupposes the existence of a comprehensive, well-oiled War Machine, plus the ideology to drive this machine in the direction of mass homicide. The beliefs of Bolshevik Communism made the tolerance of the independent peasant class of the *kulaks* impossible, the belief of the German National Socialists made the tolerance of supposedly threatening races impossible and the coexistence on an equal footing with 'inferior' races intolerable. Leaders subscribing to both ideologies invented mechanisms of mass extermination directed against elements of their own populations, which they could apply thanks to the efficient state structures and the advanced technology (not least transport) they commanded.

External war was initiated by the National Socialists and by the Japanese in order to cement their own predominance over 'inferior' peoples. Coming into conflict in this expansionist war with countries fighting to defend their own beliefs and governmental structures, the National Socialists in Germany, and running to keep up with them, their adversaries in Britain and the USA, aided by scientists from France, Italy, Norway and beyond, began a race to be the first to develop a weapon of mass destruction. The research leading to the creation of this weapon under extreme pressure of time and resources was made possible by the *shared* advanced technology, the existence on all sides of state structures which could raise the taxes and procure the resources to make this work possible. Both the Axis Powers and the Allies had the technology available to develop nuclear weapons sooner or later (and there is no reason to doubt that Hitler for one would have used them, had they been available to him). Today many states are near a partial stage of technological development in which weapons of mass destruction are within reach for their scientists, even if these states cannot devise means of containing the vital resource problems of their countries, and even if they will not act decisively to prevent further uncontrolled demographic growth.

There are enough inter-state quarrels and inter-group hatred left to make plausible scenarios of inter-state wars, particularly outside NATO territory. Sooner or later, the technology, the War Machine and government apparatus could be exploited by just about any medium- to large-sized state of the twenty-first century to develop weapons of mass destruction if their beliefs drove them to follow such a course. The crucial variable is not technology, it is the will to procure and perhaps to use such weapons. This will, in turn, is a function of ideologies, of values and beliefs. The question is thus, what are the ideologies, values and beliefs of present and future nuclear powers, and owners, present and potential, of other weapons of mass destruction? Will these beliefs encourage the use of such weapons, or militate against them?

As we have shown, the invention of weapons of mass destruction has come in a phase of human history when the hitherto fluctuating pattern of technology, social organisation and population has given way, after millennia, to sudden, unidirectional, cataclysmic change. But have human values and beliefs kept up with this irreversible technological change? First, human thinking, particularly in Europe and America, but also in Japan, developed to take technological change to its worst possible extreme, to its application in war. But has it adapted further to take into account the danger weapons of mass extermination now pose to all life on earth?

In the following, we will take another analytical cut at this question. We will address two often raised questions: first, whether human beings are genetically or socially predisposed to fight wars, or whether they can learn to settle all conflicts peacefully; and second, what chance there is, if they cannot become entirely peaceful, that they can learn, collectively, to abstain at least from the use of weapons of mass destruction.

Societal and cultural-ideological causes of war

The first question forces us to visit at least very briefly the debates among a variety of disciplines about the causes of war. Following on from much older theological debates about the sinfulness with which man is born, biologists, biological and social anthropologists have long argued about whether the tendency towards aggression is an inherent part of human nature, or whether human beings are taught to be aggressive. If aggressiveness is part of humanity, can it be controlled? If it is 'nurture', then can the transmission process of aggressive patterns of behaviour from generation to generation not be disrupted and replaced by a conscious peace education, furthering non-violent ways of settling disputes?

The 'nature/nurture' debate shows no sign of being settled. Nevertheless, the whole answer to our enquiry into *war*, as opposed to individual aggressiveness, must be sought on a different level: in the words of the American socio-psychologist Gordon W. Allport,

> The fallacy of this purely personal explanation lies in the fact that, howsoever pugnacious or frustrated an individual may be, he himself lacks the capacity to make organised warfare. He is capable of temper tantrums, also of chronic nagging, biting sarcasm, or personal cruelty, but he alone cannot invade an alien land or drop bombs upon a distant enemy to give vent to his own emotions. Furthermore, whereas national aggressiveness is total – all citizens being involved in offensive and defensive efforts – relatively few of the citizens feel personally hostile toward the enemy. Studies of soldiers in combat show that hate and aggression are less commonly felt than fear, homesickness, and boredom. Few citizens, in an aggressive nation, actually *feel* aggressive. Thus their warlike activity cannot be due solely to their personal motivations.[14]

In other words, it is not individuals who wage war, but groups, and therefore, the social dimension of the organisation of individuals for the purpose of collective aggression (or defence) is more important than the individual propensity to aggressiveness, whether the latter is inherent or not.

Here it is worth harking back to the famous experiments conducted at Yale University by Dr Stanley Milgram in the early 1970s, which tested the limits of the average person's obedience to authority. Milgram drew the following conclusion from his study:

> ordinary people, simply doing their jobs, and without a particular hostility on their part, can become agents in a terrible destructive process. Moreover, even when the destructive effects of their work become patently clear, and they are asked to carry out actions incompatible with fundamental standards of morality, relatively few people have the internal resources needed to resist authority . . .[15]

14. Gordon W. Allport, 'The Role of Expectancy', in Leon Bramson and George W. Goethals (eds.), *War – Studies from Psychology, Sociology, Anthropology* (2nd edn., New York: Basic Books, 1968), p. 178.

15. Stanley Milgram, in *Dialogue* Vol. 8, No. 3, 4 (1975), p. 20, quoted in Arthur Koestler: *Janus: A Summing Up* (London: Hutchinson, 1978), p. 90. See also Stanley Milgram: *Obedience to Authority: An Experimental View* (originally 1974, repr. London: Pinter & Martin, 1997).

Even in such an explanation, we find that apart from the influence of purely external factors – such as an economic recession, unemployment – there are cultural factors at work, in the words of anthropologist Walter Goldschmidt, 'war is a cultural phenomenon'.[16] These cultural factors, these beliefs and values, vary from culture to culture, and can differ strongly even within one state, although in societies such as National Socialist Germany and militaristic Japan, uniformity of views throughout the state were strongly emphasised. Different cultures have different levels of tolerance of violence, even on a basic level. Domestic violence is still a widespread phenomenon among the poorer sections even of Western civilisations; in Russia and Turkey, to give but two examples, it is normal for conscript soldiers to be manhandled and brutalised, something that is rare indeed in the conscript armies of countries such as France, Italy, or Germany. Corporal punishment has been banned from most European schools, but is still common practice in many other parts of the world. Many countries still enforce death sentences, and summary public executions take place in China even today. Several Islamic states include amputation of limbs among the punishments they are prepared to inflict on their own subjects.

Varying attitudes to life and personal liberty are also reflected in attitudes to birth control. Many Catholic but also Islamic cultures oppose contraception, as the suffering caused by the lack of contraception – continual childbearing, high infant and maternal mortality – are seen by them as more bearable (particularly when it is others who bear it) than the supposed sinfulness of contraception. In many of these cultures the effect has long been that abortions – which are irrefutably more questionable morally, as the termination of a nascent life is involved, not the prevention of its conception – in practice substitute for contraception. In China, laudable pressures for birth control result in female infanticide, and many staunchly Catholic societies until the twentieth century knew the practice of what in Bavaria is called '*himmeln*', the deliberate neglect of a baby born to an already very large family, so that it would die early and 'go to heaven'. Crucially, therefore, societies differ greatly even today in their attitude to death and suffering, in their willingness to bear pain and inflict it on others.

But the findings of Chapter 2 show that one does not have to search in different societies in order to find crucial differences in values. Even within one society, within one country, there are

---

16. Walter Goldschmidt, 'Inducement to military participation in tribal societies', in Paul Turner and David Pitt (eds.), *The Anthropology of War and Peace: Perspectives on the Nuclear Age* (Granby, MA: Bergin & Garvey, 1989), p. 24.

differences. Democratic, humanitarian Britain thus produced a Trenchard and a Harris, while National Socialist Germany produced a Wever. Moreover, faced with an enemy imposing Total War, and faced on its own side with technology that made it impossible to wage war in a more humane way, the USA, notwithstanding previously developed moral constraints, drifted steadily towards an increasingly inhumane conduct of war. Where the US Air Force had hoped to bomb only war industries or other (predominantly non-human) targets essential for the enemy war effort, it was they who finally took city bombing to its most hellish extreme. In a protracted war, and faced with an enemy prepared to go to the ultimate extreme, self-imposed values and restrictions are difficult, perhaps impossible, to uphold.

A factor related to values and their importance on a lower scale for the conduct of war is what Allport has called 'expectancy', that is, what models there are in particular cultures for resolving disputes and clashes: does 'England expect every man to do his duty', i.e. to fight, and worse, does every young man know that his parents, peers, and girlfriend 'think he ought to go', to paraphrase a popular British song of the Great War? Or is a politician expected to 'go the extra mile for peace' (as the US administration put it on the eve of Coalition intervention in the Gulf War of 1990/91)? These questions show that there can be a wide variety of different cultural attitudes to violence even today, and far from all cultures, and far from all groups and individuals in one society, have developed the abhorrence for violence, war, and particularly major war, that we think of as a civilisational *acquis* in most Western countries.

THE SURVIVAL OF THE FITTEST SOCIETY

For over a century sociologists have tried to compare such cultural factors and to assess their importance for the fate of a particular society. Darwinism, applied by some nineteenth-century sociologists, became largely recast as an analysis of which society was fittest to rule over all others. This argument is sometimes expressed in terms of a 'group selection model of evolution'; hinging on actual genetic changes.[17] In the era of the apotheosis of nationalism and of the 'nation-state', several influential sociologists, in Germany, Austria, but also in other countries, used Darwinism to construct theories of the struggles of nations for supremacy. Social Darwinists tended to

17. Corning and Hellyer Corning, 'An evolutionary paradigm', p. 369.

argue that the most aggressive nations were also the fittest to dominate, which in good part explains the almost universal enthusiasm for war in the two or three decades leading up to the First World War.[18] The Austrian sociologist Ludwig Gumplowicz, for example, foreshadowed some of the arguments of Huntington's much debated 'clash of civilisations'.[19] Gumplowicz firmly believed that wars would be as unavoidable in the future as they had been in the past, and that in these wars, larger 'races' (what he in fact meant was cultures) would absorb smaller 'races' (cultures) until continent-wide 'races' had been formed. In Europe in the late nineteenth century, he saw three 'races' or three cultures, the Germanic, the Slav and the Latin.

> Can one imagine what horrible national and world-wars will have to take place before these three cultural worlds carried by three races . . . will have exhausted themselves in war and before a single European cultural area, one single European race, can step into the place of the Latin, Germanic and Slavic cultural area?[20]

Prophetic words indeed, looking back at the twentieth century.

One can, however, turn the Social Darwinists' theory on its head and show that with human societies, another process is at work. Societies are more than the sum of their biological parts. The anthropologist Ashley Montagu, for one, has argued that most 'Social Darwinist' writing has ignored the possibilities of collective survival (and prosperity) due to co-operation.[21] Taking this view one step further, one might emphasise that societies are 'conditionable'. Societies undergo learning processes, giving humans an enormous advantage over animal species. According to Darwin's findings, the latter take hundreds and thousands of generations to adapt biologically to environmental changes. In the process of this adaptation the species themselves are transformed through the survival and multiplying only of those members of the species who, through mutation, are by genetic accident more adapted to the new environment, while all those animals in the species (and their progeny) which have not undergone this mutation, or do not interbreed with

18. Hegelian adulation of war was thus mixed in generous measures with Social Darwinism and chauvinism in the writings of the sociologists Friedrich Ratzenhofer, *Die Soziologische Erkenntnis* (Leipzig: 1898), but see also William Graham Sumner, *War and Other Essays* (New Haven, Ct.: Yale University Press, 1911).

19. Samuel Huntington, 'A clash of civilisations?', *Foreign Affairs* Vol. 72, No. 2 (Summer 1993).

20. Ludwig Gumplowicz, *Der Rassenkampf* (Innsbruck: Verlag der Wagner'schen Universitätsbuchhandlung, 1883), p. 345.

21. Ashley Montagu, *The Nature of Human Aggression* (Oxford: Oxford University Press, 1976), pp. 43–5, 137–92.

mutants, die out. Human societies, however, can change the beliefs
and values which are central to their culture within one generation
or less.

Two arguments are possible: one, that cultures come into being
like a random natural mutation, and that like a mutation, any culture can either harm or further the fortunes of a society, condemn-
ing it to decline and go under in a particular environment (like
thin-skinned cold-blooded animals in an ice age) or to flourish
(like animals with thick furs in an ice age). The second argument
runs that human beings, being rational, can objectively analyse the
changing circumstances and rationally adapt and change their culture and their beliefs to take them into account. An example would
be that of the majority of Germans at the end of the Second World
War, who did not follow their leaders into suicide, abandoned the
National Socialists' racist ideology and became enthusiastic supporters of private enterprise and threw all their energy into the
Wirtschaftswunder instead.

There are arguments supporting both cases. Either way, a proclivity towards war has harmed some societies and benefited others,
just as a proclivity towards a pacific conduct of business has harmed
some and benefited some. The Germanic and Slavic warrior tribes
which in the third to fifth centuries invaded the Roman Empire, or
the Turks who invaded the Byzantine Empire during the tenth to
fifteenth centuries were less sophisticated than the empires they
vanquished, and flourished due to their bellicosity. On the other
hand, societies such as that of the Netherlands in the second half
of the seventeenth century, or of Germany and Japan since the
1950s, benefited hugely from propagating a peaceful conduct of
trade, and grew in strength as they abstained from squandering
their forces in wars. But the question remains to what extent one
can steer the process whereby a culture adapts itself to new circumstances. A doctrine, a system of beliefs, tends to be tenacious, and is
rarely totally abandoned without a cataclysmic event forcing a society
to do so; historic examples abound of societies clinging to cultures
which brought them doom, whether these were too pacifistic for
their good, or too bellicose. Even sudden abandonment of one
belief system for another can go to a dangerous extreme. The Jewish
populations of Europe were clearly too little organised, too civic,
and too pacific for their own good between 1933 and 1945; their
heirs in Israel may have gone a notch too far in the opposite direction from the perspective of their own long-term safety in an area
of acute scarcity of vital natural resources (particularly, water). The

suicide of the inhabitants of Masada in the first century who refused to give themselves up alive to the Romans may not be entirely reassuring as the basis of the national myth of a country believed to own nuclear weapons.

None of these speculations about the adaptability of collective beliefs to changed circumstances on the basis of objective evaluations seems very relevant, if societies collectively are driven by unalterable biological laws rather than by beliefs, and if these biological laws include the drive to wage war. For there are a host of factors which could continue to drive human societies into war. Wars for vital resources such as food and water are increasingly likely in large areas of Africa and the Middle East, where rising birth rates make competition for these scarce commodities fierce, and where the expansion of the population itself contributes to the desertification of some of the very food-growing areas on which they rely. Not all the classical biological incentives to go to war, listed by biologists and anthropologists, are of ageless application (for example, the idea of men going to war to find wives for themselves, of which there are examples even in Europe in classical antiquity, sounds quite implausible today).[22] But large-scale war over food or water seems a more likely cause of war in the twenty-first century than in the twentieth. In such a fight for survival, how do weapons of mass destruction, coming on top of revolutionary technological change and population increase, enter into the equation? We must assume that within the next few decades, many countries that are struggling to feed their exploding populations will be capable of acquiring the technology to produce weapons of mass destruction. The latest members of the nuclear club, India and Pakistan, are notoriously plagued by famine, and North Korea, where food shortages reached catastrophic proportions in the late 1990s, used the threat to develop nuclear weapons as a lever to secure international aid. Competition for scarce natural resources militates against peacefulness, and is likely to form a lethal combination when added to the possession of weapons of mass destruction.

22. Examples include the Romans' abduction of the Sabine women, or the abduction of the Trojan womenfolk by the Danaic conquerors (not exactly welcomed by the wives of the latter, who sometimes, as in the case of Klytemnestra, took bloody revenge). By the twentieth century, however, these cases, still known apparently among the tribespeople so popular with anthropologists, seem to have given way to the atrocious maltreatment of women as a side-effect of wars: such cases include the mass rapes committed by Soviet and Japanese soldiers in the Second World War, and by Yugoslav men against those who used to be their own countrywomen in the early 1990s.

How likely, then, is it that all human societies capable of producing weapons of mass destruction have adapted to the dangers posed by them? Are they at least in the process of adapting to the fact that these weapons, used even just singly, can create an environmental catastrophe? And that used massively, they can eradicate all higher forms of life in very large areas, affect others horribly, and possibly even make the entire globe uninhabitable for humans?

HAVE NUCLEAR WEAPONS ABOLISHED MAJOR WAR?

Since the First World War, international norms have moved towards the recognition that war should be outlawed. War was specifically rejected as a means of settling disputes in the Briand-Kellogg Pact of 1928, that is, before the nuclear age. But this statement of good will did not protect its signatories from those who refused to sign it. The United Nations, who adopted their Charter some five weeks before Hiroshima and Nagasaki, explicitly outlawed war, except in self-defence. Neither was thus directly influenced by nuclear weapons.

Indeed, Britons, Frenchmen and Americans were on the whole pleased when their own countries acquired nuclear weapons (and many NATO members were and are glad that the USA had them). This can be reconciled with their growing distaste for war: as Richard Crossman pointed out, nuclear weapons could be interpreted as obviating the need for large conscript forces, which were very unpopular in Britain and the USA, making reliance on nuclear deterrence all the more popular. Crossman thought this must be the case in any 'affluent society' in general, accounting for the difficulties 'of turning the citizen of a modern democracy into a fighting soldier'. Moreover, in Crossman's view the Korean War showed that

> most Western soldiers are unwilling to fight on level terms with a Communist enemy. Indeed, one of the moral problems of Western defence is our reluctance to be killed, compared with the stoic fatalism of a Chinese or a Russian soldier. That is why no Western army can sustain a casualty rate such as the Russians sustained in the Second World War and the Chinese in Korea. . . . The truth is that the nuclear weapon was developed in the West as a substitute for the fighting soldiers, and nuclear annihilation came to be regarded as a means of avoiding the long, evenly matched slaughter of battles of position.[23]

23. Richard Crossman, 'Western defence in the 1960s', *Journal of the RUSI* Vol. CVI (August 1961), pp. 334f.

The Anglo-American defence academic Laurence Martin argued that in the West, the belief in the 'utility of force' was waning:[24] he saw 'consensus' on this tenet stemming on the one hand from the rise of the 'gods of welfare economics' and the rejection of martial glory, and from the conclusion 'that trade, investment . . . are the route to success, rather than conquest and mercantilist rivalry', conclusions typical of industrial societies. This assumes that 'the chief national purposes are economic', and that in societies with mass politics and with mass media clamouring for steady economic improvement, this goal is immutably fixed. On the other hand he saw

> changes in the instruments of conflict and in particular to the self-defeating nature of the supreme nuclear power wielded by the great states. Just as the modern goals of states are no longer to be sought by force, so military means have become incommensurate with any conceivable rational end. Between nuclear powers, . . . victory would be neither necessary to destroy one adversary nor sufficient to preserve the other, still less to achieve the victor's purpose. By fear of the process of escalation . . . the inhibitions of strategic nuclear power reach down to inhibit the use of lesser force for lesser ends.[25]

Views along these lines, noting as dangerous Western societies' increasing distaste for war, or deploring it in view of the unabated martial spirit elsewhere in the world, can be found throughout Western societies. Oddly, nuclear weapons were thus to a large extent the symbol of the rejection by many Liberal democracies of major war, not the expression of any bellicose intentions or attitudes. Nevertheless, these same states have been involved in many wars, including some with considerable escalatory potential (Korea, Vietnam), and were never made desperate enough to contemplate the use of nuclear weapons seriously after 1945, even though the USA, for one, used chemical weapons in several wars. How differently might events have unfolded if their opponents in these wars had reacted less prudently? And what about the possession of weapons of mass destruction by other powers? What can we say about their future behaviour in crises and wars with a strong escalatory potential?

Essentially, there are four schools of thought with regard to the question whether nuclear weapons have abolished wars. One is the

24. Laurence Martin, 'The utility of military force', in 'Force in modern society: its place in international politics', *Adelphi Papers* No. 102 (1973), p. 16.
25. *Ibid.*

school of those who believe this to be the case for war in general –
a school that was very short-lived. In 1954 Sir John Slessor, who had
been a chief of the Royal Air Force, confidently proclaimed 'that
war has abolished itself because the atomic and the hydrogen bombs
have found their way into the armouries of the world. So the greatest disservice anyone could do in the cause of peace would be to
abolish nuclear arms on either side.'[26]

All too early, it became clear that nuclear weapons had certainly
not abolished *all* war. But the question to this day remains whether
nuclear weapons have abolished *major* war, as a second group of
thinkers argued. The restriction to total or major war, rather than
all war, had become obvious to another Briton even earlier. Immediately after the atomic bombardment of Hiroshima and Nagasaki,
at the same time as Bernard Brodie and Admiral Castex wrote their
first remarkable comments on the new age, the retired naval officer
and former MP Sir Stephen King-Hall wrote, 'Total War has reached
its ultimate and absolute physical development, it has made political and economic nationalism a meaningless thing and so *Total
War has abolished itself.*'[27] Many other British military men and
politicians thought nuclear war 'unthinkable', 'because nobody can
have the slightest hope of gaining anything in a nuclear war'. Therefore, besides thinking it totally 'impracticable' that nuclear weapons could ever be abolished worldwide, some of them thought until
the end of the century that it would be disadvantageous to give
them up, as such an act would open the door again to major *conventional* war.[28]

Among this school of thought which we might call that of the
nuclear optimists must be counted also those extreme optimists
like the French air force general Pierre Marie Gallois, who even in
the 1960s argued that the more members there were in the nuclear
club, the stabler the world would be – nuclear deterrence could be
made multilateral, he thought, and could benefit the entire world.[29]

26. Italics in original: Marshal of the R.A.F. Sir John Slessor, *Strategy for the West*
(London: Cassell, 1954), p. 15.

27. Newsletter of 16 August 1945, cited in King-Hall, *Defence in the Nuclear Age*
(London: Victor Gollancz, 1958), p. 11, my italics.

28. Sir Dermot Boyle, 'Thoughts on the nuclear deterrent', *Journal of the RUSI*
Vol. CVII (Feb. 1962), p. 12; Peter Blaker, 'Das Kräfteverhältnis zwischen konvention-
ellen und nuklearen Streitkräften und die Rolle der neuen Technologie', *Europäische
Wehrkunde* Vol. 32, No. 4 (April 1983), p. 160; Michael Quinlan, 'Nuclear weapons –
the basic issues', *The Ampleforth Journal* Vol. 91, part 2.

29. Pierre M. Gallois, 'New teeth for NATO', *Foreign Affairs* Vol. 39, No. 1 (October
1960).

It is from Gallois that the American political scientist Kenneth Waltz took this idea, and who passed it on to one of his pupils, John Mearsheimer, who proclaimed nuclear proliferation – even in Europe – to be inevitable, and manageable, in view of the respect on all sides for nuclear weapons.[30] A late, classic statement of the importance of nuclear weapons for the banning of war is that of the American political scientist Robert Jervis, who, as the Cold War was drawing to a close, once again enumerated all the reasons why nuclear weapons made major war unprofitable.[31] This begs the question to which we shall return presently whether a society measures profitability in terms of economic gain, or numbers of martyrs' crowns in heaven, or the flourishing of one's own race or social system despite high casualty figures on all sides. Who in the West would have imagined during the Second World War that the National Socialist régime would give priority to the extermination of Jews over other parts of the war effort, even though the former in many ways detracted scarce resources from the latter?

A third school of thought doubts whether nuclear weapons have produced the stability in which, to quote the by now hackneyed words of Churchill, peace is the 'sturdy child of terror'. They would point to the danger of fatal errors (Kennedy's famous 'There is always some so-and-so who doesn't get the word' when he heard that one of the American U-2 spy-planes had overflown Russia during height of the Cuban Missile Crisis and was shot down);[32] they pointed to pre-emptive war options (striking pre-emptively in the expectation of an enemy attack – a real danger when both the USA in the 1960s, and the USSR long thereafter maintained a counter-force strategy);[33] and they pointed to the possibility of accidents (for example, a flock of geese being mistaken by the American early warning system for an incoming missile attack,[34] or an announced Norwegian missile test setting off Russian automatic nuclear retaliation mechanisms even in the 1990s, which were stopped within minutes of disaster).

A fourth school of thought has held for a long time that major war has become obsolete, regardless of nuclear weapons. This school

30. John Mearsheimer, 'Back to the future: instability in Europe after the Cold War', *International Security* Vol. 15, No. 1 (Summer 1990).
31. Robert Jervis, 'The political effects of nuclear weapons', *International Security* Vol. 13, No. 2 (Fall 1988), pp. 80–90.
32. Quoted in Jervis, 'The political effects of nuclear weapons', p. 88.
33. See Chapter 2.
34. Cf. Peter Pringle and William Arkin, *SIOP: The Secret US Plan for Nuclear War* (New York: W.W. Norton, 1983).

goes back to Auguste Comte, who wrote in 1842, just before the rise of 'nation-states' with their centralised governments throughout Europe, before the spread of the Industrial Revolution and the technological innovations which together formed the basis for the constitution of the War Machine, and before Social Darwinism seized Europe like a mental illness, 'At last the time has come when serious and lasting war must disappear completely among the human élite'[35]. Unfortunately, subsequent events proved him very wrong indeed. Raymond Aron commented almost a century later, that objectively seen, Comte *should* have been right, if only the European leaders had seen the cost-benefit calculations in the same way as Comte, if only they had calculated on the basis of economic gains, exports, trade interests, and social welfare costs in times of peace in relation to the cost of war in terms of losses of productivity, manpower, etc.[36]

After Aron, a number of people came back to this idea in the Cold War, including John Mueller and Carl Kaysen in the USA. Carl Kaysen in his review of Mueller's celebrated book *Retreat from Doomsday*[37] sums up the main problem with this argument: not unlike Comte, Mueller's thesis is that 'major war was already becoming obsolete by the time of the First World War; World War II repeated and reinforced that lesson' (Kaysen's words).[38] In other words, it was quite irrational of the powers involved to go to war in 1939, which they should have known even in 1919, and yet they *did* go to war in 1939, however unreasonable this option looks from the perspective of John Mueller's analysis. Yes, certain economic interpretations of the situation of Germany in 1939 should have led Hitler to conclude that he stood more to lose than to gain from antagonising the major powers, and that the territory of Germany could easily support even a growing population (it has done since, as the population density after 1945 was greater than it ever had been before, and continued to grow for some time). But for whatever reasons, Hitler believed only in a Malthusian interpretation of the world in which Germany needed more 'living space' if its population grew, and if anybody tried to persuade him to think otherwise, he or she remained singularly unsuccessful.

35. Quoted in Raymond Aron, *War and Industrial Society* (London: the London School of Economics and Political Science, 1958), p. 3.

36. *Ibid.*, pp. 4–8.

37. Mueller, *Retreat from Doomsday*.

38. Carl Kaysen, 'Is war obsolete? A review essay', *International Security* Vol. 14, No. 4 (Spring 1990), pp. 42f.

Thus the most objective of interpretations of a situation may not necessarily be shared by the crucial leaders who will decide on war and peace; they only need to base their reasoning on different beliefs, and August Comte's arguments, like those of John Mueller, will simply be brushed aside. As the anthropologist Anderson Nettleship has remarked, 'Man's environment . . . is largely conceptual and as such is subject to endless imaginary manipulation . . .'[39] The tens of thousands of Japanese soldiers who fought suicidally (the *kamikaze* pilots being the most famous examples of a much more general tendency), and the mass suicides of Japanese civilians prior to the American invasion of their isles, recall the self-sacrifice of Masada – only we know, while the Japanese could not imagine, that they had less to fear from the Americans than the Jews of Masada had from the Roman slave-drivers. We simply cannot count on our beliefs about the world, and our system of priorities, being shared by all other cultures or by key decision-makers.

Raymond Aron, and following him, John Mueller and Carl Kaysen, argued that it is simply not in the interest of highly industrialised societies to go to war with one another. While Aron's and Kaysen's arguments still hinged on the Cold War situation of mutual deterrence, and on the importance of nuclear weapons in this equation,[40] John Mueller has argued that nuclear weapons were essentially irrelevant to the move away from major war.[41] Aron thought the Cold War bipolar system unstable, Kaysen thought it stable, but all of them assumed that it would be highly industrialised and domestically fairly stable powers who would own the world's nuclear weapons. Their arguments may thus still hold, but with reference to certain countries and certain cultures only.

Our survey of the development of anti-war movements (Chapter 4) has shown that Aron, Mueller and Kaysen were right in as far as there was a growing revulsion against war in many Western societies in the twentieth century, that this was a minority phenomenon before the invention of nuclear weapons, but that it assumed considerable political weight after 1945. Lessons that had precisely *not* been learned fully by 1918 (for example in Germany) were well and truly internalised by 1945. Many liberal democracies, particularly those that have experienced the world wars at close hand, have

39. Anderson Nettleship, sectional introduction, in Nettleship, Dalegivens and Nettleship (eds.), *War, its Causes and Correlates*, p. 393.

40. Aron, *War and Industrial Society*; Kaysen, 'Is war obsolete?', pp. 42–64.

41. John Mueller, 'The essential irrelevance of nuclear weapons: stability in the postwar world', *International Security* Vol. 13, No. 2 (Fall 1988), pp. 55–79.

embraced beliefs which reject war, particularly major war, as a way of settling disputes, supporting the basic tenet of the UN Charter. But is this true for all societies?

Neither Aron nor Mueller nor Kaysen speculated about the consequences of nuclear proliferation to countries that were poor, overpopulated, dominated by religious belief systems with a fanatical wing, where basic resources are scarce and political systems unstable. None of them predicted a situation, in which, due to the disappearance of a bipolar framework in which the two superpowers kept smaller powers in check, the latter have – or think they have – more freedom for action, as demonstrated by Iraq's invasion of Kuwait in 1990, or indeed by India's and Pakistan's nuclear tests in 1998. As NATO governments made efforts in the wake of the Euromissile crisis (1979–83) to inform their publics about all the safety devices existing on Western nuclear systems, fewer people subsequently worried about nightmare scenarios of nuclear war by accident; little did they anticipate that thousands of tactical nuclear weapons would one day litter the former Soviet Union, with unpaid guards, rusting shelters, and decaying safety devices, practically inviting irresponsible black marketeers to come and steal them.

In the mid-1990s, as the non-proliferation treaty came up for extension (which was agreed in 1995 for an indefinite period), the 'declared' nuclear powers (the USA, Russia, Britain, France and China) displayed great commitment to stopping the spread of nuclear weapons to other states. But while the first four reduced their own arsenals considerably, they did not make any further moves to implement their commitment of 1968, when the treaty was originally signed, namely to move towards *complete* nuclear disarmament themselves. They all professed great shock, however, to see India and Pakistan attempt to join their club in 1998.

And there is not just nuclear proliferation to worry about. Algeria, Libya, Iraq have long been working on biological and chemical weapons. Again, it is worth remembering that certain chemical weapons are able, in a certain dosage, to have effects on living beings that are comparable to a low-yield atomic explosion. Scientists believe that two aircraft with tanks of Sarin, sprayed like pesticides over a city, could kill as many people as first-generation nuclear weapons, that is up to 100,000 people. Biological weapons can be even more devastating: a small aircraft with a 20 kg bomb of Anthrax, released above a large urban conglomerate, could result in 20 million deaths. The difference between the lethality of nuclear, and chemical, or particularly biological, weapons is not as clear as it used to be. Moreover, biological weapons could be produced in a moderate-sized laboratory; no nuclear power station or large plants are needed here.[42]

Unlike the non-proliferation treaty, which tolerates the possession of nuclear weapons by the declared nuclear weapons states of the 1960s, conditional upon their work in good faith towards their elimination, a 1975 convention totally proscribes the ownership of biological weapons. This convention, which was signed by 158 states (except Algeria, Sudan and Israel) was ratified by 140. Its shortcoming is that it does not include a verification régime, and experts agree that the verification of the non-production and ownership of biological weapons would be much more difficult than the verification of the non-production and non-ownership of nuclear weapons. A convention on the elimination of chemical weapons was signed by 165 states in the spring of 1997. Iraq, Libya, Syria and North Korea refused to sign this convention. Even though it would be easier to verify the observance of this treaty than of the biological weapons convention, compliance, here, is also difficult to assure.[43]

What will happen to weapons of mass destruction, indeed to war more generally, will continue to depend on beliefs at all levels of societies – the beliefs of crucial, powerful individuals (such as leaders of governments), the beliefs of influential groups, the structures and tools available to them. It is a particular characteristic of weapons of mass destruction that while it takes a sophisticated scientific apparatus to create them, once built, they can in principle be used by very few people, unless elaborate security systems are deliberately put into place to prevent unauthorised use. This means that nuclear or biological weapons, once acquired by any Third World power or indeed by a wealthy non-state actor (a terrorist group, an international criminal organisation), could be used to great effect with quite primitive means of delivery. While the 'bomb in the suitcase' or in the merchant vessel, a scenario feared since the beginning of the nuclear age, would not be the end of the world, it could be the end of a big city. It is not clear how nuclear deterrence (nuclear reprisals against whom?) could frighten terrorists or gangsters off using such weapons for blackmail on a gigantic scale. Many frightening scenarios can thus be imagined which make

42. Victor A. Utgoff, 'Nuclear weapons and the deterrence of biological and chemical warfare', Occasional Paper No. 36 (Henry L. Stimson Center: Oct. 1997), pp. 4f.
43. *Ibid.*, pp. 11–13.

it difficult to see Hiroshima and Nagasaki as the nuclear use to end all nuclear use.

It is easy to imagine, for example, that new proprietors of weapons of mass destruction are as naïve about their effects as NATO powers were until well into the 1960s and Soviet planners until the mid-1980s. (For example, in the 1950s, NATO deployed short-range nuclear missiles the lethal radius of which would have encompassed the soldiers firing them; Western plans for the large-scale use of earth-detonated 'Atomic Demolition Munitions' took little account of the particularly massive nuclear fall-out which these weapons would have generated.) It is quite imaginable that a régime might use nuclear or biological weapons on a neighbouring country or a remote rebellious region, ignoring the environmental catastrophe they would trigger, and the effects on their own country. Another all too credible scenario is that of a régime resorting to the use of such weapons if made truly desperate, seeing that they (and perhaps their families) would not themselves survive a surrender any more than Mussolini survived the end of the Second World War in Italy. While these are not necessarily doomsday scenarios for the entire world, the use of a handful of nuclear weapons might still render large regions radioactive, and bring on an ecological catastrophe for a whole continent. The effects of biological weapons are more difficult to predict, and could have wider consequences still.

Conclusions

At the end of the twentieth century, does it seem as though nuclear weapons have made a considerable impact on the history of warfare, indeed on the history of humankind in general? We can say with some relief that they contributed to preventing a Third World War being fought between the Warsaw Treaty Organisation and NATO.[44] But how confident can we be, half a century on, that they have banished major war even on the Indian subcontinent, in the Middle East where Saddam Hussein's physicists were working on a nuclear programme prior to the Gulf War, or in North Africa? The

44. See for example the fascinating study of Milton Leitenberg of the Center for International and Security Studies at Maryland, who has shown the risk-proneness, yet the moderation in the response of both sides in small-scale conflicts throughout the Cold War: 'Nuclear Weapons and 50 years of International Political History: Risks, Dangers, Threats, Crises, Proposals and Consideration of Use', unpublished MS (1997), cited with the permission of the author.

answer, it is suggested here, lies not only in technological accomplishment and state control, but most importantly in the beliefs and values of those striving to develop weapons of mass destruction, and is not exclusively linked to nuclear weapons. In European and North American societies, on the whole, nuclear weapons merely catalysed an existing revulsion of war, amplifying and strengthening it to become the basis of future policies of deterring, rather than fighting, major war. Yet it is doubtful that the belief predominating in these societies that major war must be avoided in future, will find permanent, universal acceptance, even in Western societies.

It is not accidental that weapons of mass destruction have been invented in an unprecedented period in human history, where population growth, and strife for ever scarcer basic resources, might well be the cause for cataclysmic wars of the twenty-first century. Whether or not these will become catastrophes involving the use of weapons of mass destruction depends very much on whether all societies of this world not only *can* adapt, but *will* adapt to the destructive potential of such weapons by embracing the belief that a war that might lead to the use of such weapons could not benefit them in any way. If our conviction that a 'mutation' of attitudes towards war must take place, that we must collectively learn this lesson, fails to persuade *all* cultures of the world, and all fanatical sects, cults, and the last individual with access to a biological and chemical laboratory, weapons of mass destruction could yet become a turning point, indeed a final point, of human history in a catastrophe beyond our imagination.

At the dawn of the third millennium, it is thus not easy to be confident that the sacrifice of Hiroshima and Nagasaki has once and for all banished the danger of major war for all mankind, as the peace foundation in Hiroshima hopes.

Useful Further Reading

The rôle of nuclear weapons in concluding the Second World War is best discussed in J.C. Buton, *Japan's Decision to Surrender* (Stanford, CA: Stanford University Press, 1954); Herbert Feis, *The Atomic Bomb and the End of World War II* (Princeton NJ:, Princeton UP, 1966); Gar Alperovitz, *The Decision to Use the Atomic Bomb and the Architecture of an American Myth* (1995, this edn.: London: Fontana Press, 1996); Dennis Wainstock, *The Decision to Drop the Atomic Bomb* (Westport, Ct: Praeger, 1996). Key articles include Rufus E. Miles, Jr., 'Hiroshima: the strange myth of half a million American lives saved', *International Security* Vol. 10, No. 2 (Fall 1985), pp. 121–40; Barton J. Bernstein, 'Understanding the atomic bomb and the Japanese surrender', *Diplomatic History* Vol. 19, No. 2 (Spring 1995); Lawrence Freedman and Saki Dockrill, 'Hiroshima: A strategy of shock', in Saki Dockrill (ed.), *From Pearl Harbor to Hiroshima: The Second World War in Asia and the Pacific* (London: Macmillan, 1994), pp. 191–211. On the effects of the bomb on the Japanese, see Robert Jay Lifton, *Death in Life: Survivors of Hiroshima* (New York: Basic Books, 1967); Hiroshima Peace Culture Foundation, *Eyewitness Testimonies* (Hiroshima: HPCF, 1991); Ian Buruma, *The Wages of Guilt: Memories of War in Germany and Japan* (New York: Meridian/Penguin, 1995); Laura Hein and Mark Selden (eds.), *Living with the Bomb: American and Japanese Cultural Conflicts in the Nuclear Age* (New York: East Gate Books/M.E. Sharp, 1997).

On the development of air power strategy, see the seminal George H. Quester, *Deterrence before Hiroshima: The Airpower Background of Modern Strategy* (New York: John Wiley, 1966) and Robert A. Pape, *Bombing to Win: Air Power and Coercion in War* (Ithaca: Cornell University Press, 1996). See also Malcolm Smith, *British Air Strategy Between the Wars* (Oxford: Clarendon, 1984); Richard Overy, *The Air War 1939–1945* (London: Europa, 1980); Mark Clodfelter, *The Limits of Air Power: The American Bombing of North Vietnam* (New York: the Free Press, 1989); David M. Glantz, *The Military Strategy of the Soviet Union: A History* (London: Frank Cass, 1992); Air Marshal M.J.

Armitage and Air Commodore R.A. Mason, *Air Power in the Nuclear Age, 1945–82: Theory and Practice* (London: Macmillan, 1983).

Key articles on air power strategy include R.J. Overy, 'Air power and the origins of deterrence theory before 1939', *Journal of Strategic Studies* Vol. 15, No. 1 (March 1992); Tami Davis Biddle, 'British and American approaches to strategic bombing: their origins and implementation in the World War II combined bomber offensive', in *Journal of Strategic Studies* Vol. 18, No. 1 (March 1995); Klaus Maier, 'Total War and German air doctrine before the Second World War' in Wilhelm Deist (ed.), *The German Military in the Age of Total War* (Oxford: Berg, 1985); W. Hays Parks, ' "Precision" and "area" bombing: who did which, and when?', in *Journal of Strategic Studies* Vol. 18, No. 1 (March 1995); Williamson Murray, 'A tale of two doctrines: The *Luftwaffe's* 'Conduct of Air War' and the USAF's Manual 1-1', *Journal of Strategic Studies* Vol. 6, No. 4 (December 1983); Williamson Murray, 'The Luftwaffe before the Second World War: a mission, a strategy?', *Journal of Strategic Studies* Vol. 4, No. 3 (Sept. 1981); David Chuter, 'Triumph of the will? Or, why surrender is not always inevitable', *Review of International Studies* Vol. 23 (1997).

On the development of nuclear strategy, see Lawrence Freedman, *The Evolution of Nuclear Strategy* (2nd edn., London: Macmillan, 1989); Beatrice Heuser, *NATO, Britain, France and the FRG: Nuclear Strategies and Forces in Europe, 1949–2000* (London: Macmillan, 1997, ppb. 1999); Beatrice Heuser, 'Warsaw Pact military doctrines in the 70s and 80s: findings in the East German archives', *Comparative Strategy* Vol. 12, No. 4 (Oct.–Dec. 1993); Beatrice Heuser, 'Victory in a nuclear war? A comparison of NATO and WTO war aims and strategies', *Contemporary European History* (special issue on NATO's 50th anniversary, April 1999) and again David Glantz, *The Military Strategy of the Soviet Union.*

On Total War, the defining book is Erich Ludendorff's *Der Totale Krieg* (Munich: Ludendorffs Verlag GmbH, 1935), translated by Dr A.S. Rappoport as *The Nation at War* (London: Hutchinson & Co., 1936). Key literature on 'total war' includes Hannah Arendt, *The Origins of Totalitarianism* (New York: Harcourt, Brace, n.d. {1949}); Raymond Aron, *Les Guerres en Chaîne*, translated as *The Century of Total War*, trans. E.W. Dickes and O.S. Griffiths (London: Derek Verschoyle, 1954); Lucy Davidowicz, *The War against the Jews, 1933–1945* (Harmondsworth, Penguin Ppb., 1997); Eric Markusen and David Kopf, *The Holocaust and Strategic Bombing* (Boulder, Co.: Westview Press, 1995); Lothar Gruchmann, *Totaler Krieg* (Munich: dtv,

1991) and, used with some circumspection in view of the looser use of the term 'total war', Berenice Carroll, *Design for Total War: Arms and Economics in the Third Reich* (The Hague: Mouton, 1968). Literature about the development of pacifism and pacifism and general reflections on the morality of war includes Frederick H. Russell: *The Just War in the Middle Ages* (Cambridge: Cambridge University Press, 1975); Pierre Viaud (ed.), *Les religions et la guerre* (Paris: Cerf, 1991); Peter Brock, *Pacifism in Europe to 1914* (Princeton, NJ: Princeton U.P., 1972); Peter Brock, *Twentieth-Century Pacifism* (New York: Van Nostrand-Reinhold, 1970); Keith Robbins, *The Abolition of War: The 'Peace Movement' in Britain, 1914–1919* (Cardiff: University of Wales Press, 1976); Martin Ceadel, *Pacifism in Britain, 1914–1943: the Defining of a Faith* (Oxford: Clarendon 1980); Martin Ceadel, *The Origins of War Prevention* (Oxford: Clarendon, 1996); Michael Howard (ed.), *Restraints on War* (Oxford: Oxford University Press, 1979); Christopher Driver, *The Disarmers: A Study in Protest* (London: Hodder & Stoughton, 1964); Pierre Lellouche (ed.), *Pacifisme et dissuasion* (Paris: IFRI, 1983); Frank Parkin, *Middle Class Radicalism: The Social Bases of the British Campaign for Nuclear Disarmament* (Machester: Manchester University Press, 1968); Richard Taylor, *Against the Bomb: The British Peace Movement, 1958–1965* (Oxford: Clarendon Press, 1988); Philip Sabin, *The Third World War Scare in Britain* (London: Macmillan, 1986). On other European countries, there are two very useful articles: Hans-Jürgen Rautenberg, 'Friedensbewegungen und Nukleardebatte in westeuropäischen Nato-Staaten', *Beiträge zur Konfliktforschung* Vol. 13, No. 3 (Autumn 1983); Wilfried von Bredow, 'Sozialer Protest und Friedensbewegung in Westeuropa', *Beiträge zur Konfliktforschung* Vol. 15, No. 4 (1985).

On the industrial revolution and its consequences, see David S. Landes, *The Unbound Prometheus: Technological Change and Industrial Development in Western Europe from 1750 to the Present* (London: Cambridge University Press, 1969); Richard Sylla and Gianni Toniolo (eds.), *Patterns of European Industrialisation* (London: Routledge, 1991); Michael D. Biddiss, *The Age of the Masses: Ideas and Society in Europe since 1870* (Hassocks: Harvester, 1977). On human aggressiveness, conflict, the history of warfare and the evolution of inter-societal relations, the following works might point to the contributions made by various disciplines: Martin Nettleship, R. Dalegivens and Anderson Nettleship (eds.), *War, its Causes and Correlates* (The Hague: Mouton, 1975); John B. Calhoun, 'Population density and social pathology', *Scientific American* No. 206 (1962); Dennis L. Meadow and William W. III Behrens., *Dynamics of Growth in a Finite World* (Cambridge,

Mass.: Wright-Allen Press, 1974); Wolfgang Lutz (ed.), *The Future Population of the World* (London: Earth Scan, 1994); Leon Bramson and George W. Goethals (eds.), *War – Studies from Psychology, Sociology, Anthropology* (2nd edn., New York: Basic Books, 1968); Stanley Milgram: *Obedience to Authority: An Experimental View* (originally 1974, repr. London: Printer & Martin, 1997); Paul Turner and David Pitt (eds.), *The Anthropology of War & Peace: Perspectives on the Nuclear Age* (Granby, MA: Bergin & Garvey, 1989); Ashley Montagu, *The Nature of Human Aggression* (Oxford: Oxford University Press, 1976);

The debate about the end of total or major war includes Raymond Aron, *War and Industrial Society* (London: the London School of Economics and Political Science, 1958); John Mueller, 'The essential irrelevance of nuclear weapons: stability in the postwar world', *International Security* Vol. 13, No. 2 (Fall 1988); John Mueller, *Retreat from Doomsday: On the Obsolescence of Major War* (New York: Basic Books, 1989); Carl Kaysen, 'Is war obsolete? A review essay', *International Security* Vol. 14, No. 4 (Spring 1990).

Index

Aachen, 29
Abyssinia (Ethiopia), 52, 118
Acheson, Dean, 14
Afghanistan, 71, 164
Albigensian Crusade, 115
  see also Cathars
Algeria, 65, 78, 220–1
Allport, Gordon W., 208, 210
Alperovitz, Gar, 8–9, 15, 17, 20–3
American Civil War, 116, 190, 194,
  204
Anabaptists, 142–3
Anderson, General Orville, 64
Antwerp, 60
Aquinas, St. Thomas, 141
Arab–Israeli Wars, 65, 75–6, 131
  see also Israel
Aragon, Louis, 185
Arendt, Hannah, 111–12, 121
Armitage, Marshal M.G., 74
Aron, Raymond, 112–14, 130,
  218–20
Ashmore, General E.B., 50
Athens, 188
Attila, 115, 195
Attlee, Clement, 14
Augsburg, 29
Augustine of Hippo, St., 141, 156,
  178, 181, 189
Auschwitz, 28, 121, 131, 133–4,
  181, 190, 196
Austria, 13, 116, 145, 149, 210

Badajoz, 52
Bahr, Egon, 168
Baldwin, Hanson, 13

Baldwin, Stanley, 50
Baptists, 143
Barbusse, Henri, 148
Barcelona, 52
Barmen, 29
Barre, Raymond, 88
Baruch, Bernard, 137
Batovrin, Sergej, 161
Beach, General Sir Hugh, 139
Behncke, Rear-Admiral Paul, 38
Beijing, 52
Belgium, 38, 40, 60, 117, 151, 163,
  174, 187–8
Berlin, 29–30, 55, 57, 62–3, 120,
  168
Bernstein, Barton, 17, 22
Bethmann Hollweg, Moritz August
  von, 38
Beuve-Méry, Hubert, 185
Biddle, Tami Davis, 62
Biermann, Wolf, 161
biological weapons, 220–3
Blackett, P.M.S., 164, 167
Bochum, 29
Bogomils, 141
Bohemian Brethren, 142
Böll, Heinrich, 169
Bonhoeffer, Dietrich, 171
Bonn, 163, 166, 168
Bosnia-Hercegovina, 78–9, 174–5,
  184, 190, 201
Brandt, Willy, 168
Brecht, Bertolt, 170
Bremen, 29
Briand, Aristide, 151
British Bombing Survey, 25, 56

Brock, Peter, 140, 152
Brockway, Lord (Fenner), 165
Brodie, Bernard, 94, 100, 216
Brodin, Colonel, 65
Brunswick, 29
Brussels, 146, 163
Buchenwald, 133
Buddhism, 175, 189
Bulgaria, 14, 159
Bundy, McGeorge, 184
Burma, 125, 175
Buruma, Ian, 124–5, 176
Butow, Robert, 23
Byrnes, James, 15, 17, 22
Byzantine Empire, 203, 212

Campaign for Nuclear
    Disarmament (CND), 164–7
Canada, 195
Carter, Jimmy, 99
Carthage, 114–15, 195
Carver, Field Marshal Lord, 139
Casablanca Conference (1943), 13
Castex, Admiral Raoul, 35, 94, 216
Cathars, 141–2
Catholicism, Roman Catholic
    Church, 141, 144–5, 156, 163,
    171, 178–81, 185–9, 209
    see also Christianity
Ceadel, Martin, 136, 160
Challener, Richard, 116
Chechnya, 79
chemical weapons, 220–1, 223
Chennault, General Claire, 21
Chernobyl, 161
Chiang Kai Shek, 123
Childers, Major E., 40
China, 7, 12, 16, 21, 28, 31, 33, 52,
    63, 71, 85, 119, 122–6, 137,
    158, 175, 195, 209, 220
Christianity, 140–1, 151, 162, 173,
    189, 197
Chungking, 52
Churchill, Winston S., 14, 29, 54,
    217
Chuter, David, 82

Clausewitz, Carl von, 46, 48, 61,
    80–1, 91, 103–5, 107, 162,
    194–5, 204
Clodfelter, Mark, 73
Cobden, Richard, 104
Cologne, 28–9, 54, 63
Communism, 152, 159
Communist International
    (Komintern), 152, 158
Communist Information Bureau
    (Kominform), 159, 162
    see also Socialism
Comte, Auguste, 218–19
Constantine I (Roman Emperor),
    140, 182
Cordoba, 52
Cot, Pierre, 184
Coudenhove Kalergi, Richard
    Count, 151
Coventry, 28, 30, 63
Crossman, Richard, 64, 214
Cuba, 83
Cyprus, 188
Czechoslovakia, 71, 115, 132, 153,
    161

Darmstadt, 29
Daudet, Léon, 105
Davidowicz, Lucy, 112
Dayan, General Moshe, 74–5
Denmark, 116, 145, 174
Dockrill, Saki, 24
Dorgelès, Roland, 148
Dortmund, 29
Douhet, General Giulio, 39, 44–50,
    52, 57, 59, 67, 75, 78–82, 100,
    110, 117–18, 128, 134
Dover, 38
Dresden, 22, 26, 28, 30, 34, 55, 63,
    76, 126, 132–3, 173
Duisburg, 29
Düsseldorf, 29

Egorov, A.I., 46
Egypt, 74–6
Einstein, Albert, 154

Eisenhower, Dwight D., 9, 22, 55
Elberfeld, 29
Emden, 29
Emmerson, Ralph Waldo, 153
Engels, Friedrich, 146
Enola Gay, 18
Eppelmann, Reiner, 173
Erasmus of Rotterdam, Desiderius,
    144
Eshkol, Levi, 74
Essen, 29

Falklands War, 98, 166
Falls, Cyril, 109, 130
Fascism, 159
    see also Totalitarianism
Fat Man, 18, 155
Feis, Herbert, 8, 157
Felmy, General Hellmuth, 59
Finland, 64
First World War, 5, 36, 38–41, 45,
    48, 50–1, 60, 80, 82, 94–5,
    97, 104–9, 112, 116, 136–7,
    145–52, 154–5, 158, 174, 194,
    196, 201, 204, 211, 214, 218
Fischer, Joschka (Josef), 168
Flensburg, 29
Foch, Marshal Ferdinand, 44
Foerster, Gerhard, 105
France, 33, 38, 43, 47, 65, 81,
    85, 87–8, 94, 96, 105, 115,
    118–19, 128, 137, 145–8,
    150–1, 153–4, 160, 170, 181,
    184–7, 190, 195, 204, 206,
    209, 214, 220
Franco, General Francisco, 152,
    188
Franco-Prussian War (1870–71),
    104, 116, 204
Frankfurt am Main, 29
Frankland, Noble, 54
Freedman, Lawrence, 24
French Revolutionary Wars, 105,
    115–16, 143, 195, 204–5
Friedrichshafen, 29

Frunze, Mikhail Vassilievich,
    45–8
Fuller, J.F.C., 45–6, 67, 128

Galbraith, J. Kenneth, 19
Galen, Cardinal Clemens August
    Graf, 171
Gallois, General Pierre Marie, 79,
    216–17
Gandhi, Mohandas Karamchand,
    153
Garrison, Jim, 135
Gaulle, General Charles de, 67
Geneva Convention, 138
Genevoix, Maurice, 148
genocide, 33–4, 104, 127–34
Germany, 12–13, 15, 28–33, 43, 47,
    50–1, 53–7, 60–4, 66, 81–2,
    85, 89, 94, 97, 106–8, 112–13,
    116–22, 125–7, 132–3, 145–54,
    159, 161, 166–74, 176, 181,
    185–8, 206, 209–10, 212,
    217–18
Ghaddafi, Colonel, 81
Giono, Jean, 148
Glasgow, 38
Göbbels, Joseph, 110, 120–1
Godzilla, 27–8
Goering, Hermann, 57, 60, 76
Goldschmidt, Walter, 209
Gorbachëv, Mikhail V., 98,
    161–2
Grass, Günther, 170
Graves, Robert, 148
Gray, Colin, 98–9
Greater East Asia Co-Prosperity
    Sphere, 34, 123
Greece, 14, 74, 178, 194, 199, 203,
    205
Greek Civil War, 65
Grew, Joseph, 13
Griffin, Jonathan, 49
Grotius, Hugo, 141
Grozny, 79
Guernica, 51

Gulf War (1990–91), 32, 76–80, 83, 99–100, 166, 174–5, 184, 201, 210, 223
Gumplowitz, Ludwig, 211

Habsburg Empire (Holy Roman Empire), 203
Hagen, 29
Hague Conventions, 42, 137–8, 145, 179
Haiphong, 73–4
Halle, 173
Hamburg, 26, 28–30, 34, 53, 63, 126, 132
Hankow, 52
Hanoi, 73–4
Hanover, 29
Harbottle, Brigadier Michael, 139
Harris, Air Chief Marshal Sir Arthur, 29, 54–6, 76, 128, 147, 210
Havel, Waclaw, 161
Hawkes, Jacquetta, 164
hibakusha, 27–8
Hiller, Kurt, 150
Hindenburg, Field Marshal Paul von, 107
Hine, Air Chief Marshal Sir Patrick, 77, 80
Hirohito (Japanese Emperor), 7, 10–11, 13–14, 16, 19, 22–4, 122–3, 155
Hiroshima, 1, 4, 7–10, 17–28, 30–4, 35, 47, 51, 63–5, 81–2, 86, 88–9, 97, 99–100, 111, 125–7, 131–4, 135, 147, 157, 175–6, 192–5, 201, 216, 222–3
Hitler, Adolf, 51, 57, 60, 106–7, 112–13, 119–21, 152, 154–5, 197, 206, 218
Ho Chi Minh, 73
Holocaust, *see* genocide
Homer, 194
Hoover, Herbert, 49

Hopper, Bruce, 129
Horner, General Charles, 139
House, Colonel Edward M., 149
Hungary, 71, 159
Hunthausen, Archbishop Raymond, 181
Hus, Jan, 142
Hussein, Saddam, 77, 79, 222

Ienaga, Saburo, 122–3
India, 65, 85, 137, 153, 213, 220, 222
Indochina, 65, 74
Indonesia, 12, 125
Inskip, Sir Thomas, 54
Iran, 79
Iraq, 32, 75–7, 79, 83, 202, 220–1
Islam, 175, 177, 189, 209
Israel, 74–6, 85–6, 98, 212, 221
   see also Arab–Israeli wars
Italy, 13, 33, 43–4, 47, 51–2, 64, 105, 118, 129, 148, 159, 188, 204, 206, 209, 222
Iwo Jima, 10

Jäckel, Eberhard, 120
Japan, 5, 7–34, 63–5, 82–3, 85, 87, 119, 121–7, 130, 132–3, 155, 157, 164, 172, 175–6, 194, 206–7, 212, 218
Jaspers, Karl, 169
Jaurès, Jean, 146
Jena, 29
Jervis, Robert, 217
Jeschonnek, General Hans, 59–60
Jesus, 140
John Paul II, 180
John XXIII, 178
Johnson, Lyndon B., 73
Joliot-Curie, Frédéric, 184
Jordan, 75
Judaism, 140, 175, 177, 189, 194, 197
Jünger, Ernst, 105

Kairo Conference (1943) and Declaration, 18
Kampuchea, 131, 133–4, 196
Kanji, Lieutenant Colonel Ishiwara, 124, 128
Kant, Immanuel, 143
Karlsruhe, 29
Kassel, 29
Kästner, Erich, 170
Kaysen, Carl, 218–20
Kennan, George, 184
Kennedy, John F., 96
Kent, Monsignor Bruce, 165
Khrushchev, Nikita V., 67
Kido, Marquis, 29
Kiel, 29
King-Hall, Sir Stephen, 216
Knauss, Robert, 43
Koestler, Arthur, 103, 192
Köln-Deutz, 29
Kopf, David, 130
Komintern *see* Communism
Kominform *see* Communism
Korea, 26, 65, 71–2, 74, 76, 79–80, 90, 122–5, 131, 213–15, 221
Korean War, 9, 71, 180
Kosovo, 190
  see also Yugoslavia
Krasnovskiy, Marshal S.A., 69–70
Krefeld, 29
Kuper, Leo, 119, 126, 201
Küster, Fritz, 150
Kuwait, 76–7, 175, 220
Kyushu, 15

Lactantius, 140
Lafontaine, Oskar, 168, 172
landmines, 137
Le Corbusier, 185
League of Nations, 149
Leahy, Admiral, 20
Lebed, General Alexander, 139
Leipzig, 29
LeMay, General Curtis, 21, 76, 92
Lenin (Vladimir Illich Uljanov), 46, 89, 91–2, 114, 162

Lenz, Siegfried, 169
Leverkusen, 29
Lévi-Strauss, Claude, 198
Libya, 81, 220, 221
Liddell Hart, Captain Basil, 45–6
Lidice, 115
Liebknecht, Karl, 146
Lifton, Robert Jay, 26
Little Boy, 18, 155
Littlewood, Joan, 154
Livy, 196
Lloyd George, David, 38, 41
Lollards, 142
London, 38, 41, 50, 54, 59–60, 81–2, 97, 143, 163
Longerich, Peter, 106
Lübeck, 29, 54, 60
Ludendorff, Field Marshal Erich von, 102, 106–11, 115, 118–19, 122, 126, 128–31, 133–4, 194
Luftwaffe, 30, 50–1, 57–9, 64, 81
Luxemburg, Rosa, 146
Luzon, 15

MacArthur, Gerneral Douglas, 21, 71–2
Machiavelli, Niccolo, 204
Mackie, Air Commodore Alistair, 139
MacLeish, Archibald, 14
Maddox, Robert James, 9, 23
Madrid, 188
Magdeburg, 115, 196
Mahoney, Bishop Roger, 181
Mainz, 29
Malaga, 52
Malaya, 65
Malthus, Thomas, 201, 218
Manchuria, 12, 18–19, 28, 72, 119, 123–4
Manhattan Project, 21
Manichaeans, 141
Mannheim, 29
Marianas Islands, 20
Markusen, Eric, 130

Marseille, 60
Marshall, General George, 17, 21–2
Martens, de, 138
Martin, Kingsley, 164
Martin, Laurence, 215
Marx, Karl, 146
Marxism-Leninism, 68, 91, 98, 146, 160, 162, 169
Masaaki, Tanaka, 125
Mason, Air Commodore R.A., 74
Matthiesen, Bishop Leroy, 181
Maurice, General Frederick, 39
McNamara, Robert, 72, 96, 184
Mearsheimer, John, 217
Melos, 195
Mengele, Joseph, 124
Mennonites, 142–3, 163, 182
Messer, Robert L., 17
Methodists, 162
Miles, Rufus, 15–16
Milgram, Stanley, 208
Miller, Mark, 66
Milne, General (later Field Marshal) Sir George (later Lord), 41
Mitchell, William, 45, 47–8, 50, 60, 71, 79–80
Mohammed, 177
Molotov, Vjacheslav M. (Skriabin), 152, 158
Mönchen-Gladbach/Rheydt, 29
Montagu, Ashley, 211
Montand, Yves, 185
Moscow, 87, 95, 152, 159, 189
Mountbatten, Field Marshal Lord M. of Alamein, 95
Mueller, John, 218–20
Mühlheim, 29
Munich, 29, 59, 153–4
Mussolini, Benito, 105, 152, 222

Nagasaki, 1, 4, 7–10, 17–25, 27–8, 30–4, 35, 47, 51, 63–5, 81–2, 86, 88–9, 97, 99–100, 111, 126–7, 131, 133–4, 147, 157, 175–6, 179, 183, 190, 192, 194–5, 201, 216, 222–3
Nanking, 31, 34, 52, 124–5, 134
Napoleon, 103, 115, 204
Napoleonic Wars, 105, 116, 132, 143–4, 173, 194–5
National Socialism, 9, 31, 43, 56, 113, 115, 119, 122, 151, 153, 159, 206, 210, 212, 217
Netherlands, The, 59, 88, 142, 149, 163, 170, 174, 187
Niemöller, Martin, 171
Nitze, Paul, 19
Noel-Baker, Philip (later Lord), 49, 165
Non-Proliferation Treaty (of Nuclear Weapons, NPT), 137–8
Norstad, General Lauris, 92
North Atlantic Treaty, North Atlantic Treaty Organisation (NATO), 67–70, 85, 87, 89–91, 93–9, 132, 159–60, 168–9, 171, 173–5, 180–4, 187, 189, 192, 207, 220, 222
Norway, 174–5, 195, 206, 217
Nuremberg, 29, 55

O'Neill, Robert, 139
Oberhausen, 29
Odom, General William, 139
Okinawa, 10, 20, 125
Ollenhauer, Erich, 168
Oradour-sur-Glane, 115
Orgarkov, MarshalNikolay V., 160
Origen, 140
Orthodox Christianity, 145, 175, 182, 188
Oslo Treaty on landmines (1997), 137
Osnabrück, 29
Ossietsky, Carl von, 150
Overy, Richard, 56, 81, 100, 129, 132
Oviedo, 52
Owen, Wilfred, 145, 148

pacifism and pacificism, 135–6,
    139–91
Pakistan, 65, 85, 137, 213, 220
Pal, Randha Binod, 126
Papandreou, Andreas, 189
Pape, Robert, 71, 83, 85
Paris, 60, 146, 152, 163
Patarins, 141
Paulicians, Poblicans, 141
Peace Movement, *see* Communism
Pearl Harbor, 23, 28, 63
Penn, William, 142
Philippines, 12, 28, 33
Picasso, Pablo, 51, 185
Pius XII, 178–9
Ploetz, Michael, 169
Plymoth, 38
Pol Pot, 131, 133f., 196
Poland, 14, 31, 33, 59, 132
Portal, Air Chief Marshal Sir
    Charles, 48, 55
Portsmouth, 38
Portugal, 12
Potsdam Conference (July–August
    1945) and Declaration, 13–14,
    16, 19
    see also surrender, unconditional
Presbyterians, 143
Priestley, J.B., 164
Protestantism, 142–6, 153, 162,
    167, 171–5, 182, 187–9
    see also Christianity
Prussia, 116
Pyongyang, 71

Quakers, 142–4, 162, 182
Quester, George, 37, 94, 132
Quin, Archbishop John, 181

Rappoport, Anatol S., 111
Rau, Johannes, 168
Reagan, Ronald, 99, 168
Remarque, Erich Maria, 148, 169
Remscheid, 29
Résistance, 159
Ribbentrop, Joachim von, 152, 158

Richelieu, Cardinal Armand-Jean
    du Plessis, Duke of, 143
Riobé, Bishop, 185
Robbins, Keith, 148, 154
Rocard, Michel, 139
Rogers, General Bernard, 139
Rokhilin, General Lev, 139
Rome, 114, 163, 203, 213, 219
    Roman Empire, 140, 156, 194,
    198, 205
Roosevelt, Franklin D., 13, 127
Rostock, 29, 54, 60
Rotblat, Josef, 139
Rotterdam, 28, 30, 59
Royal Air Force (RAF), 31, 39–41,
    50, 52–5, 57, 59, 64, 72, 216
Rubenstein, Richard L., 116
Ruhr-Area, 53
Rumania, 14, 159
Ruskin, John, 104, 153
Russell, (later Lord) Bertrand, 164
Rüsselsheim, 29
Russia, 79, 119, 145, 152, 220
    see also USSR
Rwanda, 131, 134, 196

Saarbrücken, 29
Saint Pierre, Abbé de, 143
Sakharov, Andrej, 161, 167
Sanguinetti, Admiral Antoine, 139
Saragossa, 52
Sarajevo, 146
Sassoon, Siegfried, 148
Scandinavian countries, 149, 154,
    163
    see also Sweden, Denmark,
    Norway, Finland
Schelling, Thomas, 81
Schmidt, Helmut, 168–9
Schmitt, Carl, 106
Schröder, Gerhard, 168–9
Schweinfurt, 61–2
Seché, Alphonse, 105, 116
Second World War, 4, 7–34, 35,
    48, 51–4, 56, 59–66, 71–2, 78,
    80–2, 85, 94–5, 97–8, 100,

102–3, 105, 112, 115, 117, 119,
121, 127, 129, 131, 133, 136,
150–1, 153–5, 157, 173–4,
180, 188, 192, 194–7, 201,
206, 212, 217, 222
Seville, 52
Shanghai, 52
Shiro, Azuma, 124–5
Signoret, Simone, 185
Skinner, J. Allen, 164
Slessor, Marshal of the RAF Sir
John, 48, 76, 80, 216
Smith, Gerard, 184
Smith, Malcolm, 53
Smuts, General Ian, 49
Social Darwinism, 31, 44, 117–18,
121, 145, 218
Social Democrats, 146, 210–11
Socialism, 145–7, 152
First Socialist International, 146,
158
Second Socialist International,
146, 158
Third (Communist)
International, 152
Sokolovsky, Marshal V.D., 67n
Spaatz, General Carl, 18, 21, 62
Spaight, J.M., 94, 129
Spain, 52, 158, 188, 204
Spanish Civil War, 51, 58, 63,
150–2
Speer, Albert, 43–4, 57, 121
Stalin, Josef V., 8–9, 14–16, 66,
112, 131, 152, 159, 190
Stettin, 29
Stimson, Henry, 16
Stoakes, Geoffrey, 119
Stuttgart, 29
Sudan, 221
Suez Crisis, 74
surrender, unconditional, 7, 12–13,
16, 19–20, 23–4, 32, 98
Suttner, Bertha von, 147
Suzuki, Kantaro, 18
Sweden, 10, 19, 115, 173, 175,
194–5

Switzerland, 12, 19
Sykes, Air Vice Marshal Sir
Frederick, 41, 45–8, 118, 130
Syria, 75, 221

Taiwan, 122
Talmon, J.L., 116, 205
Tedder, Air Chief Marshal Sir
Arthur, 55
Tel Aviv, 79
Tertullian, 140
Thirty Years' War, 115, 132, 143,
195–6, 201
Thompson, E.P., 165
Thoreau, Henry David, 153
Thycidides, 194, 196
Tirpitz, Fleet-Admiral, 38, 82
Tiverton, Major Lord, 39
Togo, Shigenori, 19
Tokyo, 9, 17–18, 25–6, 28–30, 34,
63, 76, 133
Tolstoy, Leo, 145–6, 153
total war, Total War (in
Ludendorffian sense – *see also*
Ludendorff), 4–6, 34–5,
101–34, 179, 181–2, 189–90,
192, 196, 210, 216
totalitarianism, 111–14, 131, 205
Trenchard, Marshal Sir Hugh
(later Viscount), 41–8, 50,
52–4, 76, 118, 128, 130, 134,
210
Trotsky, Leon, 46
Troy, 115
Truman, Harry S., 8–9, 14–18,
21–4, 127
Tucholsky, Kurt, 170
Tukhachevsky, General Mikhail,
46–7, 70

Ukraine, 161
Unit 731, 124
Unitarians, 143
United Kingdom, 7, 13–14, 16–17,
25, 29, 31–3, 37–41, 43,
46–51, 53–7, 60–6, 82–3, 85,

87–90, 94–6, 112–13, 117–21,
126–32, 137–8, 142–3, 147–50,
152–4, 159–60, 163–6, 168,
170, 174–5, 185–6, 194, 206,
210, 214, 220
United Nations (UN), 72, 83, 104,
126, 137, 181, 214, 220
US Air Force (USAF, until World
War II: USAAF), 9–10, 18,
30–1, 57, 61, 64, 66, 71, 78–9
US Strategic Bombing Survey
(after Second World War), 10,
15, 19–20, 22, 64, 72, 82–3
after First World War, 60
USA, 5, 7–34, 37, 45, 57, 60–5,
71–4, 77–92, 95–9, 112–13,
116, 119, 125–33, 137–8,
142–3, 155–7, 159–60, 163,
173, 175–6, 180–4, 188, 190,
206, 210, 214, 217–20
USSR, 7, 9, 14–18, 20, 23, 33,
46–7, 50–1, 57, 61, 63–4,
66–71, 75, 87–93, 95–9,
112–13, 118, 125, 137, 152,
156–62, 164, 166, 190, 201,
217, 222

V1 and V2 Rockets, 60, 80
Vatican II, Council, 178, 185–6
Vershinin, Air Marshal, 66
victory, 40, 97–100
Vietnam War, 8–9, 32, 65, 72–4,
78–9, 81, 98, 100, 131, 180,
183, 190, 215
Vinci, Leonardo da, 199

Wainstock, Dennis, 13, 29
Waldensians, 142

Waltz, Kenneth, 217
War Machine, 103–4, 110, 114,
116–18, 126–7, 130, 134, 145,
195, 207, 218
war
limited, 103, 194
absolute, 103, 194–5, 204
see also Franco-Prussian War,
Arab–Israeli Wars, French
Revolutionary Wars, etc.
Warsaw Treaty Organisation
(WTO), 66, 69–70, 80, 90,
96–8, 132, 159–60, 192,
222
Warsaw, 30, 59, 63
Webster, Sir Charles, 54
Weinberger, Caspar, 99
Wells, H.G., 116
Wever, General Walther, 57, 76,
210
Weygand, General Maxime, 128
Wieman, Henry, 135
Wilhelmshaven, 29
Wilson, Woodrow, 149
Wismar, 29
Wycliff, John, 142

Xenophon, 194

Yalta Conference (February 1945)
and Declaration, 14, 16
Yugoslavia, 83, 131, 201

Zhigarev, Air Chief Marshal, 67
Zuckermann, Sir Solly (later
Lord), 55
Zurich, 142
Zweig, Arnold, 148